M000107597

DANC'N TO

THE BOSUN'S WHISTLE

FORT BIGELOW

This is a work of fiction.

Names, characters, places and incidents are either products

of the author's imagination, or if real, are used fictitiously.

Copyright © 2016 by James Krentz

Cover Illustration: Kindle Direct Publishing

DBA Fort Bigelow

All rights reserved. No part of this book may be reproduced, transmitted, or stored

in an information retrieval system in any form or by any means, graphic,

electronic, or mechanical without prior written permission from the author.

First Edition 2016

Second Edition 2019

Printed in the United States of America

"Hey Patterson! Petty Officer Patterson!"

It was Senior Chief McNulty from engineering.

"Yea, Senior?"

"The cardinal points on a compass; what do they point to?"

"The cardinal points on a compass…are you kidding!"

"Go ahead."

"Is this a joke?"

"I'm waiting!"

North…South…East…and West!"

"Negative!"

"They don't!"

"Nope!"

"What then?"

"Wind…Water…Whiskey… and WOMEN!!!

To Erlinda, Nicholas and Jason

I hope you enjoy reading this as much as I enjoyed writing it.

Danc'n to the Bosun's Whistle

Chapter 1

New Jersey

1983

Our high school graduation ceremony was about to conclude. All that remained were the dispensing of the diplomas. The ceremony was held at Wright's Stadium which is where the football team plays its home games. Straddled across the fifty yard line was a hastily constructed platform made of wood, wire and plastic. Located in the middle of the platform was the speaker's podium where people who like to hear themselves talk had gathered. Their flowery speeches fabricated for their own entertainment. It was a brilliantly clear day; the setting sun was still minutes away from disappearing below the horizon. For reasons unbeknownst to us, the undergraduates were seated facing west. As the sun's light faded, its lingering rays concentrated on an area directly above the podium illuminating the area where we were sitting. Almost immediately, tears and sweat began to trickle down the sides of our faces as we strained to hear our names over the shouts and whistles of parents acknowledging the achievements of their offspring. I had just recovered my cap and was about to exit the field when the reality of the moment crystallized the anxiety I was feeling. Instead of being "out of many one." I was now "one out of many," with no clear direction or vision; a lost ship in search of a harbor. My parents, members of the greatest generation, expected me to go to college; in fact, my dad insisted on it. Being the good son that I am, I applied for admission to a local college half way through my senior year even though I had no idea what I wanted to study. When I asked my mother about tuition, she calmly assured me they would take care of the first

1

semester; after that, it was up to me. I remembered my reaction; I stood there frozen

unable to answer. Not only did I have to go to college; I had to pay for it! Fortunately, I

had the summer to figure things out. College didn't start until September. This was June

and as I was walking down Essex Ave in my cap and gown, it hit me. The hell with

college! Hello U.S. Navy! I don't know why I thought of it right then and there but I did.

In hind sight, yea, I should have given it more consideration, but I was young and

impulsive. Initially, I decided to wait a week before signing up. Seven days was more

than enough time, but as Wednesday drew near; I developed cold feet. I waited forty

eight hours more before heading downtown to the recruitment center. When I arrived at

the center, I was greeted by Petty Officer Gary Stevens. He had wavy red hair and a

strong face. Across his chin was a pencil thin scar he probably got as a child. He looked

impressive. His dress blue uniform boasted of ribbons and medals acquired through years

of loyal service. He was trim and had the look of a runner. He told me he had just

completed his tenth year, and was looking forward to making Chief Petty Officer before

Christmas. Age wise I would say he was about thirty. We exchanged some small talk. He

told me he was born in New Jersey but had moved to Texas when he was seven years old.

He wanted to be a recruiter in New Jersey because he still had relatives there he'd not

seen since childhood. Slowly, the conversation shifted from him to me. He wanted to

know why I decided to join the Navy. I explained my situation as best I could and asked

him what job openings were available. He informed me I would be tested and my score

would determine job availability. In addition, I would be subjected to both a physical and

a background check in order to determine suitability.

"Do you have any specific questions William?"

"I guess I just want to know about the pros and cons?"

"Pros and cons?"

"Let's start with the pros and there are many. Free food, free housing, free medical, technical training if you qualify, adventure, travel, and WOMEN!"

He highlighted the word women with a nod and a wink.

"A steady paycheck and the ability to go to college, and, if you decide to stick it out and do twenty years, you're looking at a pension at thirty eight with full benefits."

"I like that, a pension at thirty eight."

"And, if you really want to do it right, after the military, go work for the government for another twenty years and then you can sit back and collect two pensions!"

"Wow, I like that even better!"

The recruiter then leaned forward in his chair and looked me square in the face. He wanted my undivided attention. "The cons. There are a few but if you do what you're told and follow orders you shouldn't have any problems. Yea, you're gonna get orders from time to time that don't make any sense but you have to obey them anyway, and, you're gonna run into officers every now and then who like to bust balls, but don't take it personally. They are under a lot of pressure themselves and the Captain is harder on them then he is on the crew, so when you get an order that seems to defy common sense, remember this conversation."

"Wow, thanks for the advice."

"There's one more thing William, and its part of the enlistment process which hardly ever gets addressed, in fact, most recruiters by pass it all together."

"What would that be?"

Petty Officer Stevens removed a cigarette from the opened pack on top of his desk and lit it.

"Deployment."

"What?"

"Underway, out at sea."

"What is it I need to know?"

"Every now and then, you're gonna run into a crew member who rubs you the wrong way and vice versa. He can be from another division or even your own. In the old days, the Navy had "smokers" which were sanctioned boxing matches between crew members. If you had a beef with someone, you could put the gloves on and settle it in a make shift ring up on the main deck, but since the Navy did away with them, you have to find other ways to vent your anger."

"So what do they do now?"

"Exercise my boy! I know that sounds crazy. Nothing like a closed fist if you ask me, but since we can't fight anymore, the next best thing is exercise. Besides, you can always talk to someone if something is bothering you. You've got your shipmates, chief, division officer, department head, executive officer and even the old man himself if need be. Plus, if its personal, you can always talk to the Doc, he's usually a pretty good listener."

"Well, I'll try to get along with everybody."

"That's the spirit Patterson! You hit the nail on the head!"

"I did?"

"You did, but listen to me carefully. When you're two or three thousand miles from the nearest land and you've been out to sea for a hundred plus days without even seeing a bird, you can become a little disoriented. It doesn't happen to everybody but it does happen. Some, especially the married guys with kids, that much time away from their families extracts a heavy toll. Others, the ones who like to drink their paychecks, and there are some, can get a little nasty going that long without a drink."

I was listening intently.

"The point I'm trying to make Patterson is this, not everyone adjusts to life at sea the same way and the guy you can't stand or can't get along with, he might be the one to save your life. Remember this William; make it your mission when you're out to sea. Try to get along with everybody, especially the ones you don't like. Life on board ship is dangerous; I'm not going to lie to you. Accidents can happen at any time and nine times out of ten, it will be the guy you least expect who will come to your aid."

I thanked Petty Officer Stevens for his honesty. I was surprised he went into such detail with someone who hadn't been sworn in yet. I considered it an honor being told; it showed he had a lot of confidence in me. Before I began to fill out the neatly stacked paper work on his desk, he asked me when I wanted to be sworn in; I told him after the summer was over.

"No use wasting valuable beach time."

He chuckled at my response and said it would probably be early September before security cleared me, and that he would contact me regarding the time and date for the physical. Once all the forms were filled out, we shook hands and I left. On the way home, I realized there were three things I had to deal with, and the first would be my parent's disappointment. They had their hearts set on me going to college.

The big announcement came on Sunday.

We had just returned from church and were preparing to sit down for our customary Sunday meal of chicken, mashed potatoes and green beans. Once seated and after my dad said the prayer, I decided to break the news to the family as we ate. Yes, I could have waited until later, but I felt compelled to get it off my chest. As I was speaking, I noticed my mom's reaction only because she sat opposite me.

You would have thought someone died.

She turned pale white as tears began to form in the corners of her eyes. My dad lowered his head in disbelief as my brother and sister practically sprang from their chairs in jubilation. Shortly after, my dad asked if it was too late for me to back out. Even though I hadn't been sworn in, I told him my mind was made up. I remember the expression on his face. It was a mixture of joy and sadness which seemed odd since he himself was a WWII Navy veteran. I was expecting something different. We finished the rest of the meal in silence which was very strange; usually we're a talkative family. I thought for sure there would be many questions but none were asked. Perhaps they were waiting for a more opportune time to speak to me. As for my brother and sister, the somber mood had no affect on them. They could barely contain themselves. My younger brother Jimmy was grinning from ear to ear, in fact, I don't know how he was able to keep food in his mouth. My sister Ruth, preoccupied with the thought of having additional closet space, hadn't even noticed the chicken stain on her white dress. Soon after, we finished our meal and went about our separate ways. I spent the remainder of the day wondering if my parents were ever going to discuss the matter with me; they never did. Later that evening, as my head hit the pillow, I let out a sigh of relief. Round one with my parents was over. Round two with my girlfriend was next. Before falling asleep, I was suddenly consumed with selfishness. Since I wasn't leaving for another three months, why rock the boat? I had all summer to tell her. Besides, if I told her now, she might want to break up with me, leaving me alone and that was not a good thing. You see, my girlfriend Diane was a passionate girl, full of emotion and very good at self expression. I wasn't ready to give that up yet. Besides, we had been together for about a year and I had gotten to know her family quite well. Her mom, a housewife, was a great cook and since she knew my mom from the food market, dating Diane was that much easier. Her dad, an engineer, liked the fact I brought his daughter home on time. He said it showed good character. Looking back now, yes, the honorable thing to do was to tell her, but the little devil inside me wouldn't have it. I wrestled with the dilemma for two weeks before making up my mind. I would spill the beans Labor Day weekend! I was on a roll. Last but not least were my maternal grandparents.

I thought they might take it the hardest, but my mom softened the blow a bit by telling them I was going to attend college out of state.

She reassured them I would be home for the holidays to see them. My mom felt it wise not to bring up the military since they both lost family members fighting the Nazi's. She also took into consideration my grandmothers health. Recently, she suffered a mild stroke and was in no condition for any unpleasant news. Perhaps they could be told at a later time, but not now.

After she finished explaining this to her parents, my grandfather said he would be dead and buried by the time I came back to visit him. My grandmother, not to be out done, said the terminal cancer she was dying from, which she did not have, would linger on for years, tormenting her with pain and suffering, lasting all the way up to one week before college graduation when she would depart this earth and be carried away by angels up to heaven.

And they say I'm the one who is melodramatic.

Anyway, June and July went by quickly. By the time August rolled around, I had completed my physical and any remaining paperwork. All that was left was the background check and the job rate. Since it was pointless to look for employment, I spent as much time as I could at the Jersey shore. Now, those of you unfamiliar with the Atlantic Ocean and the North East, allow me to fill in the blanks. The ocean water in the beginning of summer is cold, sometimes very cold. I can remember admiring my blue fingers and toes as a child. Running in and out of those frigid waves took guts. Not to mention dealing with the under tows and rip tides near the sand bars. For us, it was a badge of courage. Within weeks though, the cold water is replaced with warmer water and once August rolls around, the sea temperature is perfect, making Labor Day weekend the optimum time to be at the shore.

Not wanting to let a good thing slip by, a bunch of us decided to end the summer at the shore. We rented a couple of rooms at a motel but they were a long way from the beach. There were places closer, but they were also more expensive, and since all we had was chump change, this was the best we could do.

It was also right around this time I received the results of my background check and job rate. According to the Navy, I scored high enough to become a sonar technician and I was told to report to Newark on September 12 for the swearing in ceremony.

As a kind of a going away present and knowing it would be a while before seeing me again, my dad let me borrow his brand new Cadillac which absolutely floored me. When he gave me his car keys I got the usual "drive safe" speech but then he added "I hope Diane doesn't take it too hard," which surprised me. He had never commented on our relationship before.

Labor Day weekend at the Jersey shore is insane. It's the busiest time of year with heavy traffic everywhere. The ninety minute drive took four hours which absolutely fried my patience but it didn't seem to bother the sun worshipers. On the contrary, the champions of self expression relished the heavy traffic. As soon as we slowed down to a crawl, they got out of the car and spread their beach towels across the trunk and roof. Armed with bottles of sun tan lotion, they cautiously positioned themselves on their towels. Usually I don't mind when the girls do that, but this was a brand new Cadillac. I was worried about scratches. Tony, a mechanic friend of mine told me not to worry. He said he would buff out any imperfections.

I breathed a sigh of relief.

Anyway, not to be outdone, girls from other vehicles joined in. Within minutes, a bunch of teenagers had turned the Garden State Parkway into a big beautiful steel beach. It really was something to see. Girls in bikinis perched on top of cars or in windows exhibiting their natural attributes. And talk about the whistles!

Some of the old timers referred to it as the trophy show.

When we finally got to the motel, the parking lot was so crowded I had to triple park to unload the car. When we attempted to check into our reserved rooms, we were told they hadn't been cleaned yet even though they were supposed to have been ready

9

three hours ago. The manager apologized and gave us free tickets to go on the cable car ride which was located down the far end of the boardwalk. By 7:15 P.M. we were settled in, the girls in one room the guys in another. Around eight, we walked to the boardwalk for some jumbo pizza and root beer. After that, the group wanted to go on the cable car ride, but since I was already tired from the long drive and stuffed from the pizza; my only thought was to walk down to the ocean and have a smoke.

The wind had picked up a little so Diane and I went back to the motel to get her sweater. Once we got to the beach, we sat down on a sand dune which was elevated slightly higher than the surrounding area giving us an unobstructed view of the ocean. I lit my cigarette as Diane leaned back against my chest, her hair diverting the wind from my face. The fading sun behind us, we looked eastward across the ocean. Stars began to appear, faintly at first and then brighter as the sky darkened.

If there was ever a more opportune moment to tell her it was now, but I hesitated. Unbeknownst to me, Diane had prettified herself with my favorite perfume. Accentuated by the wind, it quickly overwhelmed my senses. This, coupled with the twinkling stars distracted me to the point of not caring. Like I said, Diane was a passionate girl, full of emotion and very good at self expression.

The holiday weekend came and went and still I hadn't told her. I don't know why I was procrastinating. I mean come on, I'm not the first guy to join the Navy and besides, I wasn't breaking up with her; I was simply relocating. I finally convinced myself to tell her on September 5th.

Do you want to know why I picked that day? The answer is pretty simple. Whatever her reaction; I only had to deal with it for seven days. Perfect! I picked Diane up around seven that evening and drove her to a local park where we could walk around and talk. I figured if she was going to do any crying, she would be conscious of the fact we were in a public setting. Just as I was about to drop the hammer, she put her hand to my lips.

"I know what you want to tell me."

"You do?"

"Yes, you're leaving for the Navy next week."

I stood there frozen unable to move.

"How...how did you know?"

"Your mom told my mom. They ran into each other at the market, and by the time they were done with the deli counter, my mom knew. You know women talk."

My mother spilled the beans, of all people, and then it dawned on me. The comment my dad made about Diane not taking it too hard, he already knew she knew!

All I could do was shake my head from side to side.

"Yes, my mom told me. In fact, I knew even before we went down the shore, and that's why I didn't say anything. I wanted to hear it from you first."

"I don't know what to say; I'm speechless."

"Well, I was upset at first, you know, walking around the house with a box of tissues, but after I calmed down, I accepted it. I realized this is something you want to do."

"What about us?"

"Yes, William what about us? That's the hard part. I know we can write to each other and call each other but, the fact is, you're going to be gone and I'm gonna be here."

"So, what are you saying?"

"What I'm trying to tell you is we're both alike. We're both passionate. Honestly, I don't think either one of us is going to be faithful to the other, and I'm not sure we should even try. Listen, I'm still your girl but if I find somebody else…"

"Ok, I get the picture."

The thought of Diane with another guy upset me, but she was right. We both suffered from R.E.S. (roving eye syndrome) and being apart, it was only a matter of time before one of us would get the urge to test the waters. Looking back now, I'm glad her mom told her. It gave her time to vent emotionally and also to gather her thoughts.

I saw her everyday that last week and thanked her for being honest for the both of us.

Chapter 2

Fall 1983

My father and I arrived at the Federal Building approximately thirty minutes before I was due to report to the induction center. The transit from our driveway to the station took exactly twenty minutes. For reasons unbeknownst to me, my dad drove his old Chevy Monza instead of his new Cadillac. I guess he was worried someone might hit him, or worse, scratch his new baby. Speaking of scratches, I had Tony go over the car like a surgeon before returning it to my father.

When we arrived at our destination, we were quickly surrounded by a sea of construction workers who were working feverously on completing the face lift the front of the building so desperately needed. My dad jokingly referred to them as plastic surgeons with hard hats!

Needless to say, parking that close to the building was impossible. The only other option was the "no parking/no waiting zone" which was located directly in front. As we pulled up parallel to the curb my dad quickly extended his right hand and said "good luck."

As I extended my hand to meet his, I looked him square in the face and said thank you. There really wasn't time for anything else.

I exited the car and quickly climbed the steps which led to the building's entrance. Before disappearing inside, I turned around to see if he was still there but a police officer had motioned for him to move on. I watched him as he drove down the street wondering

13

how long it would be before I would see him again.

After that, I made my way past security and onto the elevator which took me to the military processing floor. The swearing in ceremony would be conducted there. It was the first step of many necessary to transform the twenty or so guys with me into future sailors. Once we were sworn in, we were transported to the airport and sent to the west coast to begin training. The minute we arrived at our destination, we boarded a military bus and were ferried to the training center. No one spoke during the thirty minute ride. I remember it was close to midnight when we finally got to our barracks and told to go to sleep.

The next morning, if you want to call it that, we were awakened at 0400 by the sound of a large gray garbage can crashing onto the floor. It entered the barracks with such velocity, I thought at first it might be a missile!

The first day or two were spent processing; this included haircuts and inoculations. I remember the inoculations very well. Several of us were lined up single file and told to proceed to a mark on the floor where a medical technician holding a "nail" gun was waiting. It's difficult to describe the apparatus per se due to its many parts. Suffice it to say it was rectangular in shape and filled with short stem needles that resembled snake fangs. When it was my turn, I stood tall like a Spartan, but afterwards, nothing could shield me from the sore throat and headache that followed. Some of the guys behind me had serious reactions and were required to sit down until they were ready to proceed. The shots were followed by uniform fittings, boots and then a quick pit stop to the chow hall.

Exactly 15 minutes later I was standing in the middle of an open concrete field commonly known as the "pulverizer." It was here where we were introduced to our company commander. He was a first class yeoman and judging from the gold hash marks along his left sleeve had been in the Navy between twelve and sixteen years. My first impression was a positive one; he didn't appear to be overbearing. Strict yes, but not like the instructors you see in the movies. We were required to call him sir or commander but I could tell from his expression he was uncomfortable with that and I'll explain why. Not long after graduating from boot camp I ran into him in the enlisted club where he was having a beer. I went over to where he was seated and greeted him with "good afternoon sir," which made his eyes roll.

"What's your name again?"

"Patterson, Sir."

"Ok, Patterson! First things first; boot camp is over and done with! I'm no longer a sir or a commander, you got that!"

"Yes…Petty Officer Colmes."

"Second, now that your getting ready to go to school, make sure you salute the officers and not the chiefs, you got it!"

"Yes Petty Officer Colmes."

"We've been getting our butts chewed out because so many of you can't tell the difference. I know it's difficult because they both wear khaki, and from a distance it's hard to tell them apart, especially in the morning when the sun is in your eyes, but as they get closer, the ones with bars on their collars…they're the officers!"

He paused to take a sip of his dark beer.

"Look Patterson, you and your buddies got to learn to pay attention to detail. It's

15

real simple; the chiefs have anchors, the officers don't! Oh, and another thing, as far as busting balls go, boot ensigns are the worst, followed by the guys who went through ROTC. The academy guys are usually pretty mellow which surprises me since they're the ones with the most military bearing. Anyway, remember what I'm telling you!"

"Will do!"

"Now, please tell this lovely young lady what you're drinking so she can earn a living."

It would have been nice to drink a beer but since I was only 18 I had to settle for a coke. After I got my drink, I moved off to a small table to savor the moment. It appeared the petty officer and the bartender were friends; I felt it best not to intrude on their privacy.

But I digress, getting back to the pulverizer, it was here where we did our marching and exercises, and since we were no longer considered a group of individuals, but rather a company of men, whenever one screwed up all were punished. Yes, my new family and I enjoyed multiple sets of pushups, sit ups, leg lifts and my favorite…eight count body builders!

This was considered the first level of discipline.

Level two, commonly known as "the foots log," was an afterhours exercise party. Yes, once the setting sun had bedded down for the evening, the attendees were encouraged to demonstrate their physical prowess by completing a profusion of exercises not unlike the ones done earlier. The one positive. The heat of the day had abated; the cool night air made it just a little more bearable.

Fortunately, and I do mean fortunately, this is where the group punishment ended.

For the real hard boiled eggs, there was one more level of discipline. Level three was the final corrective measure, and depending on what part of the country you trained in, had different names. On our base, it was known as "Cut to the Bone," and according to those who went through it, a truly harrowing experience. Having never been through it myself, I can only tell you what I've heard. One of the "exercises" involved placing M-14 rifles across the tops of the knuckles of the recruits doing pushups. The instructors then stood on the rifles making sure their body weight was evenly distributing across both hands. Just the thought of that gives me goose bumps. Truly, the pain must have been incredible.

Imagine that scenario the next time you're doing pushups!

I will say this regarding the "parties," I was looking toned and trimmed. In fact, I hadn't looked this good since I was on the wrestling team in high school. Bottom line: I was in the best shape of my life and as far as the Navy was concerned…mission accomplished!

Graduation from boot camp fell on a Friday giving us forty eight hours of liberty. Across from the training base was an entertainment center equipped with all the latest games. It was great being away from the base, but after three hours of pinball, most of us yearned for something else. Some of the guys wanted to cruise the streets just for the hell of it. Others, in need of a little female companionship, decided to try their luck at the city mall which was five blocks away. As for me, I did neither. I smoked one more cigarette then headed back to the base.

Once there, I took a stroll around the complex to better orientate myself and much to my delight I discovered a nice little sandwich shop not far from where I was quartered. I ordered a tuna sub with chips which was not only delicious but cost effective. In fact, I enjoyed it so much I ate dinner there Saturday and Sunday as well.

Monday morning, I reported to my sonar class in one of the buildings perpendicular to the complex I was housed in. The small classroom came equipped with four large windows which were located on the east side of the room thus ensuring a daily baptism of warm sunshine. Before taking my seat, I did a head count. I was one of fifteen and somewhat disappointed because I didn't recognize any one from boot camp. Once again, I was surrounded by total strangers.

Our instructor entered the room carrying a clip board in one hand and a large black bag in the other. Multi colored paper protruded from one of the unzipped pouches which ran the length of the bag. The instructor was a first class petty officer named Hobbs. He had blond hair and wore a Van Dyke. Frame wise, I would say he was stocky.

My mom would have said burly, but she was back in New Jersey.

Every now and then while lecturing, he would lean back against the blackboard and press his right hand up against his left rib cage.

The gesture reminded me of Napoleon. I found it amusing.

Subject wise, Petty Officer Hobbs was competent and appeared to be knowledgeable but seemed more concerned with end of course evaluations than the actual subject matter. I will always cherish the puzzled look on his face as he read the comments I had scribbled down in the personal critique section near the bottom of the last page. It was rather lengthy and flowery and filled with words I barely knew the meanings of. No one knew it at the time, but I was delighted Petty Officer Napoleon had difficulty comprehending the subtle compliments I had given him.

Once school finished I received orders to report to my ship, but before doing so, I took leave to visit my family. True, the winter holiday season had come and gone but it didn't matter, I was going home. Once there, I tried to relax but I was nervous and apprehensive. I thought about calling Diane but I backed out at the last minute. My sister Ruth had spilled the beans. Diane had a new boyfriend. She wouldn't give me the particulars except to say he was studying to become a doctor.

Good for her.

My immediate family, along with my grandparents, relatives and friends were all fine. They had adjusted well to the separation although my mom appeared a bit tense. You know that protective look your mother gives you when she thinks something or someone may harm you; I was getting that look and the closer my departure day, the more anxious she became. After talking to my dad, I found out the cause for her anxiety. She was having difficulty coping with the unknown. I was about to enter an environment none of us knew anything about. There were no reference points to go by. True, my dad was ex-Navy, but he was stationed on an island and that was a long time ago. Her consternation was legitimate. My concern, however, was much different. I was focused on not screwing up once I got to my ship. Everyone knows first impressions mean everything. I wanted mine to be a good one.

The two weeks at home flew by quickly. I said my goodbyes posthaste and then it was off to Florida. My ship, the U.S.S. Baffles FF-1953 was pier side when I arrived. I remember nervously walking up the brow and waiting for an escort. Even though it was winter, sweat rolled down my back and down my legs. I was experiencing a minor panic attack because the bag containing my socks and underwear had somehow been diverted to another flight, and according to the airlines, would not arrive at my location for another forty eight hours!

Great! Just great!

My escort arrived. We shook hands and exchanged names before I followed him down two levels to berthing struggling with my bags the whole way. Once we reached our destination, Petty Officer Dyson pointed to the top right rack which was located next to the entrance. I realized this was probably the worst spot in the whole division and the nosiest, but it was mine just the same. With my rack assignment out of the way, my next task was to locate my locker. After a few minutes, I found it. Unfortunately, it was at least fifty feet away from where I was going to bed down. I unpacked quickly and put on the uniform of the day which was a dungaree shirt and pants. As I was changing, I looked around but didn't see anyone.

"Where is everybody?" I asked.

"Off the boat…you know…liberty call."

"What time is quarters?" I asked.

"We muster at 0800 on the forecastle. You're lucky, chow is in 15 minutes. The mess deck is straight down this corridor till you can't go straight anymore then make a left, can't miss it."

"Thanks."

"Revile is at 0600."

"Thanks."

Petty Officer Dyson exited berthing through a hatch directly above me. I think it took him to the main deck but I wasn't sure. I located the head, washed my hands and face then made my way to the mess deck. As I entered, all eyes shifted in my direction; I

20

felt as if I was being scanned. Neither a word nor smile came from any of the twenty or so sailors present. My initial guess was they were from the duty section. Almost immediately, I noticed a disparity in uniforms. Whereas my uniform was squeaky clean, their uniforms were not. They looked well seasoned and faded; I stood out like a sore thumb. I grabbed a tray and did like the others placing food where ever I could find space. I sat alone with my back to them, allowing their ricocheted stares to bounce off my head like misplaced hockey pucks. I quietly hoped it wouldn't last long, but then again, I was the new kid on the block. After chow, I watched television with a few who chose to remain behind. The TV was tucked away into one of the corners away from the serving area. I stayed there till 2100 then made my way topside to the fantail where two sailors were sitting. As was the case on the mess deck, the two kept their distance and avoided talking to me. After finishing my smoke, I went below and hit my rack.

The next morning, the quietness of sleep was shattered by revile and raucousness as members of the division spilled into berthing. Almost all of them had to change into the uniform of the day. The space around my locker became a bottle neck. Everyone and I mean everyone noticed me. Most just said good morning as they whisked by ; a few smiled and acknowledged with a head shake, but then a tall, skinny guy with a kool aid smile approached.

"Good Morning, I'm the LPO; my name is Peter Healy, welcome to the Baffles."

Peter extended his right hand and I extended mine.

 "I'm William Patterson from New Jersey."

"NEEEEEWWW JOIESSSYY!"

The fiat came from a khaki standing behind me. I turned around to face him.

21

"Another Damn Yankee!" he said smiling.

"Well, I'm Senior Chief Mark Robbins and I'm the head honcho around here. Go ahead, finish what you're doing and I'll talk to you after quarters, and by the way, welcome aboard. "

The Senior Chief exited berthing through a port side hatch which led to a long corridor.

"After a few days, once you get to know the guys, things will settle into place," said Peter.

"You know where the mess deck is?"

"Yes."

"Quarters is at 0800 on the forecastle, ok."

"Ok."

The leading petty officer disappeared through a labyrinth of rack curtains. I watched him navigate the maze until he was gone. Quickly I finished dressing then made my way to the mess deck. As soon as I got in the chow line, the shunning continued.

No one looked at me or spoke to me.

Fortunately, I recognized two guys from berthing who were five heads ahead of me.

I let out a sigh of relief.

I quickly filled my tray then hurried so I could sit opposite them. One of the guys happen to recognized me and we started talking.

At that moment, I was the happiest man alive!

I ate quickly then made my way to the forecastle. Since I was fifteen minutes early, I grabbed a smoke and was just about to flick it overboard when the rest of the division arrived. We lined up in two rows. Standing in front were Senior Chief Robbins, Leading Petty Officer Healey and our Division Officer, Ensign Carson, who began speaking.

"Before I get started, I want to introduce our newest shipmate, Petty Officer William Patterson who will be assisting Petty Officer Healey in maintaining the Nikason Acoustic Processor."

I swallowed hard; what luck, the senior Nikason tech was also the LPO! Right then and there I knew what had to be done. In order to impress him, I needed to keep the system operational at all times. I was looking forward to the challenge.

Senior Chief Robbins spoke next. His focus was on what needed to be accomplished that day. Petty Officer Healy followed up with neatness of uniforms and breaks. After that, Mr. Carson spoke again.

"Just want to let you know the Captain was very pleased with the results of the inspection last week." Everyone involved performed admirably."

The guys nodded a thank you. Once quarters concluded, I followed a third class petty officer to a compartment which housed the acoustic processor. It was one deck below the forecastle and three spaces aft. Within fifteen minutes, Petty Officer Healy arrived and immediately began to go over the maintenance requirements. I was given a "to do" list which outlined all the scheduled maintenance necessary to keep the Nikason operational. During that first week, the only time I left the space was to eat, sleep and stand watch; I was that excited!

Also, during that first week, I found out we were scheduled to deploy to Europe which meant I had a lot to learn in a short amount of time. Number one on my to do list was learning how to get around the ship. Now, moving around a vessel tied to a pier is one thing. You can compare it to walking through someone's house for the very first time. You're cautious because of the unfamiliarity. The same is true on board. However, getting around that same house when you're rolling from side to side or pitching up and down is something else. I lost track of all the black and blues and the number of times I had to catch myself during those first days at sea. I even managed to jam my left ear against a bulkhead rivet which required drainage and antibiotics.

Once I got the walking down, I concentrated on mastering the ladders. Actually, to be honest, moving up and down a vertical ladder is worse than walking through a ship. If you don't have your "sea legs" don't even try it, especially if you have to carry something that blocks your vision. How do you get your sea legs? Very simple. Walk the entire length of the ship holding a full cup of coffee. If you can do it without spilling a drop while you're out bouncing around the ocean you've got your legs!

However, as an added precaution, and especially in the beginning, count the number of rungs on the ladder before descending. This serves two purposes. One, it keeps you from toppling over and looking like an idiot, and two, proves to the crew you're ready to join the family! Oh! And there's one more thing I had to learn and it had nothing to do with ladders but everything to do with my recruiter. He told me to avoid the ball busters and boy did we have our share of those!

After two weeks, I was comfortable travelling through the main compartments. After a month I was confident enough to perform complex maintenance procedures unassisted. It was also right around this time I received a letter from my kid brother

Jimmy asking me questions about the ship. He wanted to know how it was laid out. I struggled at first trying to come up with the words to describe the Baffles. I didn't want to burden him with all the military terms because I knew it would be confusing.

One night it came to me.

I told him to think of the Baffles as a floating puzzle. If he could imagine that, then it would be easier to visualize the many compartments and spaces as merely pieces to the puzzle that had to be assembled correctly in order for the ship to work. I explained in my letter the Captain was the puzzle master and his job was to make sure all the pieces fit and worked together. The final ingredient was successfully dealing with all the personalities that contributed to the success of the mission. Without that, the puzzle would remain unfinished.

In ending my letter to my brother, I told him I was lucky having grown up on the streets on New Jersey. I pointed out living so close to New York City gave me the adroitness to think quickly on my feet. A key component necessary to be successful, not just in the Navy, but also in life.

Chapter 3

First Deployment:

1400 Hours

"NOW SET THE SEA AND ANCHOR DETAIL!"

A big booming voice resonated from the ship's intercom system.

I quickly hurried from sonar control to my sea and anchor station. I was assigned to Line 4 which is the after quarter spring located just aft of amidships. It was an important mooring line, but its thickness couldn't compete with the larger hawser lines. A second order to single up all lines came from the boatswain mate stationed on the fantail. He was the communication liaison between the various stations and the bridge. Those of us assigned to Line 4 were responsible for preventing forward surging. We accomplished this by coiling the line through steel bitts forming figure eight patterns.

Under normal conditions, Line 4 is looped several times to avert slippage. When the order came to single up, it took all of us assigned to keep the line in place. Camels and fenders were positioned to help protect the ship from the pier but the stern wind had stiffened making the water choppy. The normally docile camels reacted swiftly by pushing the ship away from the pier, adding strain to an already difficult situation. The other end of the line, the "eye" was secured to a steel bollard. A dock worker was assigned to remove the eye once the word was given.

The underway procedure was running smoothly, however, we were struggling to keep Line 4 in place. Honestly, we couldn't wait to let go!

"LET GO ALL LINES!"

The order came from an officer standing on the starboard bridge wing which was unusual. Normally, we get our marching orders from the "duty boats" on the fantail. Even though the line was slackened, the dock worker struggled lifting the eye off the bollard. It may have gotten heavier after absorbing salt spray and splash kicked up by the camels. Next to be lifted was the bow line followed by the stern line. The last umbilical connecting the Baffles to the pier was the forward spring line. Once the forward spring was lifted we heard the following:

"TAKE IN ALL LINES!"

The order was given! Those of us assigned to line stations began pulling mooring lines up through designated chocks. The goal, of course, was to keep the lines as dry as possible. Granted, the eye is expected to get wet, but an experienced sailor knows handling wet mooring lines can be both difficult and dangerous. Once the tangled coils had returned home, they were transformed into beautifully flemished works of art. A welcomed addition to any deck!

"UNDERWAY…SHIFT COLORS!"

The flagstaff ensign was lowered; the gaff ensign raised.

The U.S.S. Baffles was underway!

Once we secured from sea and anchor, I walked forward along the starboard weather deck until I came to a ladder. After climbing to the next level, I continued walking forward until I hit another ladder, but before ascending, I stopped to look up at good Captain Stewart. He was standing on the starboard bridge wing waving his arms and shouting orders to someone below on the forecastle. For a second, I thought he was the one who gave the order to let go all lines, but I was mistaken. It was The Officer of the Deck. Anyway, I couldn't quite make out what the Captain was saying. The wind had

27

picked up to where it was hallowing past my eardrums so I climbed up one more deck which put me on the 0-3 level. The highest part of the ship!

"Freedom!" was the only word that came to mind.

As I looked around, I was surprised to find just the duty signalman on station. I thought the view and the solitude would have attracted a larger audience. According to Kenny, the signalman on duty, the 0-3 level was the least traveled area of the ship which didn't make any sense. It was the perfect spot to get away from all the noise and commotion and since privacy on board is a premium, you would think it would have been packed.

Anyway, besides the solitude and freedom, the 0-3 level was home to a huge pair of binoculars the crew affectionately referred to as "Big Eyes." It was primarily used to identify objects and shoot bearings, but it was also great for star gazing! A passion of mine I will explain in greater detail later on.

So, there I was, strolling around the signal deck taking in the view when a dark shadow in the shape of a cross appeared at my feet. I looked up and hovering above me was a large white albatross. Its wings were motionless as it swayed like a pendulum moving from port to starboard and back again. Every now and then it would rise up to a height of fifty or sixty feet then quickly descend. I marveled as this exquisite, aerodynamically superior creature moved about. During one descent, it flew so close I was able to discern a small black diamond on its chest. Had I been a hunter it would have been the perfect target. Suddenly, the bird positioned itself directly in front of me. It moved neither left nor right. It just hovered motionless, like I was looking at a postcard. And then something strange happened. For a split second our eyes locked on to each other. I must admit I was startled by the exchange. The bird had the blackest eyes I have ever seen. They were lifeless and still; like looking into a black hole.

Lord knows what he thought about me!

After exchanging glances, the albatross tilted its head towards the ocean. I believe the gesture was an invitation for a look see. My curiosity heightened, I leaned over to look at the water line. Swimming in the bow wake were three dolphins. Normally, this happens out at sea but here they were just outside the harbor. The three dolphins moved from side to side and sometimes they would bump each other as they jockeyed for position. Gliding just above them was the albatross. After several minutes, the bird lost interest and flew away. Apparently, the dolphins were playing and not fishing.

No meal to be had here.

After a few minutes the bird reappeared briefly only to rise up and disappear into low flying clouds which had snuck up from the west. The dolphins, following the bird's cue, swam away from the ship. Soon they were no longer visible. The green blue waters of Florida provided the perfect camouflage as they made their departure. My mind though, was still focused on the bird. I hoped it would reappear, but even if it didn't, no big deal. The bow dolphins were the real stars. They were considered a good omen and good omens are what sailors live for.

Soon, the diminishing land mass known as Florida disappeared. Not even Big Eyes with its powerful focus could find it. Also, it was around this time the calm tranquil waters of home had turned dark and foreboding. Scuttlebutt had it we were to steam into the Caribbean to test out new equipment before heading across the Atlantic. I thought the areas surrounding Bermuda or the Bahamas might be chosen. After all, they were within arm's reach and had we the opportunity to go ashore, had plenty of things to do and see. Unfortunately, they weren't on the itinerary.

Our orders stated we were to move as quickly as possible from where we were to where we had to go.

Talk about specifics!

Chapter 4

The Caribbean

Tranquil waters! Islands of enchantment! Fortresses! Cannons bursting with fire! Ocean's red with blood! Sharks! Rum! Women as sweet as mangoes! Buried treasure! Pirates! Davey Jones!

And…and…I was letting my imagination get the better of me.

I couldn't help it though, all those pirate movies I saw as a kid. To me the Caribbean was synonymous with adventure; the words were interchangeable! I was hoping we would get the chance to explore some of the islands we were passing, but I tempered my enthusiasm with caution.

No use getting excited over something that might not happen.

My first day underway was fortuities; I didn't have to stand watch at all. Rather than spend time inside the ship, I returned to the signal bridge. As usual, the panoramic view was breathtaking. A distant merchant, travelling perpendicular to us, appeared as a black speck on the horizon. Above, an empty blue canvass transformed into a beautiful easel in search of a master artist. Feeling somewhat adventurous, I imagined I was a famous painter commissioned to create a beautiful work of art. The inspiration would be love, but how does one paint love? I began by sketching the faces of those dearest to me. My grandparents, I would place in the top corners. My two siblings, Jimmy and

31

Ruth, the bottom corners. In the middle would be my parents. Mom to the right, dad to

the left. I closed my eyes to savor the moment. For the first time in my live I felt alone,

completely alone. The separation was taking its toll. When I opened my eyes again, the

image was gone. I stood there trying to recreate my masterpiece but I couldn't. The

inspiration had passed. It was around this time when I noticed something odd about the

wind. Besides strengthening in intensity, it tasted somewhat salty.

Scented gusts of sea spray descended upon me like snowflakes.

It wasn't long before I was saturated in its aroma. Encouraged by this strange

sense of awareness, I directed my curiosity towards the proprietary sounds of the

engines. The strengthening wind had masked their normal signature, resulting in subtle

discrepancies in the vibrations I had become accustomed too. I breathed deeply to clear

my head but the unfamiliar balm made me nauseous.

Something wasn't right.

The exclusive odors unique to the Baffles were gone. In its place, an

unrecognizable stench so foul I nearly vomited. Within seconds, I was engulfed in a

whirlwind. Had I not shifted my weight and grabbed a life line, I would have been swept

overboard. The wind pushed and swirled with such intensity, I was forced to lay on my

stomach. Even my ball cap wasn't immune. Had it not be firmly positioned would have

blown overboard. The surge came from the west just as the setting sun was inches above

the horizon. The "rogue wind" departed just as quickly as it arrived.

Afterwards, I spoke to one of the more seasoned squids on board, but even he couldn't explain the phenomenon. It was a sobering moment, one which coalesced in my mind. From that moment on, I never took the ocean for granted. I was lucky and grateful. No need to tempt fate a second time.

Sorry Davey! Your guided locker tour, the tour that awaits all sailors, will have to wait another day!!!

Not long afterwards, the ship regained its composure and life returned to normal. One evening, after standing my sonar watch, I decided to revisit the signal bridge but I had difficulty moving about. I needed several minutes to adjust to the darkness before venturing aloft. Once I arrived on station, my normal field of vision was reduced to twenty feet. The forecastle and the fantail were invisible to me. As I stood there in total darkness a chilling thought overcame me.

If someone were to fall overboard they would never be seen again. Now you know why cruise ships are lit up like Christmas trees!

Regarding the Sons of Lenin.

On occasion, we had the opportunity to cross paths with members of the Soviet Navy. During daylight hours, both the Soviets and the Americans concentrated their energies on completing the proprietary duties specific to each.

In other words, we left each other alone.

However, once the sun went down that's when things got interesting. Without delving into loquacious detail, let me sum it up this way.

33

Think of a giant game of tag played by aggressive alpha males.

Eventually someone wants to be top dog. That pretty much describes our relationship. I will say this though, on two occasions, I had the opportunity to see the Russian sailors up close, and both times they gestured for the same items. A bunch of them would gather on the forecastle or fantail and lean over their life lines as far as possible.

 Honestly, I don't know how they didn't end up in the drink!

Anyway, they would flick their thumbs in the air lighting imaginary cigarettes. Others would lift their berets off their heads in hopes of making exchanges. They always seemed interested in collecting things American.

I wonder why?

Anyhow, even though the "game" had the potential to get out of hand, I believe both our Navies benefited from the encounters. I'm sure the Kremlin and Washington had official names for these exchanges. I'm also confident opinions varied regarding the usefulness of these exercises. Nonetheless, regardless of the outcome, I always thought it was a step in the right direction.

Cold War 101 at its finest.

Oh, and before I forget, I like to mention two benefits while steaming in total darkness. First, you get to witness the miracle of bioluminescence. Imagine millions of luciferins forming protective glow rings around your ship. Most of the time they appear green but on occasion can be other colors as well. Some of the old timer's referred to them as "floating rainbows". Whatever they're called, I felt it reassuring that our mission and vessel were important enough to garner the attention of these tiny little creatures, even if it was just for a moment.

The other benefit, the one I really care about was star gazing! I don't think there's a planetarium anywhere that can compare to the oceans night sky! Before deploying, I purchased an astronomy book but found it difficult to comprehend. What were especially challenging were the star patterns. I couldn't connect the dots to form any figures. Fortunately, I befriended a quartermaster who was more than happy to give me a few pointers.

We started with one of the biggest and most recognizable star patterns available, the Orion constellation, and I remember it vividly. It was during the 0400 to 0800 watch when he called down to sonar control from the bridge and asked to speak to me. When I got on the horn, the only thing he said was "Orion is up on the port side" and hung up. That was my cue! I immediately requested permission to use the head.

Once outside the compartment, I made a bee line to the closest weather deck and, after stepping outside, looked directly up at the night sky. I was amazed at what I saw. Everything was crystal clear. There were no clouds or moon, just beautiful stars. The first thing that caught my eye was the planet Jupiter because of its brightness. It moved across the night sky like a lonely rider on an ecliptic roller coaster. Next came the constellations. I scanned the port side but I didn't see Orion. He was nowhere to be found!

The book figure had Orion standing straight up like a normal person but this was not the case. I was about to return to sonar control and call my friend back when, by accident, I happened to stumble across three stars in close proximity to each other. I believed I was looking at Orion's Belt but I wasn't sure. What threw me off was the position of the stars. Instead of pointing from left to right horizontally, they pointed from top to bottom vertically.

Then it dawned on me!

Orion wasn't standing up at all; he was lying on his back and staring at the ceiling! No wonder I couldn't find him! Honestly, he looked nothing like the figure on page 119 in my book but it didn't matter! I was ecstatic! Worse than a kid in a candy store! I remember the moment distinctly because that was the first time I was able to correctly identify a major constellation. Orion had become my Rosetta stone. It now holds a special place on my galactic key ring. The following day the ocean took on new life. The tiresome pitching which had plagued us since the Caribbean was replaced with side to side rolling. Moving about the ship reminded me of the barrel roll we used to enjoy as kids. I didn't know it at the time, but I would sleep a lot better. I had just finished standing the 1600 to 2000 watch and instead of going topside which was customary, I decided to hit my rack and catch up on some reading. Even though I wasn't tired, before long my eyes began to close. I hadn't noticed it, but the gentle rolling began to drain me of my energy. Before long, my concentration dissipated. I put my book away and turned off my night light. As I lay there under my blanket, my body began to move to the motion of the ship. The gentle rocking brought back childhood memories. I thought of the walnut crib I once called home, and how my mom would rock it back and forth until I fell asleep. On board the Baffles, Mother Nature was matron to us all. Just before dozing off, I wondered how many of my shipmates felt the same way.

More importantly, how many were willing to talk about it.

Chapter 5

Europe

It was mid afternoon when the crew got the word. The voice over the intercom said we were transiting the Pillars of Hercules. The news could only mean one thing.

No more Atlantic Ocean!

The Straits of Gibraltar signaled the end to our open ocean transit. Awaiting the transition from rough water to calm sea was the wonderful Mediterrean. She would lay a path to our first port of call.

As soon as we were parallel to the Gibraltar coastline, I changed into a clean uniform and hurried to the fantail to wave to the local populace who obviously were gathering on the shore line hoping to exchange pleasantries. But when I opened a weather hatch for a look see, I saw nothing but water. No towns! No people and no buildings! Confused and somewhat disappointed, I flagged down Senior Chief Chesterfield from engineering. He had just tossed his cigarette overboard and was getting ready to go below when I approached him.

"Senior Chief."

"Patterson."

"A quick question."

"How can I help you?"

"Are we transiting the Straits?"

"Yep, right smack in the middle by now."

"Then how come I don't see anything? Where is everybody?"

A smile formed on his tan, cracked face, withered down from years of salt spray and engine oil.

"Oh, I wouldn't say anything. There are lots of seagulls flying about and if you look closely, you might be able to spot a harbor seal or two."

"But where are the buildings?"

"Patterson, we're maybe ten miles off the coast. What did you expect to see?"

I felt like an idiot.

Senior Chief Chesterfield just stood there for a moment shaking his head. Soon after he opened a hatch and disappeared inside the ship.

As his words sunk in, so did the reality of the moment. I couldn't help but notice I was the only one on the fantail. Nobody else was that dumb.

I wanted to go below as quickly as possible. I didn't want anyone to see me walking around in a clean uniform. Just as I was about to open a hatch, a dark shadow shaped like a black cross appeared at my feet. At first I thought it was a sea gull, but its massive wing span suggested something else. I turned around to look at it.

Just above the rooster tail, a majestic white albatross hovered motionlessly. It looked frozen as it glided above the water turbulence.

I moved in closer for a better look. Embedded in the center of its chest was a small black diamond.

Could it be the same bird?

Not likely, we were thousands of miles away from our home port. Besides, finding an albatross in the North Atlantic is very rare. Still, there was something familiar about the bird. Slowly it moved forward and away from the rooster tail positioning itself just a few feet above my head.

And then, all of a sudden like, it lowered its head and turned slightly to the right, gesturing me to follow. As before, I leaned over the side to look at the water but I didn't see anything. I concentrated on a spot close to the ship and then from nowhere, a dark shadow appeared on the starboard side followed by another. Dolphins! Two large dolphins raced past me as they made their way to the starboard bow wave.

I turned around to look at the bird and then I knew.

Not so much from the color of its eyes, but in the way it looked at me. It recognized me! Don't ask me how, but apparently we were friends. But how was that possible?

Time for a reality check.

Ok, it appears to be the same bird but why would it follow the Baffles across the Atlantic? For what purpose? Did it really recognize me, or, was it just wishful thinking on my part?

I raised my hand and waved at my new friend. Not knowing how to respond, it rose slightly increasing the distance between us. Shortly after, it circled the ship three times before returning to the fantail, and just as quickly as it appeared, it ascended once again into low flying clouds. I decided to give it a name, from now on I would refer to it as "Sun Rise" not because of the time of day, but rather how it departed, always ascending rather than flying away. As if the sun had opened up and swallowed it.

Thrice around the ship. A good omen.

As we drew nearer to our destination, marvelous architecture began to appear on the shore line. It was aged and classical but also elegant. Yes, the buildings were splendid, but my mind was focused on something else. I was thinking of a scotch on the rocks followed by a beer chaser. One of the nicest things about Europe was their liberal drinking age. Yes, I was looking forward to strengthening the bond between us. I intended to make the most out of their wonderful hospitality. It was late afternoon before we were pier side, and early evening before we were allowed to exit the ship. The brow was set up just forward of the quarter deck in order to accommodate the heavy traffic which was to follow. Once I was officially off the ship, and after taking a few steps I did something I have never done before.

I fell down.

That's right, you heard me. I feel down not once, not twice, but three times. Frustrated, I just sat there.

41

"Patterson! It's your sea legs! Ya got to get rid of your sea legs!

The outburst came from Chief Boatswain's Mate Stanley Morris who hailed from Detroit.

"Get up now; remember you represent the US of A!"

Carefully, I rose to my feet and steadied myself. Once I felt comfortable, I took two baby steps and stopped.

"What the hell is happening to me?"

"It's your land legs! You don't have your land legs yet! It takes a little time to adjust" and with that, Chief Morris walked down the pier and out of sight as straight as an arrow which only added to my misery. I stood there like a statue for five minutes. My head wasn't spinning, but I definitely felt off balance. Someone not familiar with this phenomenon would say I was drunk. The experts say it has something to do with the fluid in the inner ear. I don't know the medical term but I do know this. I've never been more embarrassed in my life. Anyway, I soon recovered and was off on my very first adventure. Now, regarding liberty, a brief history lesson.

Back in the day, the sailors of old had a simple recipe for fun. The key ingredients were wind, water, whiskey and women. Today's technology has changed all that. Modern sailors seem to derive a great deal of pleasure from the gadgets they hold in their hands.

Fortunately, I happen to be old fashioned. What was good enough for my grandfather is good enough for me!

Welcome to the Patterson Love Potion!

To begin with, enough with the wind and water! Been there, done that! My cocktail is much simpler. Pour alcohol, food and music into a blender and let the machine run for sixty seconds to smooth out any rough spots. Add a woman to the mix and voila! Mission accomplished! Pretty simple right? That's what I thought. Nothing could have been further from the truth!

Here's what Euro 1 taught me which was reinforced time and time again.

No matter the country, no matter the port of call, harbor chicks run the show. To begin with, these lovely young ladies are well schooled in the art of persuasion. They are experts at understanding and detecting the wants and needs of sailors the world over. Not only do they exude confidence and knowledge as they go about their business. In matters of the heart, they are infinitely more organized and experienced than most men will ever be. These women have honed their skills for one purpose: to separate you from our money. Foolishly, sailors believe otherwise. They think the little darlings are only interested in the one eyed trolls that grow inside our trousers but they are mistaken. It has nothing to do with sex, but everything to do with economics.

And we make it easy for them. We arrive as lambs ready for the slaughter. It's simple mathematics. The more time at sea, the lonelier the sailor. I like to think of them as human barometers. We bring the pressure; they operate the relief valves. It isn't any more complicated than that.

Yes, these modern day Sirens are world champions at what they do!

Euro 1 exposed my naiveté and it would be many ports of call in many countries before I could even hope to deal with these women on their level.

Now, if you're lucky enough to survive the Sirens, be wary of the cab drivers! Before you get into the back seat, make note of the landscape and remember street names. Cabbie's the world over are notorious for circling the same block over and over again.

Also, and this is very important, when you enter a club and women are sitting by themselves either at the bar or around tables near the bar, the yellow flag of caution needs to be raised. These young ladies work for the club and their job is to get you to buy them drinks.

I'll use myself as an example.

I like to drink scotch. The female employee will either match my drink in price or order something more expensive. You're thinking if I get her drunk, she'll be an easy score, so you spend the rest of the night buying drinks for two except she's drinking colored water. By the time you're ready to hop in bed, "escorts" will show you to the door, and if you put up a struggle you could either end up in the custody of shore patrol or worse. Bottom line: You see a group of women sitting by themselves, just keep on walking. Having been to thirty two countries and eighteen islands, I've come up with a five point survival guide for sailors the world over.

Rule Number One:

Keep your military I.D. in your left front pocket. Keep twenty dollars in your right front pocket. The rest of your money rubber band it around your ankle, or, if you have the room and you're a smoker, roll it up and put it inside your cigarette pack and then secure it to your ankle. Never carry a wallet or credit cards. Pay cash for everything.

Rule Number Two:

Never leave your drink unattended. Someone could slip you a Mickey and once you're unconscious, you can kiss your money, jewelry, military I.D. and even your clothes goodbye.

Rule Number Three:

If you decide to pick up a chick, make sure she's a chick. Nowadays, it's very difficult to tell; if you're not sure, just walk away.

Rule Number Four:

Never go back to her place. Why you ask? Many a sailor has gone back to "her" place only to find three or four guys waiting to jump you. You could end up dead.

Rule Number five:

And this is probably the most important. I believe the poorer the country, the more systemic the corruption. People in positions of authority will use that power to take advantage of you.

I'm talking about the local police.

Don't give them any excuses to arrest you. If you think you've been ripped off, you're probably right, but complaining about it only makes it worse. Many times these cops receive kick backs from the local vendors. Trying to get your money back is pointless. Complain too much and you could end up in prison, and that my friend's is a fate worse than death.

Rule of thumb:

If you feel you've been ripped off, make note of the place and leave. Spread the word that it's "sailor unfriendly" and watch how fast they change their tune once their piggy bank is empty.

But I digress.

I left the harbor area and walked about twenty minutes until I discovered a very nice little restaurant tucked away on a poorly lit narrow street. It had a brick facade but its entrance way was made of either marble or granite. It wasn't crowded at all, so I entered the restaurant and took a seat at a small round table which faced the street. I looked around and didn't see anyone from my ship which was a God's send.

Don't get me wrong, I would die for anyone of my shipmates, but, when I'm on a search and destroy mission, leave me the hell alone!

When my food arrived, I couldn't help but notice on the far side of the restaurant, a pretty blond was sitting by herself. Since this was such an out of the way restaurant, I naturally thought she was the owner's daughter or perhaps a waitress on break since it wasn't that busy. I smiled at her and she smiled back.

Again, I didn't think much of it.

After a few minutes, she got up and walked over to my table which I thought was a little odd. She couldn't speak English so I hand gestured as best as I could. I motioned for her to sit down and offered to buy her dinner. I could tell from her mannerisms she was grateful but because of the language barrier, we just smiled at each other. I was hungry and not really in the mood for conversation anyway. I offered her dessert but she gestured no by shaking her head. After dinner, we left the restaurant together and walked for about thirty minutes with my arm around her shoulder and her arm around my waist. It felt so good to feel a woman's body next to mine. However, whenever someone passed, she would bury her head into my chest and look away as if she were hiding something. We walked for a little while longer until we came to a hotel and that's when it hit me.

Siren!

I was completely taken by surprise! I thought these girls only worked the dock areas. I was mistaken. Apparently, this young lady had staked out her own territory. Who would have thought? As we approached the front door to the hotel, she made a gesture to go inside. Once inside, she walked over to the hotel clerk who recognized her. He called her by her first name which was Gina. He handed her the key to our room and I handed him the money. A small, narrow wooden stairwell awaited us. She went first and as she climbed up the old creaky stair case, her tight skirt lifted to the rhythm of her cadence. My face, just inches away, melted from the fragrance emanating from her lovely perfumed thighs. When she opened the door she walked over to the bed and sat down.

Rule Number 4 was about to be violated.

She raised four fingers which needed no translation. Forty dollars. I nodded yes, at his point, how could I say no. After we finished, I gestured I wanted to go again. She smiled and raised four more fingers. I rolled over and started laughing. No way was I going to spend another forty bucks!

I was about to get up and get dressed when the Siren reached for my right hand and placed it on her firm round breast. As I began to caress her nipple the world and all its problems quietly disappeared.

47

Chapter 6

The Capitol

I don't remember much about the trip. What stands out was the fancy white bus waiting for us by the harbor entrance. Arrangements had been made to visit the Capitol. Even though it was a four hour drive, I jumped at the opportunity to go. Our Executive Officer, Mr. Calvin, was in charge of the operation which struck me as somewhat odd since he wasn't the outgoing type. He was rigid and unfriendly and the wire glasses he wore went out of style twenty years ago. Frame wise he was small and just recently he began showing signs of a belly. His receding hair line made him look much older than he was and the small bald spot he had at the beginning of the cruise had grown significantly.

As I look back now, it was easy to criticize him. What I didn't understand was the amount of aloofness necessary to carry out his duties as second in command. I guess he did what he had to do in order to get the job done. I just pitied the next group of guys who had to deal with him. Getting back to the trip, the ride itself was relatively quick. It's amazing how fast four hours can pass by when women outnumber the trees. Every marketplace we passed boasted of exquisite beauties and the closer we got to the Capitol, the better looking they became.

Unfortunately, we could only touch them with our eyeballs.

Our bus was travelling way too fast to have a conversation with anyone. I did see a speed sign every now and then but they were very confusing. They all had multi-colored arrows pointing in different directions.

When I thought we needed to slow down, the bus went faster and vice versa. A couple of guys whose parents emigrated from here were very comfortable speaking the language. In fact, one of them offered to teach us some useful phrases but the offer came with a price.

The old one hand washes the other idiom.

His proposal?

If you were willing to stand his watches, he would turn into your personal Rosetta stone. To seal the deal, he even promised to get you laid for free. Now that's something to think about.

Funny isn't it, how it always boils down to women!

When we finally arrived at our destination, we were greeted by a short, stout, middle-aged woman with dark curly hair and thick gray glasses. She was dressed in black and draped across her shoulder was a long gray scarf. In another time and age I would have said toga. We exited the bus and quickly formed a circle around her. She greeted us with smiles and handshakes. She was about to say something to the group when she suddenly pulled back. I noticed her face became flushed. Personally, I think she was a little overwhelmed.

I don't think she's ever been in the presence of so much testosterone before. Talk about a virile audience! Slowly, she regained her composure. Once fully recovered, she began to stare at our faces one by one as if she was looking for something.

At first I thought it might be someone who either had an interest or knowledge of art, but as she continued to scan, it was obvious she was looking for something else.

In New Jersey we call them" light bulbs."

You know, people who have the ability to absorb and appreciate the finer things in life. This is what Miss Sophia was looking for. Someone capable of being more than just a walking penis.

A Renaissance Man.

Within seconds she began.

"My name is Miss Sophia and I would appreciate it if you would address me as Miss Sophia and not SO-PEE-YA, OR SOAP-EE OR SO-PIE-YA!

Her voice elevated slightly emphasizing the syllables.

Miss Sophia was to be our "culture guide" at the museum we were about to enter.

Not quite the entertainment we had in mind.

Our fancy white bus had made it into the heart of the city. The area we were in was called the culture zone and for good reason. Everywhere we looked we were surrounded by beautiful buildings. The museum itself was beyond description. On either side of the entrance way stood four ionic columns. Their aesthetic beauty reflected the very best in Greco-Roman design. Topping off the Corinthian capitals were ornate volutes of such detail, I thought they were chiseled by Michelangelo himself. Breathtaking is the word that comes to mind. Anything less would do them a disservice. Personally, I just wanted to drink a cold beer. It was hotter than hell and after four hours on that bus, the last thing I wanted to do was tour a museum.

I was in luck.

Across the street was an outdoor café which featured one of the largest bars I have ever seen. I counted twelve beer taps which must be some kind of a record! Playing softly

50

from four huge speakers was danceable music which must attract a sizeable crowd once the sun goes down.

Alcohol, food and music! The three main ingredients!

I thought about sneaking away, but before I could come up with a game plan, Miss Sophia began her lecture. She moved away from the circle stopping just a few feet from the entrance. Standing slightly behind her was Mr. Calvin who took on the role of terminator. His arms were folded across his chest and he wasn't smiling. Every so often, he would move his head from side to side as if he was looking for something.

I don't think he heard a word she said.

At first I didn't catch on but then it hit me. He was conducting a continuous head count. He knew the bar was across the street and most of us wanted to be there. Honestly, there wasn't a snowballs chance in hell I was slipping away.

Miss Sophia began her oration by describing the history of the building. Yes, you heard correctly. The history of the building, beginning with site location, drawing plans, builders, masons and so on and so forth. I must admit I was impressed. She really knew her stuff.

As I was listening, I wondered if she was a college professor and the museum job was extra spending money. Obviously, she was well educated and her posture, the way she carried herself, suggested she had either been born into wealth or had grown up around it. Perhaps she was recently widowed or divorced and had to rely on herself for financial support. Maybe she needed the money to pay for someone's education, a grandchild perhaps? Whatever her reasons, she was truly a Renaissance woman and I for one was grateful for the information.

But I'm drifting.

Outside in that hot sun, I couldn't help but notice how many groups of women were either exiting or entering the museum. As informative as Miss Sophia was, her words just couldn't compete with the birds and the bees. I almost popped a neck muscle keeping score. As soon as one group departed, another arrived to take its place. It was like standing outside the ladies room. The museum had turned into a sorority house!

Besides the neck muscles, my blood pressure must have been off the chart. True, the girls came in all shapes and sizes, but the one thing they shared was the amount of anatomy on display. Naturally, I attributed it to the heat, but, when a tourist sauntered by with similar exposure, other thoughts entered my mind.

Remember, we were young and in great shape. It didn't take much to distract us. Poor Miss Sophia.

All that wonderful knowledge about to go to waste!

Actually, we stood out like sore thumbs. I looked around to see if we had any competition. We didn't. We were the only group of men there. I'm sure we must have looked strange to the locals. Maybe they thought we were priests in training or something like that. Whatever their perception, being unique does have its rewards. Since we were the only game in town, it wasn't long before the girls came around. I don't think I've ever winked so much in my life. Exchanging glances became a full time occupation.

And then I noticed something unusual.

Every now and then, a girl would fake a faint. Yea, you heard correctly. Fake a faint. It's difficult to describe but I'll give it a go. The fainting girl, overcome with emotion, falls backwards into the arms of her friends. This ritual is repeated a couple of times before she is able to recover. I guess it's their way of expressing interest. Now, just because they faint, it doesn't mean they're ready to hop into bed. Far from it. It's simply a display of emotion, a signal if you will, letting you know they are approachable for conversation.

Unfortunately, the fainting didn't go unnoticed.

Whenever our attention strayed, Miss Sophia would simply stop talking until she was certain she had regained our focus. This happened multiple times. I believe we confirmed her worse fears. There was nothing Renaissance about us; we were walking penises and nothing more. I gotta tell you, the woman had the patience of a saint. She just stood there, expressionless, like a statue. It reminded me of elementary school. Mr. Calvin, on the other hand, reacted quite differently. His glare said it all. As soon as she finished being perspicacious we entered the museum. Remarkably, Miss Sophia continued to dazzle us with her knowledge. Minute details she found fascinating were thoroughly explained. What I marveled the most about her was her demeanor.

Not once did she look at the objects she was lecturing about.

She would simply raise her right hand and extended a finger in the direction of her lecture. It was as if she had the entire layout impressed into her memory.

Amazed, I wondered how many times she had orbited this private universe of hers. One thing I did pick up on, she always seemed excited. Like a kid in a candy store. Personally, I would have been bored to death, but not her. She treated each and every tour like it was her first.

Thirty minutes later, we had come full circle. We thanked Miss Sophia for the tour and she thanked us for being attentive. Believe me, she was being kind. Strangely, we exited the museum from opposite directions.

Once outside, we were told to report back to the bus depot by 1900 by one of the junior officers. It was close to 1600 hours so we decided to go to the outdoor café. Much to our surprise, the eatery was owned by a retired Canadian school teacher who was more than happy to have a conversation in English. His name was Richard but he preferred to go by Richie. Once we got to know each other, he said it was unfortunate we had to leave so soon. There were many historical landmarks just waiting to be explored. We were polite and didn't interrupt him as he made mention of the many buildings worth exploring as well as other points of interest the city had to offer.

After we had something to eat, about half our party began twitching for some female companionship. The sorority house had taken its toll.

Richie pointed them in the right direction and off they went. They were reminded though about the 1900 curfew.

Another bunch needed photos for the family scrap book so they took off sightseeing. As for me, I was happy where I was. I was out of the sun and the afternoon wind had kicked up enough to cool things down. I was enjoying my conversation with Richie and after my third drink, he bought me a round. The beer tasted a little flat but it was ice cold and that's all that mattered. Soon the soreness in my neck disappeared. Besides the beer, the other nice thing was the soft music. The locals hadn't arrived yet, so there was no need to crank up the volume. Yes, I was quite content where I was. There was absolutely no reason to go anywhere else. Oh, and I almost forgot. Our fancy white bus was just down the street. I could crawl to it if I had too.

Perfect!

Chapter 7

Euro 2

The following morning we said our goodbyes to Euro 1 and headed back out into the big beautiful Mediterrean. Our next destination was a country two days away. I say two days because new orders and course changes could always turn that time table upside down. When it comes to ship's movement, I learned early on to always expect the unexpected. Even though we had just arrived in Europe, it was beginning to look more and more like we were on a goodwill tour. Spend a few days here and then a few days there and so on and so forth. Mind you, I'm not complaining. Just the opposite. I was able to visit country after country and the best part was I was being paid to do so.

Show me a travel agent who can top that!

As to the visits, they accomplished two things. They reassured our allies and they made the bad guys think twice about harming our friends. Reassurance and protection. Actually, you can boil it down to one word.

Babysitting.

Imagine you have children attending school in a foreign country. As responsible parents, you make it a point to check on them at regular intervals. You do this for two reasons. First, to make sure all is well and second, to resolve any issues that may come up. It was no different here!

Countries can be bullied. Some are able to resolve it on their own but others can't and that's where we come in. Our mission is straight forward. Cut the strings of despotism whenever they unfold.

But I'm getting too political.

Rumor had it the skipper hated these little pit stops. Liberty call was one thing, but having to submit to the shackles of political correctness time and time again pushed his patience. Being a good will ambassador is important. It's to be expected. It comes with the job. However, political correctness should be left to the politicians. It's what they do. It's what defines them. One time I heard from a chief who had served with the skipper long before he was assigned to the Baffles. He said the skipper told him that given the choice of attending an official function or chasing Russian submarines, he would rather chase the submarines. Once we entered the harbor channel preparations were made for a safe mooring.

Unfortunately, the cool, dry breeze which had accompanied us during our two day transit was gone. In its place was a puff of wind so stale and weak it couldn't even blow out a match. I was already sweating just standing at my station. As we neared the port, I was able to make out faint sounds emanating from the markets stretched along the length of the break water.

Drawing closer, people began to appear from their stores and shops and I noticed right away their comportment was quite different. For some strange reason or custom, they, being the men, accentuated the end of their conversations by gesticulating with their hands. They would bring them together as if they were preparing to scoop up water from a basin. It was most unusual, but I had seen that gesture many times before growing up. Whatever concerns I may have had regarding Euro 2 were quickly dispelled. I had been to this country before, I spoke the language and my mother was born here.

56

Sensing this skill would prove advantageous, I informed Senior Chief Robbins. Although somewhat surprised, he asked if I wouldn't mind serving as the skipper's translator if need be, to which I responded in the affirmative. Well, not twenty minutes had passed when I get a call from my division officer, Ensign Carson, informing me to get cleaned up and report to the Captain's cabin in civilian clothes by 1800 hours. I was supposed to stand watch on the quarterdeck at 2000 but my name was scratched off and penciled in my place was Petty Officer 3rd class Gary Ribbel of Ohio. Needless to say, he was not a happy camper but I knew how to cheer him up. I told him I would stand his morning watch once I secured from my special detail.

I waited until it was exactly 1800 hours before knocking on the cabin door.

"Patterson is that you?"

"Yes Sir."

"I'll meet you on the Quarter Deck in 15 minutes."

"Yes Sir".

The Captain arrived at the Quarter Deck on time, but looked like he was getting ready to go to a Hawaiian Lu ow! He was wearing a long sleeve purple shirt complete with two large orange dolphins appearing underneath each armpit. Contrasting the purple shirt were bright yellow shorts, a red belt and covering his feet were torn brown sandals held together with super glue!

Needless to say, he looked ridiculous, which was rather curious since we were constantly being told to blend in and not contrast with the local populace. It seems the Captain had violated his own edict, or, perhaps it was something else. Like I said, the skipper hated official functions. Maybe the mismatched clothes were a subtle sign of rebellion. Who knows?

For one brief moment, I thought about telling him how out of place he looked, but the little voice inside me said no. He was the Captain and the Captain wears whatever the hell he feels like wearing!

End of conversation!

"The people I'm having dinner with speak English, or so I've been told, but I want you around just in case they switch to their language—understand?"

"Yes, Sir."

We left the quarterdeck and this time I made sure I had my land legs well established before departing the brow. I thought we would be taking a cab but a private car complete with a tuxedoed driver waited for us just outside the gate. We both sat in the back seat.

Talk about the odd couple.

There I was in my dress whites sitting next to Captain Lu ow from Hawaii! A photograph would have been priceless.

We travelled in our chauffeured driven vehicle for about twenty minutes before turning off the main road and into a residential area. I had spent the entire journey looking for familiar landmarks, but I didn't see any. Even though I had been to Euro 2 twice before, we were in a different part of the city. Nothing was familiar.

I was as lost as I could be.

I also have to tell you I was rather nervous at this point. Yes, I spoke the language but I was concerned that it might not be good enough to fully understand everything being said. What if I made a mistake?

What if I didn't understand all of the latest jokes or slang words?

As we entered a well to do neighborhood, our chauffeur pulled up to an intersection comprised of four cul-de-sacs, or at least that was what the gold lettered sign indicated. The two storied houses surrounding us were large, as were the manicured lawns before us. Across the street, a couple of well dressed children played catch ball with their nanny as the setting sun dipped below the western sky. Wondrous smells filled my senses as families gathered together to partake in evening meals.

The chauffeur led the way up a marbled staircase to a veranda populated with people, music and food.

A party perhaps?

A man about the same age as the Captain appeared in the door well and from his demeanor looked military. His hair was well groomed and high off his ears. His frame was muscular and he was trim.

"Mike, is that you?"

Captain Stewart answered in the affirmative. I was a little surprised because the man spoke with hardly an accent.

"How was the crossing?" he continued. Captain Stewart shook the man's hand before being slapped gently on the back of his shoulder.

"Ok, you know, same old ocean, same old sky."

Not knowing what to do or what to say, I just stood there.

The man eyeballed the Captain's attire.

"Mike, what the hell are you wearing? Purple shirt! Orange dolphins! Yellow shorts! Red belt! Planning on getting a job with the circus?"

(Yes, thank you, thank you, and thank you I said to myself quietly.)

"Yea, yea, yea….your just jealous 'cause you don't have an outfit like this. Picked all this up in Japan last year; practically got it for nothing!"

The military looking man could barely contain himself.

"They should have paid you for buying it!"

Mike, I mean Captain Stewart chuckled.

"Is this one of your officers?"

"No, actually, he's one of you, or should I say half of you. Brought him along just in case things get political."

"So he speaks our language?"

"So, he speaks your language."

Captain Stewart turned around in my direction.

"Patterson, looks like things are ok for now. Why don't you grab some food but stay close just in case I need you."

"Yes, Captain."

"Patterson? What kind of name is that?" the military looking man asked.

This is the reaction I get whenever I mention my last name and it's been that way since I was a kid. For reasons I don't fully understand, my last name "Patterson" doesn't quite match my profile and bringing it up in my mom's country has always been detrimental. In fact, it hurts my ethnicity and that's why I don't use it. Many times I've deferred to my mother's maiden name just to avoid confrontation. Yes, it's a bit of a copout, but when you've had to explain your life's story as many times as I have, well, you'd understand.

"The name was changed when my grandfather immigrated to America"

I lied.

My father's father came from Scotland and my mother's father from Euro 2. In fact, they weren't even the same religion. He was listening but his focus had shifted.

"What do you have to drink?" asked Captain Stewart as he and his friend made their way into the house. I looked around for a place to sit down but all the chairs were taken. I did see a stool off to one corner but I hesitated. It was barely two feet off the ground and it was covered in shellac. I think the shellac was used to keep the remaining wood from splintering any further. As for the legs, stress fractures ran from the floor up to the seat and some were so wide you could have stuck your finger inside. I decided to stand.

A young, homely looking girl came outside to where I was. She was one of three servers hired for the party. There were other women there as well but I think they were entertainers. They mingled with all the guests exchanging smiles and glances as they made their way from room to room. At first I didn't catch on, but after a few minutes it hit me. They weren't entertainers at all. No, these women were call girls and by the way they were dressed they appeared to be very high maintenance. They wore expensive dresses and some of the rocks around their necks were as big as hand grenades. All I could do was smile back. It would take a year's salary just to keep them happy for a weekend.

The server smiled and asked me in my mother's tongue if I was hungry. I answered yes. She turned and walked away and returned with a plate filled with local delicacies that rivaled the very best my mom had ever produced. As I sank my teeth into the appetizers, images of my family filled my mind.

For a moment I stepped out of myself and returned home.

I saw my sister on the back porch talking on the phone while balancing several dishes of food. Her face strained from the conversation she was having. My father was in the den fussing around the record player. He was cursing to himself out of frustration. The red wine he was drinking had taken its toll. His focus was gone. His mint conditioned 45's were spread out on the floor. He was trying to put them back in alphabetical order but he wasn't having much luck. I leaned in to help him but I couldn't lift the records. And then it was over. Slowly my mind drifted back to reality. The white wine handed me was no mirage. I sipped it slowly reminding myself I was still on duty.

Soon word got around I was one of them.

Curiously, several guests approached and engaged me in conversation. I obliged as long as the questions were about me. I was not there to discuss the ship. The conversation was somewhat personal but I didn't mind. We talked about the usual. Where I was from? Where my people were from? Did I have a girlfriend? How long was I in the Navy? How long did I plan to stay in the Navy? Things like that. Of course I answered like I was one of them.

This was not the time or place to discuss the Scottish history of the Patterson family. I had established a nice rapport with several of the guests and damage control was the last thing on my mind. If the military looking man wanted to spill the beans after we left then so be it. They weren't going to hear it from me.

It had been a long day. It started with the midnight to 4 watch followed by sea and anchor at 7 and now it was 2300 and I still had to stand Ribbel's watch in the morning. At around 2330, the skipper appeared on the veranda and motioned for me to notify the driver we were leaving. He had spent the entire evening inside the house with his friend. In fact, I hadn't seen him at all.

"Captain, you just made my day!" I whispered under my breath

The driver opened the back door; the Captain entered first. While driving back to the ship my mind focused on three things. One, I hadn't translated a single word the entire evening. Neither my presence nor my language skills were needed. Two, the name of the Captains friend was never revealed to me which piqued my curiosity and three, the whole evening just seemed surreal. It looked like a party but the skipper hadn't mingled with anyone. He just stayed inside the house with his friend. If I had to grade his good will report card he would have received an F. As for politically correctness, I'm the one who gets the A. I had to answer and dodge questions for more two hours. Perhaps this is why I was there. Not so much for translating but for conversation. To represent The Baffles colloquially. To speak to them not so much as an American sailor, but on a more personal level. To make them feel more at ease. I had many questions but no answers. Still, it was intriguing. Noon the following day, as I was preparing to depart the quarterdeck, Senior Chief Robbins showed up like the God Hermes with an important message.

"Patterson, stay in your dress whites, you're going back out with the Captain!"

"Again?"

"Yea, but this time he said something about three days."

"Three days, are you kidding me? Senior, I'm dead tired!"

Senior threw his hands up into the air.

"What are you bitching about? You volunteered didn't you? And look how lucky you are? Uncle Sam is putting you up in a big fancy hotel with all the trimmings. You'll have room service, your own bathroom, clean towels and a big ass bed that can probably handle three fat chicks all at once!"

I busted out laughing just as his right hand landed on my shoulder. He felt it necessary to accentuate the word "chicks".

Then he said something unusual, as if he were reminiscing back to when he was a much younger man. Perhaps he was thinking about a certain adventure? For a brief moment, he let his guard down.

"Yes Willie," he said with his head slightly elevated and eyes closed.

"Show me a woman with thick thighs, a firm ass and a warm smile, and I…..I"

"You'll what Senior?"

His eyes opened; his head leveled.

"Never You Mind!" he said, somewhat embarrassed.

"So, I need to pack?"

"Pack?"

He was still reminiscing.

"Of course you need to pack! You need to pack for three days and you better make sure your uniforms are clean! You never know where you're gonna end up, and one more thing. If I were you, I'd throw in a little kiwi as well! Gotta keep those buster browns smiling!"

Chapter 8

At 1400 hours, I met Captain Stewart on the Quarter Deck and we exited the brow together. A military vehicle was parked just yards from the ship and it was huge. It was the size of a small tank and stenciled on its door panels were black triangles indicating armor plating. Around the wheel wells were small red markings which could only mean one thing. The tires were bullet proof and impenetrable. It was reassuring knowing we were so well protected.

As for the driver, he was a serious looking young man dressed in a military uniform and attached to the left side of his belt was a holstered pistol. I couldn't tell if the safety was on or off, but if I had to guess I would say it was off; after all, this was Europe not America. He didn't speak to us at all but was very polite and patient.

Like the driver, the Captain and I were also in uniform. Adorning the skipper's dress whites were rows of ribbons and medals some of which I could not identify. The Captain truly looked impressive. I, on the other hand, had a squeaky clean uniform with nothing to show except the rating badge on my left arm. I looked about as impressive as a bell hop.

Our personal belongings were placed in the rear of the vehicle by the driver who continued to remain silent. Perhaps he was given orders not to speak to us. I will say this, the guy was very professional. Once we departed the harbor area, he requested the name of the hotel where we were to rendezvous. He knew where we were going, but his orders required confirmation. As soon as I provided that information we speed away. The skipper had previously confided in me we were to meet with several military people from the region. I was to be his interpreter. The good news; over the next three days, most of

the official business was to take place during the daytime hours leaving the nights free.

Of course, there would be a dinner or two thrown into the mix. That was to be expected.

However, unbeknownst to the Captain, I had my own agenda. Whenever the opportunity

presented itself, I was going to squeeze in as much fun as possible. After all, this was my

mother's country and I wanted to make the most of it. As to the assignment, I was most

curious. I was particularly flummoxed regarding the orders. Three days off the boat to

meet with military personnel? Why three days? Something didn't seem right. Were these

activities pre-planned or were they assigned to the Captain because I was there? What if I

hadn't been assigned to the Baffles would he still be meeting with these officers?

Shouldn't the State Department be handling this?

I had nothing but questions and I was beginning to develop a headache when

suddenly I realized I was over thinking the whole situation. I was off the boat and that's

all that mattered. Let the scrambled eggs guys figure it out. After all, they're the ones

who make the big bucks!

We arrived at the hotel and immediately the skipper was met by two junior

officers. They spoke English but their accents were so thick, the Captain motioned for me

to come closer. I did the introductions and translated as best as I could before the four of

us walked into a large ball room just north of the lobby. The room was filled with

military men wearing different uniforms and speaking in different languages. If I had to

guess, I'd say it had something to do with NATO. Eventually, I was asked to leave. I

didn't have the clearance to stay. A British Officer escorted me from the ballroom. I

remained in the foyer approximately forty five minutes before the doors opened allowing those in attendance a chance to mingle and get acquainted. It was several minutes before Captain Stewart appeared and the first thing he wanted to know was the location of any pay phones. I hadn't seen any so I quickly made my way to the lobby where I was able to flag down an employee. I motioned for the skipper to follow.

Once he got to a phone his whole demeanor changed. He seemed more relaxed and at ease. You see, the skipper was a "phone home" guy. Whenever he got the chance, he would communicate with his wife and kids. Now remember, this was the age before cell phones, so communication with loved ones had to take place on a land line usually located in a building. The good news, the more time he spent on the phone, the more free time I had to roam!

The meeting concluded about an hour after the initial break. The Captain exited the room accompanied by the same British Officer who had initially escorted me from the ballroom. The officer looked me square in the eye and said the following:

"Your services are no longer required petty officer. I am quite comfortable in the language and would be delighted to translate for Captain Stewart should the need present itself."

"Enjoy the rest of your evening Patterson. I'll see you in the morning." "Wow! I was a free man!" I said to myself.

The two decided to go out to dinner and take in some of the sights, but I knew the skipper. He would find a way to call home and talk to his family. I found out the next day the British Officer had been stationed in Euro 2 for three years. Captain Stewart was in good hands.

I checked into my room and changed my clothes as quickly as possible. Back down in the lobby, I inquired about drinks and was directed to the roof which not only had a bar, but also a swimming pool. Since this was a fancy upscale hotel, well to do visitors from all over Europe patronized it. As I made my way around the bar area, I heard many different languages. The pool section was filled with scantily clad women adorned in swim wear not suitable for American beaches.

Eventually, sporadic groups of officers arrived, but I had already zeroed in on a horizontal beauty that was lying face up on three white towels she had managed to sandwich together. Although I could only see the top of her, I deduced she was wearing a blue string bikini. Next to her was a handbag and hanging from the top pouch was a key chain imprinted with the Romanian flag. I maneuvered around to her left side in order to get a better look. She had black hair, red lips and covering her eyes were dark sunglasses. She looked young, somewhere between twenty and twenty five but no older. On her right index finger was a huge silver ring resplendent in odd symbols and attached to her left wrist was a stunning gold bracelet covered in small diamonds. I moved closer towards her and that's when she lifted her head and looked in my direction.

I froze in my tracks.

For a second I thought she was looking directly at me but she wasn't. Something happening behind me caught her attention. Slowly she gathered herself and rose up to resettle into a collapsible chair.

And that's when I saw the full her.

She was flawless, cover girl perfect. Her body was firm and the area where her butt and thighs came together was completely void of any cellulose. I was now standing about ten feet away and building up courage to approach her when some guy wearing a gold chain the size of a garden hose cut in front of me carrying two frozen daiquiris. He quickly sat down in the empty chair next to her.

I cursed to myself softly. She had a damn boyfriend! What was I expecting? A vision like that would always have an escort. I was beginning to accept my fate when all of a sudden the guy turns in my direction complaining to one of the staff about not having a pool towel. And that's when I saw all of him.

Hello Quasimodo!

For lack of a better word, the guy was abhorrent. Besides being short, fat, ugly and bald, he was much older than her and whenever he stood up he tilted to the left. Obviously some kind of birth defect. But the sad thing is, if he weren't so grotesque looking, the tilting wouldn't be so noticeable. But there he was, the Leaning Tower of Pisa complaining about pool towels. But that's not all. He had beady little eyes, if you want to call them that. Set deep within their sockets, they looked lifeless and were so dark they gave off a purple sheen.

I'm not done yet.

Highlighting his teratogenesis were razor thin eyebrows and protruding cheek bones so aberrant they made the Carpathian Mountains look like valleys in comparison! Completing the hideousness were yellow stained teeth accentuated by pock marked skin. Obviously, the result of bad hygiene, poor diet and unfiltered cigarettes.

But the icing on the cake was the undersized Speedo he was wearing. It was at least two sizes too small forcing his corpulent stomach to hang over the top of the waist band. Whenever he bent over, the bowling ball he was carrying looked like it was ready

69

to give birth!

Reluctantly, I retreated to a small table away from the pool area but close enough to the bar where I could continue to admire her.

Wow! What a letdown! How could she stand being so close to that ogre! For a moment I tried to visualize them together in bed but the thought made me nauseas!

As I collected my thoughts, the first thing that came to mind was the guy was loaded. What else could it be? Anyone that ugly with a chick that beautiful had to be rich. There could be no other explanation.

Doesn't say much for a good looking guy in his twenties does it? I mean I was an Adonis class sailor in terrific shape and full of energy. But who winds up with the girl!

Despondent, I turned away, lit a cigarette and waited for the scotch I had just ordered. A few minutes passed when suddenly someone tapped me on the shoulder. It was the same staff member who had given Quasimodo a towel.

"This is from the lady in the blue bikini."

"Blue bikini! Wow! She had noticed me after all!" I said to myself. He handed me a folded napkin which I immediately unfolded.

The napkin read:

"It's not what you're packing in the front of your pants that's important. It's what you're packing in your wallet that counts!"

She had me pegged from the get go. Not only had she seen me coming, she had me figured out even before her head hit the cushion. Once again my expectations would not come to fruition. I turned around in my chair to acknowledge the napkin but they weren't there.

Apparently they had taken the service elevator. I turned around to take a sip of my scotch which had just arrived. As I sat there alone contemplating what had transpired, it occurred to me she was absolutely right. She had confirmed what I had been thinking, and then it dawned on me. These Europeans chicks were different. Maybe it was cultural or maybe economics, who knows? The important thing to take away from this was outside the states, money was everything, everything and everything.

I moved to a chair at the bar and sat there alone for quite awhile. In fact, even the bartender found time to wander away. Before leaving though, he made certain I knew what to do in case I needed a refill. Located near the register was a small brass bell. Attached to the bell was a thick metal chain which had turned green from the weather. I was instructed to ring it three times; that would be the signal for him to return. Shortly thereafter, I rang the bell and within minutes a young woman appeared carrying a black pail of ice. I call it a pail because it was small in size, a bucket would have been much larger. She seemed to be struggling with it so I offered to help.

Surprised, she turned and said "Ah! You speak our language!"

I answered in the affirmative.

"What would you like to drink?"

"Scotch and water and heavy on the water."

Even though I was done working for the day, the night was young and I wanted to keep my wits about me—just in case.

"Were you born here?"

"No, in the states."

"Are you one hundred percent—one of us?"

"No, half of us."

"Who, your father?"

"No, mother."

This back and forth continued for some time. Unfortunately, I couldn't tell if she was just being polite, curious or if she was attracted to me. One thing I did know, she was very good at verbal volleyball. Obviously, a skill she picked up working in the hotel. As soon as the sun went down, traffic around the bar picked up. I was hungry and asked her if I could eat at the bar.

"Yes, you can eat here or at a table. I think a table might be more comfortable."

I grabbed my drink and smokes and walked over to a corner of the roof which afforded me a little more privacy. The table there was small and shaped like a pyramid. I was surprised it only had one chair. Within moments, a male server approached with a menu. I waved it off knowing exactly wanted I wanted to eat. Two drinks later the food arrived. I dug in immediately. The waiter was a little surprised I was eating such a heavy meal so early in the evening. I guess he just assumed we both marched to the beat of the same drummer but he was incorrect. One of the drawbacks or pluses, depending on one's point of view to military life is the necessity to adhere to rigid schedules. On board ship, we rise to revile each and every morning. Meals are served exactly the same time each and every day with few exceptions. The Europeans, civilians in general, don't live their lives this way. Normally, they sleep late, eat late and go to bed late. Many of them take naps in the middle of the afternoon in order to recharge their batteries. Since we are not extended this luxury, we always appear to be in a rush. The public just doesn't understand we live our lives according to someone's clock.

72

Liberty call usually commences at 1600. Ever the optimists, we exit the brow filled with vim and vigor only to find deserted restaurants, bars, and clubs. All of Europe seems to be the same. As for the women, most aren't even up and about until nine in the evening. In fact, most places don't really come alive until 2200 which is the time most of us are getting ready to saw wood. I can remember walking down the streets in Euro 1 and not seeing a soul. It is particularly noticeable during the early afternoons. Why even the Capitol looked deserted; the contrast in cultures is striking.

I finished my meal and asked for the bill which also included my bar tab. While waiting, I was appreciative they hadn't insisted I pay my bar tab before moving off to a table. Perhaps because I was "half of them." It was nearly 2000 hours and I was about to exit the roof when the girl I had helped earlier with the heavy ice pail came over and asked me if I'd like to go out after she got off work.

"What time is that?"

"Two in the morning."

I hesitated for a moment before nodding my head in agreement. I knew I would be dead meat the next day, but, she was pretty and friendly and, being the optimist that I was, how could I say no?

"What room are you in?" she asked.

"315."

"Ok, go sleep. I'll put a call into your room at 1:30 A.M"

"Your name?"

"William Patterson."

She giggled and the she gave me a puzzled look.

73

"What kind of name is that?"

Here we go again I said to myself.

"It's my other half, and you are?"

"Pennie."

"Pennie!"

"Too bad you're not a dime; if you were, then, you and I could rub nickels together!"

"What?"

"Yea, I know, never mind."

I exited the roof using Quasimodo's service elevator.

Chapter 9

At first I didn't hear the phone, but after the fifth or sixth ring I reached for the receiver.

"Sir, its 1:30 in the morning."

"Thank you" was all I could muster before returning the receiver to its base. I hopped in the shower, dried quickly and was just about dressed when I heard a knock at the door. As I walked over to open it, I remembered the safety tips Ritchie the Canadian had given us.

The yellow flag of caution was raised.

"Who is it?" I said in English.

There was no answer so I tried again in my mother's tongue.

"Pennie? Is that you? Are you by yourself?"

"Yes, William, it's me and I'm by myself."

My hotel door had one of those "I can see you, but you can't see me" peep holes.

As an added precaution, I took a moment to look through the clouded glass. I gazed left then right then up and down straining my eyeballs the whole time. After I was convinced she was alone, I opened the door.

My jaw almost hit the floor.

She looked amazing. No longer confined to her blue and white uniform, she stood there in a tight black skirt and white blouse. Naturally, all the right spots were accentuated, but what caught my eye were the thick dark sandals covering her feet. Heavy straps coiled around her ankles and calf muscles like an impenetrable guardian.

Had she been a Roman soldier she could have walked the entire length of the Appian Way.

I kept my opinions to myself.

"Did you eat?" I asked.

"I'll eat later."

I grabbed my hotel key; put my smokes inside the sock of my right leg just above the ankle so as not to give the appearance I was carrying anything. An excellent way to transport something inconspicuously. We rode the elevator down to the lobby but instead of going out the front door, we took a short cut through the kitchen and out the back. The reason for that, hotel policy frowned on guests and staff socializing together, and since she needed the job, I acquiesced. She hailed a cab and off we went. Once settled, she asked me my preference: Bar or club?

"Club."

We rode for ten minutes until we came to what looked like a factory. I paid the driver and as we exited, I noticed several men smoking cigarettes while their "girlfriends" waited patiently by their side. Picture that in the states. Exactly.

"It's called Pharos, in case you were wondering" said Pennie.

We proceeded to the door, and yes, there was a cover charge. After we went inside, Pennie motioned to a waiter to find us a table away from the dance floor. The music was very loud making conversation difficult. After we sat down, she asked for a menu. I wasn't hungry so I ordered cheese with bread. She ordered a chicken with a house salad and for drinks we both had red wine. Europe was different from America in this regard. State side it was almost impossible to find food in a club; here, it was

76

expected. It was late, almost 0230 but the club was packed which surprised me since it was a week night. Again, I had to remind myself the people in this country didn't start work until 10 in the morning or later, and besides, they were used to it.

The small talk Pennie and I made with each other was occasionally interrupted by sudden trips to the dance floor. At around 0330 I told her I was going back to the hotel, thanked her for her time and asked her if she was available for lunch that afternoon. She told me she wasn't sure but would let me know by 1100. I leaned over and kissed her on the check. She kissed me back and said she didn't live far from the club. She assured me she would be alright walking home. She knew quite a few people in the club and some of them also lived in her neighborhood. I hailed a cab and went back to the hotel.

At 0600 the phone rang. It was the Captain.

"Patterson, meet you in the lobby in half an hour."

Christ, you've got to be kidding, I said to myself.

As I prepared to get ready, I realized I wasn't going to be able to have lunch with Pennie, so upon arriving in the lobby, I phoned the roof bar. A guy answered and I told him to please tell Pennie I wasn't going to make lunch. I didn't give my name and I didn't say I was staying at the hotel because I didn't want her to get in trouble. I assured him she would know who it was. The Captain arrived shortly thereafter dressed in civilian clothes so I knew our outing was unofficial.

"We're going fishing."

"Fishing?"

"Remember the guy I was visiting the other night…well, he has a boat and he wants to take a bunch of us out fishing!"

But he speaks English, I whispered to myself.

Anticipating, the Captain added…

"and the reason you're tagging along is because I need someone to deal with the questions. I don't want to have to second guess what someone is saying. Christ, I'm having a hard enough time dealing with all the accents as it is."

Captain Stewart looked me right in the eye.

"Look Patterson, these are your people, you know them, and you speak the language. If something important comes up that you can't handle, then send them my way. If not, then don't. I came out here to spend time with my friend who I haven't seen for quite a while. He wants to fish and drink some beer. I plan on joining him. You can understand that, can't you?"

"Sure, Captain, whatever I can do to help."

"Alright, then."

The first thing that came to mind was the British Officer he had befriended. He speaks the language I told myself and would probably enjoy a little ocean excursion having been stuck in an office for the last three years. Why couldn't he ask him to translate? Made sense to me.

"Go and get us a cab. No government transport today. We'll leave as soon as I am finished with this phone call."

With that, the Captain made his way over to where the pay phones were located.

Scuttlebutt had it we were to get underway in a couple days and I couldn't have been happier. This was supposed to be the highlight of my deployment but it wasn't. I was supposed to be spending time with relatives and friends, relaxing, taking in the sights, the beaches, the women!

Hell, it's been anything but relaxing, and I have no one to blame but myself! Mistake number one was volunteering to serve as an interpreter; I should have kept my mouth shut. My linguistic talents were completely unnecessary; everyone the skipper came in contact with either spoke English or was bilingual! More importantly, all this running around with the Captain was taking time away from Pennie.

The opportunity to drop my anchor was diminishing rapidly.

Chapter 10

The "fishing boat" was anything but. It turned out to be a big beautiful yacht complete with its own helo pad. I would say it was about seventy five feet long and maybe twenty feet across. Below the main deck the hull was classic white but the super structure above contained blue highlights which accentuated its overall appearance. A small Jacuzzi underlined the fantail. Once on board, a crew member escorted us up a ladder and forward to the wheel house where the military looking man was standing.

"Mike, you made it."

"Teo you have a beautiful boat! Ah! Must be nice to have money."

So his name was Teo. I made a mental note.

"Yes, being rich does have its advantages, something to drink?

"Not right now."

"And you?"

Mr. Teo spoke to me in my mother's tongue.

"No, thank you," I answered softly.

He continued.

"I understand your mother is from my country. What about your father?"

"My father is from a Nordic country and I'm sorry I told you he changed his name when he immigrated to America. He is not one of us."

"I knew that the moment you told me your last name. Apology accepted. So, do you also speak your father's language?"

"No, just the two languages. My father was born and raised in the states and so

80

was his father. Whatever language my paternal ancestors brought with them to America ended there."

"I see. Too bad. In any case, your mother taught you well, in fact, I don't even here an accent."

Captain Stewart joined the conversation.

"Mr. Teo's father and my father meet each other during World War II. Teo's dad was a member of the resistance fighting the Nazi's and my dad was the Executive Officer of a destroyer. Mr. Teo's dad along with his resistance fighters needed a lift out of a hot zone. My dad's ship provided the transport."

Mr. Teo, switching back to English added.

"They remained close friends and after the war would vacation at each other's houses from time to time and that's how we got to know each other. I told Mike he's more than welcome to buy into my business once he's finished with the Navy, but we'll see." I was grateful for the information but not sure why they confided in me. It did answer a lot of questions though.

"Captain, is it ok for me to wait on the fantail?"

"Sure, just don't fall into the Jacuzzi."

The two friends laughed.

"You're not going to fish?" inquired Mr. Teo.

"Perhaps later" was my reply.

We left the harbor and headed out into the Mediterrean. After forty five minutes the boat slowed. We were barely making enough headway to maintain steerage.

"This is the spot I was telling you about," said Mr. Teo as he powered down the engine. Immediately, the boat began to rock from side to side. Within seconds, the twenty or so invited guests made their way forward towards the forecastle. Black and brown fishing rods appeared out of nowhere. The hooks, baited with small shrimp, were carefully lowered into the sea. Everyone was particularly careful not to make any splashing for fear of scaring off the fish.

Accompanying me on the fantail was an elderly couple. The man's windbreaker displayed a French flag which appeared to be hand sewn. They had the look of tourists but I wasn't confident enough to say that out loud. After all, they could be foreigners who decided to retire in Euro 2.

It was a mystery that didn't need solving.

Whatever their situation, I will say this. They looked cute together. Decades of companionship had truly turned two lives into one. They neither ate nor drank but rather seemed content to huddle next to each other whispering in French. Not wishing to intrude on their repose, I decided to focus on Pennie. Anyone wishing to talk to the Captain could go through Mr. Teo since he obviously was fluent in both languages.

Again, I asked myself the question: why was I here?

We returned to the hotel later that evening. I immediately went up to the roof bar to look for Pennie but she wasn't there. Surprisingly, the bartender called my name as he motioned for me to come closer and when I did, he handed me a note. The note said Pennie was going to wake me in the morning and that I should be prepared to spend time with her on the beach. She had a hunch that today would be my last day in her country and she was right. At 0800 I heard a loud knock on my hotel door followed by two more loud knocks. Pennie? It had to be her. I called out her name and she responded.

"Give me 5 minutes," I said.

"Just put on your swim suit and brush your teeth."

"Yes mam."

When I opened the door, standing in front of me was a woman adorned in a white bikini so sheen she had to wear a long tee shirt to protect her vulnerable spots. Tucked behind her left ear was a red and white carnation. The flower, which served as a lure, had been seductively scented in perfume. Thin white sandals highlighted the shape of her legs adding to her over all mystique.

I had to kiss her; I had to have her.

I drew her close and was about to embrace her when the softness of her fingers brushed up against my lips preventing me from doing so.

"Not now." I exhaled.

"Why?"

"Not now. I have the whole day planned out. Besides, plenty of time for that later."

She accented the word later by pressing her index finger to my lips.

We left the hotel and made our way down to the beach which was within walking distance. I bought breakfast from a beach vendor who was nearby. The morning sun was rather hot so we sat next to each other under a huge white umbrella looking at the ocean. I knew it was nice for her but looking at the ocean was the last thing I wanted to do. At around 1000, I suggested we go for a walk.

"Why William, don't you like it here?"

"Very much so, but I thought we could go shopping."

Good move on my part.

"You want to buy something?"

"Yes, I want to buy you something!"

Over the years, I have discovered one certainty about the female of our species. With very few exceptions, most women like to shop and they especially like to shop when the word "sale" induces from a store window.

"I'll go change," was all she said before sprinting back to the employee changing room at the hotel.

"I'll meet you out front!"

I yelled as I hurried behind her. Back in my room, I quickly changed into a blue shirt which sported a white collar. Recently ironed white shorts would accompany the blue shirt and, choosing comfort over style, I decided on an old pair of white loafers before heading back downstairs. While waiting outside, I lit a cigarette and thought about the gift. I decided to buy her a necklace which required a cab ride to the jewelry section of town. I really liked Pennie and even though I would never see her again, I wanted to get her something to remember me by. I know it sounds silly, but sailors can be silly when it comes to women. The cab ride took us to a street consisting of nothing but jewelry stores. For a moment, I thought I was back in New York's Diamond District. The place was packed with every kind of bauble imaginable. Fortunately, hidden amongst the glitter were reputable establishments. We walked past three or four stores when a green jaded necklace pressed up against one of the store window caught my eye. I thought the color of the jade would complement the hazel in her eyes.

"Let's try in here," I said.

"OK."

Once inside, the aroma of burning incense, accompanied by soft R & B music emanating from ceiling speakers cajoled us, making the necklace all the more appealing.

"Do you like it?"

I said pointing to the jewelry. Pennie's eyes widened.

"I LOVE IT!"

"Then it's yours."

Usually, I inquire if the item is on sale or if the price could be lowered, but for some reason I didn't.

"Is it on sale?" asked Pennie.

Ah, thank god for women.

"Yes, we've taken twenty five percent off."

"Make it thirty and my boyfriend will buy it." I smiled but said nothing.

There are times when it is prudent not to interject oneself when two women are haggling over an impending sale.

"Is it real?" Pennie continued.

"I'll show you."

The sales woman lifted the piece from the window display and then pulled a small magnifying glass from her pocket.

"Look here."

Pennie took the glass and held the necklace up to the light.

"Show me something less expensive so I can compare."

The sales woman complied.

After a few moments, a smile appeared on Pennies face.

"Satisfied?" I said.

"Yes, it's beautiful William."

I handed the associate the money; she handed me the necklace which I immediately placed around Pennies tanned neck. As predicted, the color of the stone accentuated not only the hazel in her eyes, but also her olive skin which was an earmark for all the Mediterranean's.

I stood there looking on in awe.

Pennie had my mom's color; in fact, they were remarkably similar in many ways. As she turned to face me, a burst of sunlight beamed through the display window. The reflected image captivated and highlighted her facial features.

She glistened in its glow.

"My turn!"

"What?"

"My turn to get you something."

Na, that's ok. I'm good."

"C'mon now, let me," she said as she drew my body close to hers.

"Let me get you something," she whispered the words in my ear.

I gave in.

"OK, OK!"

"I know. I'll give you a choice. Would you like a gift or would you like to have lunch in a nice romantic setting?"

Doesn't the word lunch always go with romantic? I said to myself. Without giving it another thought, I said lunch.

"Good, I know a nice place where only the natives go…no foreigners."

"Excellent, let's go there."

In retrospect, Pennies suggestion solved my dilemma. I was looking for a way to spend time alone with her. The restaurant would give me the privacy I needed. In fact, this would be the perfect venue and the thought that no one from the ship would be there thrilled me to no end. The cab ride, which began on flat city terrain, quickly changed to a steep mountain climb. We were headed out of the city, and unfortunately, only one road was available to take us to the restaurant which was built into the side of a cliff overlooking the ocean.

The route was almost vertical.

Fortunately, the cab recently had an engine overhaul and the driver assured us the rebuilt diesel powered Mercedes was more than a match for the treacherous incline which lay before us. What was particularly captivating, and what I remember most about the drive was the amount of wind. We were several hundred feet above sea level, yet strong ocean currents had somehow managed to extend upwards to our location. Small pieces of paper which were present on the floor began to rise and circle like confetti. As a courtesy, the driver rolled up the windows and turned on the air conditioning. The wind's intensity, however, continued unabated as it made its way up and over the mountain summit.

Once we arrived, Pennie immediately instructed the seating hostess to give us a table which had a panoramic view. As we approached our table, I noticed the strong winds had subsided. The man-made barriers, which had been installed when the restaurant opened were still operational. Once seated, I was able to recognize the outline of small fishing boats below. What was particularly pleasing was the effect the shimmering water had on both natural and manmade objects.

All looked surreal.

For reasons unknown, a bond formed between the battered wooden boats and myself. Tied to weathered decks along the causeway, the small boats tossed and turned like children yearning to be free. Perhaps it was that yearning which drew me to them in the first place. Not being free was something I could relate too. Unfortunately, the little boat rebellion drew many brightly colored fish to the surface where legions of hungry sea gulls dispatched them effortlessly. Pennie ordered for both of us. She said it was going to be a "wonderful surprise."

What arrived was a cornucopia of my favorite dishes! Pennie had somehow managed to combine a myriad of wonderful delicacies. I don't know why, but at that moment, I thought about my mother. I knew my mom would like Pennie and I'm sure Pennie would like my mom. They were similar in so many ways. Too bad they will never meet each other.

It was nearly 1600 when we finally left. We made our way down the perilous road the same way we came up. As we descended, Pennie instructed the cab driver to takes us back to the hotel. Before going inside, she convinced me to take a walk on the beach which was located behind the hotel. Once there, we removed our shoes and sandals and began squeezing sand between our toes as we walked hand and hand through the surf. After half an hour, I stopped and kissed her softly on the lips. I pulled back slightly awaiting her reaction. She offered no resistance.

"I want to make love to you," I said.

"I want to make love to you too but I am afraid."

"Afraid of what? Afraid of getting pregnant?"

She smiled.

"No, afraid of falling in love."

I took a deep breath.

"Listen, if you don't want to that's ok. I understand, but I'm leaving tomorrow."

"When was the last time for you?"

"The last time for what?"

"You know, the last time with a woman?"

"Four months ago."

I lied. It was two weeks ago.

"And you."

"It's been a while?"

I repeated.

"Listen, if you don't want to that's ok. I understand."

"But I do want too."

"Ok then. Let's go up to my room."

"OK."

It was nearly 0200 when we finished. We were both exhausted but satisfied. I cuddled her as she rested her head on my chest.

"Will I ever see you again?"

Ah! The dreaded question!

"I don't know; all I can tell you is I will write you."

"I love you, you know," she said quietly.

"Well, I care for you."

Pennie lifted her head as she rolled onto her side.

"You care for me! How do you care for me?"

Here we go; another round of volleyball!

"I care enough to write you. Look Pennie, I'm a sailor and I'm leaving your country in a few hours. In fact, we should be lifting the brow before the sun reaches its high point."

"How soon before I get your first letter?"

"The next time we pull into port, the mail will be taken from the ship and delivered to the nearest post office. From there it will be delivered to you. How long before you get the letter? I honestly don't know."

"Will you miss me?"

"Of course I will."

"You promise to write me?"

"I promise to write you."

Pennie paused slightly before continuing. Her smile diminished as she became more emotional.

"I don't think we will ever see each other again!"

"Where the hell did that come from?"

"It's true!"

"You don't know that!"

Pennie could no longer hold back the emotion building inside her. She buried her face deep inside her pillow. The soft material which held it together was a washed in tears. I said nothing more because there was nothing more to say. Besides, I was getting tired of the back and forth. What the hell more could I say? I was honest with her. I didn't mistreat her. Why the hell is she crying?

I quickly dressed and ventured out to the balcony which overlooked the main entrance to the hotel. Standing there, I lit a cigarette and tried to clear my mind. When I returned to the room, Pennie was gone.

She was of course correct. We were getting ready to leave for our next port of call and we had no plans of returning. This is the life of a sailor. Master Chief Bolger from Operations once described it to me this way:

"Patterson, it's like this. We live our lives according to someone else's clock. Being sailors, we don't have the luxury of time to do the things we want to do properly; you know, the way we were raised, so we take shortcuts. One of the biggest shortcuts we take involves women. Now, if you don't feel like a challenge, there are always harbor chicks, but if you feel like testing yourself, then you have to stick to the game plan."

"What would that be Master Chief?"

"The plan is this. Think of a baseball field. You got four bases right? Well, before you can score a run, you have to touch the other three bases, right?"

"Right."

"So, this is what you do. You go out and find a girl who is willing to spend some time with you. When you can accomplish that, you've made it to first base. Now, I'm not

91

saying you're a couple, but at least you're together, right?"

"Right."

"Ok. You tell her how lonely you are and how much you miss your mother. The trick is to sound and act convincing. If you can't pull that off, game over and you need to start the process over again with somebody new.

"My mother!!"

"That's right, your mother!!"

"After that, tell HER how much SHE reminds YOU of YOUR MOTHER."

"And then what?"

"Well, if she doesn't start laughing or walk away and she seems interested then hold her hand as your talking and walking with her, and if she starts warming up to you, then go ahead and put your arm around her. If all that happens, then you've made it two second base."

"Second base?"

"Yea, second base. Now, tell her you're hungry and would like to eat something. Take her somewhere where they serve alcohol. Ask her if she wants a drink. If she has a drink, chances are she'll have another, but don't let her get tipsy or drunk, that will ruin the next step… so Patterson, are you following me so far?"

"Yes, Master Chief."

"So… just picture the situation…there you are…just the two of you; and you're sitting there with your arm around her or you're holding hands, the point is, you're softening her up for the kill."

"Then I've made it to third base?"

"No not yet! Listen to what I have to tell you!"

"I'm sorry."

"Patterson. Now comes the hardest part. Getting her into bed. The key is to get her to feel sorry for you. Tell her again how she reminds you of your mother. Tell her again how lonely you are. If you can fake a tear or two—all the more better. Ask her if she would like to go to a quiet place where the two of you can talk. Tell her you'd like to open up to her but you're uncomfortable talking in such a public setting.

Now listen carefully Patterson; this is very important.

SHE has to think SHE is in CONTROL. If she even suspects the only reason you're with her is because you want to get laid. Game over. But if she leans over and whispers in your ear about going someplace quiet to talk, you've made it to third base.

Now, don't forget the rules, especially Rule Number 4. You don't go back to her place. You take her to a place of your choosing.

Very important Patterson.

That is probably the golden rule when it comes to picking up women."

"So that's it?"

"That's it…game over... you scored...you won... you reached home plate... nothing more to say."

A harsh reality, but, reality nonetheless.

I truly cared for Pennie, but I wouldn't and couldn't promise her the "I'll come back for you" fairy tale so many sailors tell women the world over, and I couldn't tell her I was going to marry her, because I knew that wasn't going to happen either.

I have heard horror stories, about virgin farm boys falling in love with the first foreign girl they have sex with. And what happens after that? A lot of these guys feel compelled to marry these women and then bring them home to the states to meet the family. Sadly, and I have witnessed this first hand, as soon as the sailor ships out, the wife also ships out, not to a ship, but to bar or club where she meets and sinks her hooks into her next victim.

Here's the problem.

These relationships are based on lust and that is why they fail. Separation is followed by divorce, and in a lot of cases, alimony and child support. As for the woman, she establishes residency, and then slowly but surely finds ways to bring the rest of her clan to America.

I'm not saying this was going to happen with Pennie, but it was a possibility. I promised I would write her. Anything beyond that would be foolish, dangerous and stupid.

Chapter 11

Euro 3

Underway again and heading to our next country.

Word spread quickly throughout the ship that several members of deck division had caught the "crabs" while on liberty call. Apparently, they had frequented the same establishment and shared the same woman. Although they exhibited much discomfort scratching themselves as they went about their business, the rest of the crew made lite of their predicament. The fact that they shared the same woman did not surprise me. The Captain ordered we stay together while ashore, and, by golly, stay together they did! I guess in their minds, staying together also meant sharing with one another!

Ah! Boatswain Mates! Ya got to love 'em!

I can tell you from personal experience pubic lice are no joke. I once suffered from this malaise, not through intimacy, but through infected clothing not properly washed. In my situation, the ship's laundry service didn't do a good enough job.

Euro 3 consisted of several small islands surrounding a larger land mass which was within visual range from the main deck. We were told by those who had previously visited the country to anticipate a plethora of tourists from the Nordic regions of Europe.

In other words: Vikings.

As we pulled into one of the mainland harbors, a very alert signalman noticed a topless beach to our starboard. Needless to say, every available man not on watch was vying for "Big Eyes" and, as I recall, pushing and shoving their way for a look see. When someone fell down, an order was given to clear the signal bridge. As we descended to the main deck, a few stragglers remained above on the 0-3 level.

One of the last to leave was a guy named Bartholomew Jones.

The Bart man was born in Trinidad but moved to the states when he was fifteen years old. Whenever he spoke, his rich Caribbean accent underlined his words. His voice was unmistakable, and I believe his accent contributed greatly to his overall popularity. He was an excellent cook and after his Navy experience, was planning on opening his own restaurant. Just as he was ready to step back from the binoculars, he began jumping up and down and waving his arms.

"Hey now! The girls are waving, they're waving at us!!!"

Bart had zeroed in on a bevy of topless Nordic beauties sunbathing near the shore line. We learned later that the girls had taken notice of the small group of sailors concentrated on the signal bridge. The wave was simply their way of saying hello. Well, the Bart man got so excited he did the unthinkable. That's right; he dove into the ocean and started swimming to shore. Three people witnessed the dive. One was the Officer of the Deck, the second was the Duty Signalman and the third was Senior Chief Chesterfield who had just ventured out to the starboard bridge wing searching for a signature to complete an engineering report. All three stated, had they been judges, would have scored the dive a perfect ten! In fact, Senior Chief Chesterfield even went so far as to make a medal which he spray painted with gold.

Fortunately, there were several boaters nearby and one was kind enough to pull the Bart man out of the drink and return him to the boat. Needless to say the punishment was severe, but it had no effect on Bartholomew. He was a rock star! Everyone was either talking to him or about him. Even the old timers, the chiefs who had been around for twenty five or thirty years, not only had they never seen someone dive from the 0-3 level, they never even heard of anyone attempting it. Although he was on restriction, the Bart man never lost his sense of humor or his smile.

Another memory I will take with me to the grave.

I was fortunate not to have to stand duty that first day. Unfortunately, I was exhausted so I stayed on board to recharge. However, the next day when liberty call sounded, I recalled my experiences in Euro 1 and instead of exiting the ship with the rest of the crew; I hit my rack and slept until 2300. I wanted to rest first, shower then go out. Quarters wasn't until 0730 so I still had plenty of time to enjoy whatever lady luck had in store for me and the best part was: no translating!

Twenty three hundred hours came quickly. When I opened my eyes, berthing was pitch black except for a small red light near the compartment hatch which separated our division from supply. When I rolled out and stood on the floor, I was alone. Everyone not on duty had either left the ship or was standing watch. It was strange being alone in berthing. Usually there is always someone listening to music or reading a book but not tonight. Curious, I walked around the maze of curtains to see if any rack lights were turned on but none were. After a quick shower, I made my way up to the quarter deck and as I began walking down the brow someone behind me yelled out my name.

"PATTERSON!"

I turned around.

"WHERE THE HELL ARE YOU GOING THIS TIME AT NIGHT?"

It was Senior Chief Robbins. I don't know if it was by chance or fate, but he always seemed to be around the quarter deck when I was either leaving the ship or returning. In fact, I heard similar stories from other guys in the division. Apparently, Senior had taken on the role of surrogate father. In a way, it was reassuring knowing someone was looking out for our well being.

"Senior, just gonna catch a bite to eat, maybe have a couple of beers and a couple of smokes."

"And a couple of women?" He began to laugh.

"I'll be careful. Besides, I know a few key phrases. I'll be alright."

"Quarters is at 0730. Don't be late."

"Roger that."

As soon as I stepped onto the pier, Senior yelled at me once more from the fantail.

"PATTERSON! YOU'RE LIKE A DAMN SHIP IN SEARCH OF A HARBOR! SURE WOULD FEEL BETTER IF YOU HAD A BUDDY OR TWO!"

"I promise to be careful."

I turned around and continued walking. Soon after, I hailed a cab and told the driver to take me thirty minutes away from the ship. I really didn't care in what direction as long as it was thirty minutes. I was tired of looking at water. Before taking off the cabbie looked at his watch.

"You want woman?"

The thought had crossed my mind.

"Not right now, maybe later. I just want to go someplace that has restaurants and music but away from the harbor...far away."

The cabbie smiled and turned around but not before I saw the gold filling in his front tooth. There was a design. It looked like someone had cemented an initial to the enamel. To do something like that in the states cost a fortune. I wondered what it cost here. Anyway, as we departed the waterfront area, I paid particular attention to the landmarks. I heard from other sailors who had been here, the cab drivers like to jack up the fare by circling the same blocks over and over again. I only had so much money with me. Instinctively, I shoved two tens down my left sock. This was ETM. Emergency transportation money. Being stranded and broke in a foreign country is no joke, especially if you are in the U.S. military.

You might as well paint a bull's eye on your back.

Luckily, my guy was honest. Traveling alone and at night, and dressed the way I was, he either thought I had been here before or that I was crazy.

He didn't ask and I didn't tell.

Whatever the reason, we made our way up a small mountain and as I looked back through the rear window, the ship and everything connected to the harbor had vanished. Twenty minutes later, we pulled up to a restaurant that had a separate entrance to the bar.

Perfect.

I paid the fair and entered the restaurant from the bar side. Once inside, I took a seat near a small table close to the coat check room. A waiter approached; I ordered a scotch and asked for a menu. Several single, rather good looking women were sitting by themselves, but Euro 1 had taught me well. These were bar girls, girls hired to get guys like me to spend twenty or thirty dollars on colored water. I took comfort knowing this scam was universal. Fortunately, I had learned my lesson well. As I continued to look around, I noticed there weren't any guys from my ship there, in fact, I didn't see anybody

99

who even resembled a sailor. Good news for me. My drink came and so did a request. Yep. One of the girls sitting at the bar wanted to have a drink with me.

"No," was my response.

"NO!" said a very surprised waiter.

"NO!" I repeated it again, but this time a little louder.

I quickly glanced at the menu and ordered chicken with salad, and then I lit my cigarette. The waiter walked away a little pissed off but, like I said, this wasn't my first rodeo. Just as my food arrived, a few more people, mostly couples entered the bar. Half way between the restaurant and the bar was a dance floor. Two bar girls were dancing with each other but no one was paying them much attention.

So, there I was.

Sitting alone with my scotch and cigarettes and enjoying a very good meal. One other bar girl ventured over to my table but I responded the same way. I was on to them. They knew it. After that, they didn't bother me anymore. An older shipmate once told me the best way to get rid of bar girls is to threaten to drink someplace else. Fortunately, I didn't have to take it to that level. Around one in the morning, the restaurant side of the club was packed. I sat there shaking my head in amazement. I had no idea people could eat dinner so late and still be able to sleep afterwards.

Ah! Europeans!

Around two in the morning, a couple of girls entered the restaurant, did a quick look see then made their way to the bar. They noticed me but I didn't give them much thought. Something inside me said they were waiting for their boyfriends and about ten minutes later that's exactly what happened. Two well to do guys showed up and parked themselves at their table.

Well that's it for tonight, I thought to myself.

I went outside and walked over to where caravans of taxis had lined up waiting for patrons. I motioned to the driver of cab number one. Immediately, we headed back down the mountain. Final destination would be the harbor. All of a sudden though, the driver slammed on his brakes, hurling me towards the windshield. Fortunately, I was able to position my left hand against the glass preventing any serious injury.

"WHAT THE HELL ARE YOU DOING?" I screamed.

"Two girls...two girls walking?"

He was pointing in front of the cab.

"YEA, WHAT ABOUT THEM!"

"Give ride."

The driver moved ahead slowly, matching their cadence. He called out to them which caught their attention. The three had a brief conversation and then the girls got in the cab. No one said anything but I did notice a baby bottle sticking out from the bag of one of the girls. They were laughing quietly to themselves and then the other girl, the one without the bottle asked me in her language if I wanted to have a drink.

"Tonight?" I asked.

"No, tomorrow around 9 P.M.?"

Such a sweet voice. Like I was talking to an angel.

"Where?"

She pointed to the mountain.

"Same place!"

Even her smile was perfect.

The attraction was instantaneous. She had my undivided attention! Before answering though, I took a good hard look. Why a drink? She just met me. Maybe something else was going on? I tried to look at it like analytically. She was maybe 20 with short black hair and olive eyes. I didn't get a real good look at her body before she entered the cab, but I knew she wasn't fat and she appeared to have nice legs. She was modestly dressed; didn't have the look of a hooker at all and there seemed to be an air of sophistication about her. Street smart yes, but also schooled. No yellow or red flags with this one. I decided to give it a try.

"Ok, 9:00 P.M."

"Ok."

And with that, the cab stopped at the location the three of them had agreed to. The girls got out but before leaving, olive eyes turned to me and said:

"Are you from that American ship?"

How perceptive of her, I thought. We had reached a point in the road where you could barely make out the harbor. I decided to be evasive by answering the question with a question.

"Are you the girl with the baby?"

"If you're a sailor from that ship that arrived yesterday, then I am not the girl with the baby."

Impressive and quick on her feet. Beauty and brains—all in the same package. I was definitely interested.

"Your name?"

"Ana."

"You? "

"William."

"Do people call you Bill?"

"Yes, but I prefer William."

How intuitive.

"See you tomorrow then?"

"Yes, I'm looking forward to it."

And with that, the two girls exited the cab and walked up a small tiled staircase. The girl with the baby bottle held on to the railing as she climbed. Ana opened the door, and then called out to someone. An older woman holding a small baby appeared near the entrance. Immediately, she handed the baby over to the girl with the bottle. Before closing the door, Ana waved goodbye and smiled. I waved back like a love struck school boy. What the hell was wrong with me?

The cab continued down the mountain and stopped at the harbor entrance. I paid the fair and got out. The cab sped away leaving me alone with my thoughts. All I could think about was Ana; the girl had mesmerized me. Whatever thoughts or feelings I had for Pennie were gone!

As I contemplated the reality of the moment, a thought came to me, was it really the girl or was it just a case of horniness? Something was overpowering my senses. I felt weak, vulnerable. I was moving into new territory and I was scared. Was this, should I dare say it…LOVE!!! Better not be! Not for this player!

Whatever it was I was going to sleep on it and hopefully understand it better in the morning. A friend once told me, whenever he sneezed, for that one split second, he couldn't see, hear or feel anything. He said it felt like he was in his own private universe!

That's how I felt about Ana. Even though we just met through a chance encounter, whenever I thought about her, I was oblivious to everything else. One thing I knew for sure walking up the brow. I was going to have a special dream tonight.

Chapter 12

From the time revile sounded till knock off ship's work, Ana was all I could think about. Yea, Pennie was around, tucked away in my memory banks, but I had moved her to the back of the bus. Ana was new and refreshing. Like a summer shower over a field of scented flowers.

The "love" word kept creeping up though, but each time it did, I pushed it back down. I asked myself again and again. What the hell was wrong with me? Still, I had no answer. One thing for sure though, logic was out the window. This was all about chemistry. No matter how hard I tried to block the rumination, nothing could placate the bells and whistles carilloning in my mind. Even if I wanted too, I didn't have the strength to raise the yellow flag of caution. I was as weak as a baby.

Nine P.M. couldn't come quick enough.

"William?"

I swiveled around on my bar stool. Standing in front of me was a vision of beauty. Besides the perfect hair, face and perfume, Ana was adorned in a tight white blouse and close-fitting jeans so snug they could have been spray painted on. Covering her gorgeous feet were white sandals with matching white toenails that accentuated her olive coloring.

I needed all my will power to remain a gentleman.

"Let's grab a table," she said as she motioned for me to get up. I picked up my lighter and smokes. She carried my drink but as we approached the table, she called out to one of the bartenders by his first name and then she waved to several bar girls.

"Hi Ana!"

Girl after girl acknowledged her presence.

"Questions? I can see from your face you have many questions. Let's see if I can answer some of them for you."

We sat down at a table away from the entrance. The night breeze had stiffened slightly. Fortunately, Ana's selection shielded us from its affects. She held my hand softly, explaining the familiarity.

"Yes, I work here. I'm a bar girl," she said pointing to her co-workers.

"I am also a university student studying to become a chemist. My family is poor. We don't have a lot of money, so I work this job to help with the expenses."

She squeezed my hand firmly as if to make a point.

"The woman who opened the door last night was my mother. The girl with the baby is my older sister. My father and three brothers are fisherman. They own their own boat and when they're not fishing, they make extra money repairing diesel engines."

I lit another cigarette and took a large sip of scotch.

"I am not married, I don't have a boyfriend and I don't have any children."

I smiled from ear to ear.

She continued:

"I'm not a prostitute, if that's what you're thinking, and I don't sleep with my customers."

The girl was a mind reader.

"My job is to get you to spend as much money as I can on drinks, but, (turning to the bartender) tonight, (and elevating her voice slightly) you are my guest and not a customer and that's why my cousin is not going to over charge you like he would another tourist. Tonight, you pay what we pay for drinks and tonight you pay what we pay for food."

Is this chick amazing or what!

The "cousin" rolled his eyes as he gazed towards the ceiling.

"Now, if you are expecting something else, you are mistaken. Drinks, food and conversation are what I have to offer."

She let go of my hand and sat back in her chair. She took a sip of her colored water which had just arrived along with a plate of plain mozzarella sticks. She looked somewhat relieved, as if a weight had been lifted off her shoulders. As I sat there digesting all that was said, the thought of getting up and walking out crossed my mind. I was angry but I didn't know why I was angry. In fact, I grabbed my smokes and lighter and motioned to get up when it occurred to me she hadn't done anything wrong.

What the hell was wrong with me? I never reacted like this before. I was crazy about the girl but wanted to leave! Does that make any sense? We sat there starring at each other in silence. I had no reason to be upset with her. I was angrier at myself because I hadn't seen it coming. How could I have known she was a bar girl who worked in this particular club? I hadn't met her here. How could I have known?

"Ok," I said.

"We'll give it a try."

"So you're not mad then?"

"Mad no, hungry yes! What do you recommend for dinner? I had chicken and salad last night but I'd like to try something else tonight."

"Do you like fish?"

"Yea, but not too many bones."

"Let me surprise you."

"Ok."

Ana motioned for the waiter.

"Another cousin?"

"No, co-worker," she said with a demure smile, although for a second I thought she was going to burst out laughing. She motioned for the waiter to come closer before whispering something in his ear. While waiting for the food Ana and I actually had time to get to know each other. She wanted to know all about me but I let her speak first. She told me she was nineteen years old, and if everything went according to plan, should graduate from the local University in three years. She paused briefly before continuing.

"Have you been with a lot of women?"

Wow! Where did that come from? I was caught completely off guard.

"A few."

Good recovery.

"When was the last time?"

Persistent isn't she.

"Last month."

"Did you use protection?"

Direct and to the point!

"Always."

"That's good, you should always be careful."

The waiter showed up just in time.

"I'll have another scotch with a glass of white wine and please bring Miss Ana another glass of colored water."

The waiter acknowledged with a nod and a frown. Yea, buddy, I'm on to you.

Shortly after, he returned with the drinks and the surprise Ana had ordered.

The food smelled delicious.

The scent seemed to emanate from the floor as it wound itself around me, delectably teasing my senses. The serving consisted of Mahi Mahi, baked potato filled with sour cream topped off with something from the spinach family although I'm not exactly sure what it was except to say it was long, green and delicious. Mahi Mahi had always been a staple at our dinner table. In fact, it was my mom's favorite dish.

As I was finishing my third scotch I asked for the check. Ana was good to her word. The bill was considerably lower than the night before. I could have made a big stink about getting ripped off, but I know this happens all over. A couple of guys had complained about it during our last port visit. It was getting late and I had duty in the morning so I decided to call it a night, but, before I left, I asked her if I could see her again. She told me the nights she worked but I wanted to see her outside of the restaurant.

"Would you like a tour of the ship?"

"Really?"

"Really!"

"When?"

"How about two days from now? I have duty tomorrow but I'm free the following day. Besides, I'm not sure how many days we have left here so the day after tomorrow would be good."

I noticed she grimaced when I mentioned the word "left."

"What time?"

"1600 hours, I mean 4 P.M. would be good."

"Ok. Can I bring someone?"

"Sure."

"Ok."

On my way back to the boat I thought about the questions Ana had asked me. You know the ones about sex. Had I been with a lot of women? When was my last time? Did I use protection? Curious things to talk about on a first date. I guess it was a plus for me. At least she was thinking about it. Still, this was a very smart girl. Best if I let her maneuver the relationship. At least she was entertaining different scenarios.

Hopefully, in one of her stratagems she had us positioned next to each other horizontally.

Chapter 13

"STG3 Patterson report to the Quarter Deck!"

I recognized the voice. It was Seaman Wilson from deck division. How'd I know it was Wilson? There was only one Messenger of the Watch who spoke as loudly and as clearly as Doug Wilson. His voice was unmistakable. I didn't know what his plans were after the Navy, but if he chose to become a radio announcer or a game show host, he would have excelled at both. Doug was from Wisconsin but that's not what he told everyone. On the contrary, home to Doug was the small piece of land he grew up on near Lake Superior. Wisconsin just happened to be the name of the state.

I was in berthing when I heard the announcement. Out of a force of habit I quickly gazed at my wrist watch. It was 1545. Ana had arrived early. I sprang into action. It took me exactly thirty seconds to get to Doug Wilson. Standing next to the watch podium was Ana and standing next to Ana was her cousin the bartender. She looked beautiful but a little under dressed. She was wearing tight white shorts, a loose fitting green top and covering her feet were high top green sneakers. I smiled to myself. Perhaps she thought we were going hiking.

"Welcome to the Baffles," I said as I leaned over to kiss her on the check. Before I could say or do anything else, her cousin grabbed me with two hands and proceeded to kiss me on both sides of my face, as was customary.

"Thank you for inviting us," he said.

"You're welcome."

The three of us left the quarter deck through the same small hatch I had appeared from. I went first followed by Ana and then her cousin. Once through the hatch we proceeded down a vertical ladder to the second level. It seemed like an eternity waiting for them to reach the bottom. Once we were together again, I led them down a small narrow corridor which brought us to the mess deck.

"Hungry?" I said.

Ana answered first.

"Maybe a little thirsty."

"And can I get a candy bar?" asked her cousin.

"Two cokes and a candy bar coming right up!"

Unfortunately, the vending machines weren't located on the mess deck. In order to reach them I had to vacate the space through an after hatch then travel down a long passageway until I got to engineering. The machines were located just outside their berthing area. I got the cokes and candy bars as quickly as I could. There is a strict rule about leaving guests unattended and I was a long way from where they were. I hurried back as fast as I could but it was too late. Standing at our table with arms folded was the Master-at-Arms, Senior Chief Thompson.

His face said it all. He was pissed.

"Petty Officer Patterson, whenever you have guests onboard this vessel; you are required to be with them at all times."

"Sorry, Senior."

He placed his right hand on my left shoulder gently squeezing as if to make a point.

"Don't leave guests unattended."

"Understood Senior Chief, and since you're here, I was wondering where exactly can I take them?"

His eyeballs rolled left then right.

"Mess deck, fantail and the quarter deck and that's it."

"Understood."

The MAA left the mess deck through the after starboard hatch. He had an established route and didn't like to veer off into areas not on his watch list. The problem was anyone up to no good could probably time their shenanigans to avoid ever getting caught. The corridor he was in led to the ship's store. Past the ship's store was the laundry area and scuttlebutt had it Filipino crew members were playing poker and gambling late at night. Only the space behind washer number three was large enough to accommodate such activity. The Senior Chief would definitely be checking out that area tonight.

"Let's go topside" I said, breathing a sigh of relief. The Master-at-Arms could have written me up sending me to Captain's Mast, but he didn't. I was lucky, besides I should have known better. It was my fault; it won't happen again. We exited the mess deck following the same path as the Senior Chief except instead of walking past the ship's store; we climbed a portside ladder which put us back on the main deck near the fantail.

Just to digress for a moment, the fantail is probably the most popular spot on board ship. Small metal bitts allows one to lean back on life lines and coke, smoke and

113

talk till your heart's content. Another plus, it's always windy so lighting your cigarette takes a little bit of practice. All in all, the fantail was one of my favorite places to hang out. I could tell from her expression she was enjoying herself. We were standing on the wind ward side of the ship just forward of the camel cushions. Several visitors were present and quite a few of them felt relaxed enough to lean against the life lines. Ana told me she had been out to sea on her father's fishing boat, but never on anything as large as this. Occasionally, wind gusts swept through her partially opened blouse filling it up with air. The ballooning influence would on occasion cause her to falter slightly. She would correct this by taking hold of the life line. On one such occasion, I moved behind her anticipating an unforeseen bobble. Ana hesitated slightly before leaning into me. The combination of her hair swirling around my face and the smell of her perfume was more than I could bear. I kissed the back of her head.

No one saw, not even her cousin. I knew she liked it because she pressed her body against mine appreciatively. We stayed that way for a few moments until the fantail became saturated with new visitors. I released her as we sat down on the bitts. I was definitely aroused and she knew it. We sat there for quite awhile until her cousin finally spoke up.

"Well it's time to go. Thank you for showing us your ship. We really appreciate it."

"So soon?" I asked.

"Yea, I got to work tonight and I want to get some rest before I have to report."

"Understood."

"Why don't you stop by tomorrow night? I think you will enjoy the special: pasta

114

and fish. My way of saying thanks."

"Yes!" added Ana.

"And I will treat you to dessert!" she said.

Ana leaned over and kissed me softly on the lips.

As she pulled back, I looked directly at her cousin but there was no reaction.

"Tomorrow then?"

"Tomorrow."

I shook the bartender's hand.

"Tomorrow."

I escorted them to the quarter deck and watched as they departed the ship. I followed them down the pier and even moved forward towards the forecastle until I couldn't see them anymore. Ana caught me by surprise with that kiss. So much for drinks, food and conversation! Things were indeed looking up and what made this especially nice was the fact I really had strong feelings for the girl. I thought about Master Chief Bolger and his baseball diamond but this went way beyond scoring. For the first time in my young life, I was in love.

Chapter 14

Rumors confirmed what I already knew. Today was our last day in port. Tomorrow we would head out to our next destination which was just a hop skip and a jump from where we were. Ana continued to remain the focus of my attention. The truth is I just couldn't stop thinking about her. Yes, I was looking forward to spending time alone with her but as I began to scrutinize the details of our chance encounter; a bizarre thought crept into my mind. I had fallen in love with Ana but look how easy it was to throw Pennie under the bus. Didn't I have feelings for her too? How could I just toss her by the wayside like that? The truth is, I would still be thinking about Pennie if I hadn't met Ana but all that changed when she walked into my life. If I had to compare the two I couldn't. It would be like comparing a tidal wave to a baby pool.

And the worst part of it all, Pennie wasn't three months ago or even last month, she was two weeks ago! Hell! I hadn't even written her a letter yet! A pattern was developing and I didn't like it. Pennie was the new Diane and I was worried Ana would one day replace Pennie. Perhaps I should just forget their names and refer to them simply as Diane 1, 2, 3…etc. It certainly would expedite things. You know the phrase out of sight out of mind, well, it was written for guys like me. Apparently, all it took to throw me off balance was a jaunt across the Mediterrean and another pretty skirt.

Talk about being shallow!

It was around this time when I decided to have a conversation with myself. The first thing on my mind was also the most troubling. Was I becoming a deviant? Had the traveling changed me? Second, what was happening to my morality? I certainly wasn't raised to treat women this way. Sure, I could blame it on being young or on the Navy, but deep down I knew it was something else.

The experts say sons who have rocky relationships with their mothers don't make good husbands. I was definitely a candidate. Although I respected my mother and did as she asked, I was always closer to my father. Perhaps it was a guy thing. Who knows? I will say this. The rift between my mother and me was real and the only way I could successfully deal with it was by telling her what exactly what she wanted to hear.

It was like a game. With me it was happy mom all is good, let's keep it quiet in the neighborhood! And the best part was it wasn't difficult at all. Unfortunately, I became so good at it I tried it on other people.

You want proof?

Let's start with Diane. The girl was my high school sweetheart. She was someone I cared for and trusted yet look how I treated her. Why did it take me three months to tell her about the Navy? Why did I procrastinate? And I tell her a week before I ship out! Surely the girl deserved better.

Pretty cold now that I look back.

Selfish and insensitive? Absolutely. I used her to please myself. I could have told her in June when I enlisted but then I would have been cut off. The thought of being deprived sex for the whole summer was unacceptable. Like I said, Diane was very good at self expression. Besides, why rock the boat when you don't have too. When it came to sex, it was all about my pleasure and my satisfaction and nobody else's. I knew it wasn't right but I didn't know how to change. I was hoping I'd be a different person when we arrived back in Florida. This is what I was thinking about on my way to Ana's restaurant.

Just like Pennie, I knew I would never see Ana again but this time it was different. This time it hurt. Deep down inside I didn't want her to end up just another notch on my belt but the little voice inside me prevailed.

It said do yourself a favor and let it go.

"William!"

It was the bartender cousin.

"Ana had to deliver something for the boss; she'll be right back. You want a scotch or something else?"

"Yes, I think I'll have some white wine served in the biggest glass you've got."

I sat down at a table close to the bar but before I could light my cigarette, a waiter unknown to me approached with the biggest glass of wine I have ever seen.

"510 grams!" He said proudly.

"Thank you," was my reply.

I lit my cigarette and sipped the wine slowly and, as I was about to extinguish my smoke, Ana appeared from what looked like the kitchen area.

"Hi!"

"Hi Ana, how are you?"

"Good...but I missed you!"

"I missed you too!"

I repeated the words silently to myself. Man, if she only knew how much I missed her. I had fallen for the girl hook line and sinker. Saying goodbye would be the hardest thing I would ever do. Thoughts about commitment, family and children flashed in my mind. I was even contemplating marriage; I was that far gone.

"Ana, do you think we can spend some time alone with each other?"

"Why do you want to spend time alone with me?"

"I think you know why."

"I do. But I'm not sure I can. Remember, food, drink and conversation."

Even though she said the words, her conviction was eroding. I could see she was beginning to change her mind.

"We're leaving tomorrow, and I just thought...well I thought...hell! I just want to hold you and kiss you!"

I never said those words to Pennie and certainly not to any of the other women I had met on this cruise. I said them because I felt them. Ana paused to answer...thought about the words and then replied:

"Maybe at 11...I take my break then. Maybe we could go back to my

place. Would you like that?"

"Would I like that? That would be perfect!"

"I need to get back to work. Enjoy your meal and I hope you like the dessert I picked out for you," she said.

"Whatever you picked will be perfect."

Ana left and returned back to the kitchen. The waiter who brought me my wine also delivered the pasta with fish, and to say it was delicious wouldn't do it justice! It was quite possibly the best meal I've ever eaten in my life! The food literally melted in my mouth. It was like the whole meal was cold butter on a hot baked potato. In fact, the meal was so good; I couldn't even talk to the girls who were trying to strike up a conversation. All I could do was a smile, besides, word was out, I was Ana's guy so hands off! The piece de resistance was the dessert Ana had promised. Positioned in the middle of a huge white plate was a large transparent plastic cup. Inside the cup was a cornucopia of delightful treats. I recognized most of the assorted fruits and some of the different colored ice creams occupying the bottom half of the cup. Topping off this magical creation was an overabundance of ice cubes. Accompanying the large, transparent cup was a very long spoon the likes of which I have never seen. The spoon, according to the waiter, served two functions. The first, for mixing all those marvelous ingredients together; the second, for reaching those hard to get to spots at the bottom. By the time I had finished my meal it was close to eleven o'clock. Ana reappeared from the kitchen sans apron.

"Ready?"

I motioned for the check, paid the bill leaving the waiter a nice tip. I shook hands with the cousin bartender one last time and waved goodbye to some of the girls sitting at the bar. Before leaving, I did a look see one last time. I scanned the restaurant thoroughly, savoring every image; I did not want to forget what happened here.

Once outside, we quickly turned right then proceeded down a narrow, somewhat dangerous stairwell, in that, it didn't have any handrails, making the descent somewhat threatening. Just as we were about to reach the street, we passed between two Roman columns which served as sentinels. I turned around to get a better look. As I starred at them, I was carried back to the museum I had visited in Euro 1. An accumulation of thoughts transpired into vibrant images.

A dozen or so Roman children were playing tag with each other. Some, not wanting to be touched, disappeared up a marble staircase. Others had removed their sandals hoping the coolness of the morning stone would provide relief from the heat.

Then came merchants with small carts lined up at the foot of the columns. Soon, well to do Patricians flooded the street as they went about their business. Yes, these columns had stories to tell that spanned not just centuries, but millennia.

"I usually don't work in the kitchen, but two girls didn't show up tonight and since the boss knows I can cook, he assigned me the job."

Ana's voice broke my concentration. The day dream was over. The children vanished as quickly as they had arrived.

"How long is your break?" I asked.

"Oh no, I'm done for tonight, I'm sorry, wrong choice of words."

I put my arm around her and speaking softly said "I understand."

We walked for about 15 minutes and then we stopped.

"Here we are."

She gestured towards the same building I had seen the night before in the cab. I recognized the front door and the long cement stairwell which wound its way up to the landing.

"William, listen, my family and I live in a three bedroom apartment.

I nodded.

My sister and I share one bedroom, my parents another and my three brothers share the last one."

"I understand."

"And…And… you're very lucky! My dad and my brothers won't be back until tomorrow night. They're trying out a new location, somewhere closer to the Straits of Gibraltar, I think. They said the fishing will be better over there."

"I understand."

All I could say was I understood. I wasn't listening anymore. The thought of sinking my teeth into her gorgeous thighs consumed me.

"And remember, my sister has a baby."

"Yea, I know all about babies...my sister has two."

Another lie. My sister Ruth is fourteen years old. I drew Ana in close and kissed her on the lips.

"Not here silly!" she said giggling.

As we entered the apartment building, someone who looked familiar yelled out to me.

"PATTERSON! WHAT THE HELL ARE YOU DOING HERE?"

It was Boiler Technician Martin Drieden from engineering.

"SAME AS YOU BUDDY!"

Hanging on to him for dear life was an older woman with firm round breasts, a tight butt and shapely legs. She looked to be about forty but it was difficult to distinguish her facial features due to the poor lighting and her disheveled makeup. The two of them had been drinking heavily and both were a little unsteady. It was pretty obvious they had just come from the sack.

This is Rosa."

"Please to meet you," I said.

She acknowledged with a smile.

"Hello Ana."

"Hello Rosa."

122

The two women knew each other.

"Sea and Anchor going down around 0600 I think?"

"That's why you're heading back now?"

"Yea, I know me. I'm dead tired and I've been drinking all night and if I fall asleep here, I'll miss ship's movement…you should head back too!"

"WORRY ABOUT YOURSELF SNIPE!" I yelled back.

Snipe is an acronym for Standard Navy Issue Propulsion Engineer, or at least it was on board the Baffles. It's a word that describes all who work in the engineering spaces. This includes fresh-air snipes (engineers who don't work in the engine room) and A-gang (engineers who work on auxiliary equipment such as air conditioning units, emergency diesels, hydraulics, etc).

"YOU TOO TWIDGET!" he shouted as he and Rosa made their way out the door and down the winding staircase. For a moment, I thought they were going to fall over and injure themselves. Fortunately, Rosa had the good sense to walk behind him knowing full well the petty officer's body would serve as a cushion breaking her fall.

This definitely wasn't her first rodeo.

Ana shouted something to Rosa. At first the older woman resisted and appeared upset, but when the cab arrived she acquiesced. Rosa accompanied Drieden back to the ship. I let out a sigh of relief and thanked Ana for her help.

Regarding twidgets.

Twidgets are technicians who operate and maintain electronic equipment on board ship. In the old days, electronic technicians were called twidgets because they often carried a tweeker in one of their shirt pockets. This was a tool, usually a small fine

123

screwdriver used to make modulation adjustments. Notice I said electronic and not electrical because electricians are part of the snipe family and not the other way around. On board the Baffles, twidgets usually worked above the main deck and snipes below the main deck so you can see how a certain degree of animosity coalesced. Besides the physical separation, snipes are always dirty, sometimes filthy dirty working with oil and grease and such. Twidgets, on the other hand, hardly ever break into a sweat. They work in air conditioned spaces and usually the heaviest thing they have to pick up is an oscilloscope. Snipes, on the other hand, are constantly hoisting motors, gears and heavy machine parts in very hot conditions. They often worked in spaces where the air is filled with smoke or steam.

The dissimilarity between the two groups is striking.

This separation, coupled with a general disconnect, lends itself to a certain degree of resentfulness and jealousy. I know for a fact a great many snipes felt short changed and saw us more as "babysitters" rather than workers. I will say this though, whatever ill feelings they had, they kept it to themselves. There facial expressions did all the talking. I will end with this; I served on board three ships and the animosity between the two groups never subsided, regardless of the ship or the coast.

Remember when I first reported on board? Remember how I was ignored? Do you want to know why? No one knew if I was a snipe or a twidget! It wasn't any more complicated than that.

"This is our apartment,"

Ana said opening the door after inserting her key into the lock, "and this, this is the bedroom I share with my sister."

Ana entered first, had a brief conversation with her sister who smiled at me as she and her baby made their way down the hall disappearing into another room. Ana gestured for me to enter. As I walked into her bedroom, I noticed several books lined along the wall on two shelves. The top shelf consisted of biology and anatomy books, but the bottom shelf seemed to be filled with only chemistry books. I took great comfort knowing she had spoken the truth about her quest to become a chemist. Between the book shelves and her bed was a small desk used for study and scotched taped along the inside of one of the desk shelves was the periodic table of the elements. Ana had drawn colored circles around certain proton and electron configurations as well as around even numbered atomic numbers. She said the red circles represented positively charged elements and the blue negatively charged. The yellow marker was used exclusively for the atomic numbers. Which was all fine and dandy but I wasn't there to discuss agitated protons. The thought of making love to her was driving me crazy. I felt like every hormone in my body was about to burst in anticipation. I couldn't wait to get naked and get busy, but something lingered in the back of my mind. I needed to know why she was breaking her rules. How many times did she tell me no sex? How many times did she remind me about the restaurant policy? Yet here I was; in her apartment and alone with her in her bedroom.

"What made you change your mind Ana? Why have you broken your own rules?"

She sat on the edge of her bed, and after removing her shoes she laid down on her back placing her head on the far side of her pillow obscuring my view.

"It's because…because…you made me weak. I know your leaving but I need to take something to remember you by. I also know you want to take something to remember me by. It's not that complicated. We want to touch each other and that's ok with me; I can handle it now because I feel for you."

I wondered how many times she had given that little speech…at this point…it really didn't matter.

"The only thing I ask, the only thing I hope for is, please don't get me pregnant."

"No way…I have plenty of condoms, not a problem!"

"I only hope and pray nothing happens."

That was my cue, besides I couldn't take it anymore. I was ready to blow a gasket. Ana said something about taking a shower but I shook my head no. I ripped off my clothes as fast as I could and got on top of her. A short while later, we were both naked. We made love until 0430 and as I was preparing to leave I promised Ana the same thing I had promised Pennie. I promised I would write. I also made a promise to myself to never make that promise again. First Pennie and now Ana, that was enough. On the way back to the boat, I thought deeply on what had transpired. Yes, I believed whole heartedly that I was in love with Ana. I really believed it, but the reality of the situation was no different from when I left Pennie. I was unable to commit to a relationship with her just as I am unable to commit to Ana. Feelings aside, it just wasn't possible. The letters we would write to each other would do one of two things. Either bring us closer together or end us. Time, time will solve that mystery.

Wind, water, whiskey and women.

I was beginning to see the wisdom in those words.

Chapter 15

The crew was finally smiling.

For the first time in eight months the weight of deployment was lifted from our shoulders. We had completed all of our commitments and were preparing to sail home, but before weighing anchor and heading west across the Atlantic, we had a change of command ceremony. Good Captain Stewart, the cigar smoking, beer drinking skipper who enjoyed wearing purple shirts with orange dolphins was about to be replaced by a sour puss of a human being named Commander Whitehead.

I will remember Captain Stewart for one particular thing. Yes, you guessed it, the translating. It is now clear why I had to tag along. I was the Captain's PR spokesperson. I was there to talk to and deal with the locals so the Captain could spend as much time as he wanted with his friend Mr.Teo. Yes, I will remember good Captain Stewart and how he cleverly concealed his true intentions from me.

The ceremony was held on the helicopter flight deck and I was fortunate to be standing directly in front of the speaker's podium. I was able to see and hear everything. The only drawback, it began at noon and boy was it hot. The sun was shining brightly through a cloudless blue sky. My good friend the wind, who usually can be relied on to provide a steady breeze, picked one hell of a day to take off. In a vain attempt to provide some shade, helicopter nets were lowered but they failed miserably. It was like being covered in stockings made out of fish net. Yes, it was a real scorcher and had I been in charge, I would have had it either earlier in the day or after five when things cooled down.

127

But I wasn't in charge so we all had to suffer.

Speaker after speaker approached the podium drenched in sweat, everyone that is, except Commander Whitehead. There he stood, cool as a cucumber. Like he had an air conditioner stuck up his ass. Not only was he not perspiring, there wasn't even a wrinkle in his uniform! He looked like he just stepped out of a damn catalogue. His immaculate attire was adorned with ribbons and medals and around the front of his waist was a polished belt buckle so bright, it nearly blinded us. If the Navy ever needed a new poster boy, Commander Whitehead was it! By contrast, our uniforms looked worn and tattered. Many months at sea had taken its toll on them. Even the white piping on our dress uniforms was beginning to turn yellow.

When it was time for the new skipper to speak, and after the usual pleasantries, he got right down to business. He said he loved being underway and hated being in port. He also said the Baffles would best serve the nation out at sea and since this was his first command, he felt it prudent not to let Uncle Sam down!

Seriously?

The Baffles just spent the better part of a year either preparing for or on deployment. To say we were a tired crew doesn't quite cut it. We were exhausted, physically and mentally. Our batteries needed recharging. One good way to accomplish that was by spending time with family and friends back in Florida. What we needed was rest and relaxation not more deployments but that was not to be. No, instead of getting a Captain sympathetic to our situation, we got Captain Bligh.

The new skipper was bursting with energy and after three years of shore duty parked at a desk, was ready to take on King Neptune himself! I believe Captain Stewart

128

sensed this in him and did his best to placate the Commander but, the son of Bligh, a nick name he would soon earn, wouldn't hear of it.

And he was no Boy Scout.

Scuttlebutt had it he had been passed up for promotion once before. If he didn't make Captain this time around, he would never make it and that was unacceptable to him. Commander Whitehead would become Captain Whitehead, and to that endeavor, the officers, crew, the ship itself, were subservient to his needs. In ending his speech, the Baffles new master emphasized three words.

Preparedness…Volunteering...Recognition!

Preparedness: From this moment on, all equipment will operate at peak efficiency.

Volunteering: The Baffles will, from this moment forward, volunteer for all future assignments not yet posted at Headquarters. Any mission not completed by other squadron vessels would be assumed by the Baffles.

Recognition: Both Headquarters and the Command Center will take notice the example set by the Baffles. By raising the bar, she will receive the recognition she deserves!

Are you kidding me?

Sounds great doesn't it? Just one problem. Although achievable, it's not sustainable. Allow me to explain.

Equipment breaks down and needs to be serviced. Down time in port provides technicians and mechanics the opportunity to take systems off line, perform delicate maintenance, replace parts, tweak new software, etc, etc. Requiring all equipment to be

129

"on line" and working at maximum efficiency all the time is unrealistic. Think of your own automobile. When your car needs an oil change or brake job you have to service it. Servicing means taking the car "off line" in order to perform said maintenance. The same is true with equipment on board ship. Unfortunately, the new Captain didn't see it that way. According to the skipper, the reason for having spare parts is to eradicate downtime. Something breaks down; you pull the old piece out and replace it with a new one.

Problem solved! Simple, right? Wrong again!

What happens if a turbine cracks or you have problems with equipment installed underwater? Then what? The more Commander Whitehead spoke the more out of touch he sounded to the crew. Even then, many of us began to question his fitness for command. How could a Commander, someone with years of naval experience think this way? Hell, not even a boot ensign straight out of school would make those kinds of demands! We found out later that even before the ceremony, Whitehead meet with some of the department heads in the wardroom. It was there where he informed his senior officers that "all repairs" were to be done at sea. That way, the ship would pull into port always ready to tackle her next assignment.

Allow me to interject.

I was a sonar technician; some of our equipment was literally underwater. If a malfunction occurred, what was I supposed to do? Jump over the side and repair it? Commander Whitehead finished his speech, wished Captain Stewart good luck in all future endeavors then retired to his new cabin. The rest of us, officers and crew alike, gave good Captain Stewart a proper send off. As he departed the ship, all of us to a man saluted him. He disappeared into a military vehicle which was waiting for him on the pier and drove away from the ship and from us for the last time. The next several hours were uneventful. The mood throughout the ship, however, was dour. Most of us felt like a family member had passed away. We all liked Captain Stewart and it was painful watching him depart. Taps sounded at 2200 hours and as I was getting ready to hit my rack, a voice over the 1MC ordered us to report to our sea and anchor stations!

We were leaving Europe in total darkness? Why? For what purpose? Getting underway can be a dangerous operation. The best way to reduce danger is to adhere to strict safety precautions. That means you set sail while the sun still shines. Captain Stewart understood this and that's why he always set sea and anchor detail when there was enough light to operate. Getting underway in the middle of the night was unnecessary and dangerous. We didn't know it at the time, but Whitehead's penchant for disregarding safety procedures was a harbinger of things to come. We cleared the harbor around midnight but didn't secure from sea and anchor until 0200. I finally hit my rack at 0240 and was just about to fall asleep when someone keying the 1MC yelled "General Quarters!

General Quarters! All hands man your battle stations!" Exhausted, we did as ordered. Approximately one hour later, the order was given to secure from general quarters. Many of us stood around looking at each other in utter amazement but no one said a word. Exactly one hour later, we had another drill but this time we were on station until the sun came up.

This continued every night until we were pier side in Florida.

Exactly two weeks later, the Baffles received orders to get underway again. This was unprecedented. Never before had a deployed vessel received such a quick turnaround. The crew was in disbelief.

Count them. There were four other ships in our class who could have handled that assignment but didn't. None of the four had recently deployed and all were operational so why the Baffles? Then it hit us, the speech he gave at the ceremony. You know; the one about preparedness and volunteering? Yea, that one. I will say this for the new skipper. He was true to his word and he did give us fair warning. Now he was following through on implementation. In fact, he was so eager to get underway; he would make daily trips to the command center. He wanted to be present whenever new assignments became available. No other Captain in our squadron did this. Whatever assignment came up, no matter how lousy, he would volunteer the Baffles and god help the officer, chief or enlisted man who's equipment wasn't up to the task! Down time was a thing of the past. If we weren't standing watch, we were troubleshooting and repairing equipment, and just to make matters worse, a few crew members were sent to Captain's Mast for falling asleep while on duty. Morale amongst officers and crew deteriorated rapidly. "Blanket parties" were becoming common place. A blanket party is the crew's solution to someone who becomes too unbearable to deal with. In most cases, the "party" corrects the malfunction. If it doesn't, the individual eventually gets transferred off the ship.

Here's a common scenario.

The "party guest" is brought to an area known as anchor windlass. It is a small compartment one deck below the forecastle in the forward most part of the ship. The space contains, amongst other things, a large motor which is used to raise and lower the anchor. Due to its narrowness, there is little room for maneuvering and very few of the "khaki clad" (chiefs and officers) ever venture there. As for the "guest" sometimes he comes voluntarily, sometimes he doesn't. I will say this, the more he struggles the more painful his experience. The windlass is chosen precisely because of its exclusivity. Noises emanating from the space are quickly drowned out by powerful waves striking the boat. Someone standing one deck above would not be able to hear the whaling and screaming below.

It was the perfect place to beat the hell out of somebody.

I don't know why, but the parties always took place early Sunday morning. As a precaution, lookouts were posted two compartments aft of windlass just in case a "khaki" happened to wander off the reservation.

The "guest" would be surrounded by his peers and then covered with a blanket. Punches would emanate from everywhere; and the more the resistance the more the pounding. Sometimes it ended with a knockout, but that was rare. Usually, the sailor just ends up black and blue but more importantly, he gets the message and all of a sudden like, the malfunction corrects itself. The reason for the blanket is simple. If he complains or presses charges and it ends up in Captain's Mast, and he's asked who hit him, he can't answer truthfully. Even if he names those in attendance, all they have to do is deny being there. How could he prove otherwise? Besides, if he snitches, he would get another invite to another party and this time his dance card would be full.

Remember what my recruiter said about "smokers?" A quick review. In the good old days, the Navy allowed authorized fights between enlisted men. If two sailors had a dispute which needed resolving, they were allowed to box each other in a make shift ring usually located on a weather deck. The fights were well supervised and broken up if

133

serious injury was imminent. Unfortunately, the Navy won't allow us to fight anymore; they consider it hazing.

Hello blanket party.

The stress, by the way, was not limited to just the enlisted personnel. Mess cranks assigned to Officers Country reported hearing numerous disputes between senior and junior officers. In fact, on two occasions, loud thumps were heard coming from the Chief Engineers cabin. If anyone was assaulted, it wasn't reported. The Captain had no tolerance for insubordination. Imagine how bad the punishment would have been for the officers.

Not even meal time was immune from the growing malaise. Again, the officers had it worse.   You see, the Captain preferred the second meal setting. Since no one wanted to associate with him, all the other officers, including the Executive Officer, made it a point to dine during the first setting. Unfortunately, there were only so many chairs to sit down in meaning some of the junior officers had to dine with the skipper. I heard it became so unbearable that some of the officers made arrangements to eat while standing watch. As the days and weeks progressed, it became obvious to all; Commander Whitehead was obsessed with making Full Bird. Nothing else mattered, not the ship; or the morale of the officers and crew.

We were a one second blip on his radar screen.

But, like my dad always said, actions have consequences. His obsession was beginning to take its toll. Exhaustion was common place. Both man and machine were reaching their breaking points. No one spoke about it openly, but a huge rift existed between the Captain and the crew.

At first, I tried to give him the benefit of the doubt by looking at it from his perspective. Perhaps he was bitter because he had been passed over. Perhaps he was competing with someone? I wanted to think well of the skipper, but what he was doing was dangerous. It was only a matter of time before someone got hurt or worse. Efforts were being made though to ease tensions. Several Chiefs, both individually and in small groups approached the Master Chief of the Command requesting he speak to Mr. Calvin. After their meeting, the XO declined to take it any further. He didn't offer any specific reason, but I'd like to think he was aware of the Captain's obsession but didn't want to appear as an impediment to the mission. You see, Mr. Calvin was a master at political correctness and I believe he was worried about his own career. His goal was to become a Captain one day; therefore, he couldn't afford to have any blemishes on his record.

Taking on the skipper might jeopardize that.

Next, the chiefs went to the "Doc" to see if something could be done, but the "Doc" said he wasn't a psychiatrist and that's what the old man needed, in his opinion. So, nothing was done to "correct" the malfunction that festered within the skipper. As tensions continued to increase, I decided to keep a log which I kept hidden from everyone. Not even my closest friends knew of its existence. Needless to say, the volunteering continued and so did the deployments. We were in and out of port more than any other ship in our squadron, and, as a result, were developing a reputation for being unsafe.

And then it happened.

For reasons unbeknownst to both officers and crew, Commander Whitehead decided to do away with tug boats. The Baffles was to moor and get underway on her own power. I don't know if this was ego driven or an attempt to prove something but this went way beyond being unsafe. This was borderline reckless. As far as we knew, no other ship assigned to our home port was engaged in this type of maneuvering. All were using tugs coming in and out of port. In fact, we spoke to several sailors not assigned to our squadron and asked them if they were using tugs and all responded in the affirmative; all were using tugboats. Our inquiries led to questions which needed to be answered. Why would the skipper attempt something so dangerous? For what purpose? What was the point? Who was the Captain trying to impress over at headquarters? As I previously stated, the ship and crew were subservient to his needs. We were expendable, and if placing us in harm's way was a step closer to making Full Bird, then so be it. Fortunately for me, my sea and anchor station continued to be Line 4 which gave me a bird's eye view on any activity occurring on or near the fantail. Another plus, and it didn't matter which side we moored to; I had an unobstructed view of the after most part of the ship. On one such deployment, as we rounded the inlet and before entering the harbor, we were instructed to go to our sea and anchor stations.

Since I was already near the starboard quarter, I was first to arrive on station. As I was putting my life jacket on, a black cross appeared on the weather deck below me. Shielding my eyes, I turned around and as I looked up I saw an albatross hovering above me. Immediately I thought of "Sunrise" and was about to wave but I noticed something different. This bird was smaller and its color was darker. Sunrise was large and white and something else caught my eye. A small piece of its wing was missing. It didn't seem to affect the bird's flight but when it hovered, it wobbled slightly. No, this wasn't Sunrise that much I knew for sure. I was able to see it steady itself for a moment above the rooster tail but then it flew away. Still, the bird reminded me of Sunrise. I missed my old friend. In fact, I hadn't seen the bird since I gave it its name. I wondered if Sunrise was ok and when I might see it again and that's when it happened.

As we neared the harbor entrance, I noticed the sea was anything but calm. Robust winds had turned the normally docile waters into choppy waves pushing the boat towards the pier. Under normal circumstances, tugboats would be present buffering our activity, but since we were unaided, controlling the ship was next to impossible. We hit the pier hard on the starboard side. Two fenders designed to protect the ship from the impact were crushed. The collision ruptured an intake pipe in engineering causing it to burst. The ensuing rush of water not only flooded the space, but damaged one of the evaporator pumps, limiting our ability to make fresh water. As bad as that was, it paled in comparison to the utter disconnect between Captain and crew. The skipper, who was standing on the starboard bridge wing during the collision, disappeared inside the ship. Within seconds, we heard his voice loud and clear over the 1MC.

"I KNOW WHAT JUST HAPPENED! YOU DID THIS TO ME ON PURPOSE! YOU EMBARRASED ME IN FRONT OF THE ADMIRALTY! I SEE THIS AS A FAILURE IN COMMUNICATION. BUT IT CAN BE FIXED. NEXT TIME WE DEPLOY, ALL WATCHSTANDING WILL INCREASE FROM FOUR HOURS TO TWELVE HOURS AND I EXPECT THE SAME LEVEL OF EFFICIENCY FROM ALL OF YOU! THAT IS ALL!!"

Strike one!

The very next day, the Master Chief of the Command along with Senior Chief

Likenhood, the ship's senior medical person, paid a visit to Fleet Command

Headquarters. They went there for two reasons. First to inform headquarters about not

using tugs, and second, to relay to command exactly what transpired during the collision.

Now, notice I said enlisted personnel. Not one officer accompanied the master chief or

doctor to headquarters which seemed incredible since we knew the officers were just as

fed up with the skipper as we were. The meeting concluded and they returned to the ship.

Whatever transpired at headquarters was not discussed with any of the crew, although

I'm sure some of the officers were given a heads up. A month passed and we still hadn't

deployed. Many of us believed the Admiralty had accepted what was told them and were

considering some kind of punishment.

For the crew, it was a God's send.

We were finally able to catch up on our sleep and perform critical maintenance to

various systems which had been neglected. However, once the second month had passed,

we were back out at sea and, unbelievably, continuing to operate without tugboats! The

punishment we so desperately wanted for Whitehead never came. We were about to give

up all hope but then we had another mishap. On our first attempt at docking since the pier

collision, we collided with another ship offsetting their collision alarms! The noise was

so loud and piercing I thought my ear drums were going to burst. I can only imagine the

debilitating pain my shipmates had to endure on board the effected ship.

Once again, nothing happened to the Son of Bligh, but this was strike two. Not

long after that, we attempted to dock after a brief deployment and crashed into another

pier. Again, the reason was bad weather. We just couldn't control the ship. However, this

crash damaged the pier forcing two other ships to tie up elsewhere. That was it. That was the straw that broke the camel's back. Headquarters had had enough. Whitehead was summoned to appear before the Admiralty where he finally received his comeuppance. Did I actually say comeuppance? I don't think that word quite captures the moment. How does this sound?

WHITEHEAD GOT HIS ASS CHEWED OUT!!!

Does that work for you? It does for me. Yes, Commander Whitehead was instructed to never again pull in or out of port without the use of tugboats.

STRIKE THREE; YOU'RE OUT— YOU SON OF A BITCH!!!

Needless to say the crew was elated but the victory was bittersweet. The question on everyone's mind. Why had it taken the Admiralty so long to react to the mishaps? And what about Whitehead, was he finally punished? Who knows? He wasn't relieved of command which surprised all of us. If anybody deserved to be canned it was him. Yes, life went on as usual and so did the deployments. The Baffles continued to accept assignments other ships didn't want but the meeting at headquarters had changed him. Granted, he was still a ramjet but the encounter had taken the starch out of his uniforms. Whatever transpired at the command center had affected him. I'd like to think he got his own "blanket party." All in all, I had my feet on dry land sixty-six days during my first sixteen months on board! Sailors like to whine, on board this ship and with this skipper; these sailors had something to whine about!

Chapter 16

The Caribbean

The First Island

According to the latest weather update, the island we were scheduled to visit was dealing with the end stages of a storm. Heavy winds and rainfall were causing significant damage. Debris was everywhere. The cleanup, once started, would take several weeks to complete and it would be a while before the island was fully functional again. As we entered the channel, howling winds made it difficult to maintain steerage. The helmsman, a former boxer from Los Angeles, was ordered to don grip gloves to help steady the wheel. Even with this added precaution, the Baffles was tossed about like a toy boat in a bathtub. On several occasions, the ship's roll indicator passed the 25 degree mark making topside conditions extremely dangerous. In a final attempt at improving the safety for those assigned to weather deck stations, First Division was ordered to rig mooring lines around the main deck.

The purpose?

They were the final backup to the existing life lines. We all knew the seriousness of our situation. Anyone going over the side in these waters would be lost forever. Had I been the Captain I would have cancelled the port visit. There was a very real possibility the Baffles could have been damaged. The storm hadn't subsided and according to the weather track, we would need at least two more hours before attempting to moor.

Conditions like these would certainly raise the yellow flag of caution, and any normal person would have steered clear of the island, but Whitehead was not a normal person. On the contrary, Captain Ramjet, even now, was trying to figure out how to get the Baffles pier side. You see, this was just another opportunity for the Son of Bligh to demonstrate his seamanship abilities. I heard from a reliable source, who was on the bridge at the time, Whitehead's face was void of any emotion. His blank stare not only increased the overall nervousness of the crew, it also affected the Officer of the Deck. According to my source, the OOD was sweating profusely. Not because of the weather, but because of what Whitehead might or might not do next.

And then something wonderful happened.

The bridge received a crackly radio message from the Harbor Master. He stated unequivocally, it was unsafe to proceed. All of us to a man, including the officers, let out a sigh of relief. Whitehead was out of luck. Thank God. The Harbor Master had spoken and his word was the final word. Even if Whitehead had received the go ahead, he was still out of luck. There weren't any tugboats around to assist us. They all had the good sense to move to the leeward side of the island where they sat out the storm. I know in Whitehead's mind he was still thinking about going in solo but to disobey a direct order from the HM would be a death sentence. At that point, you could kiss your Navy career goodbye. One would have thought the ass chewing he received at headquarters was motivation enough, but apparently not. The only other option was to drop anchor and hope for the best. We knew there would be some bottom drag, but we were the only ship in the harbor. For now, swinging at anchor wouldn't be a problem.

The worse thing about the storm was the driving rain. Each time it hit my face I felt like I was being stung. It reminded me about the time I fell down on an ant hill trying to retrieve a baseball. Instead of coming up with the ball, I came up with a face full of fire ants. I remembered the waves of pain from the stinging and the biting. That's how it felt now. The only protection we had was turning away from the water. It may not have been full proof, but it was the best we could do. As for the ship, fenders were deployed every ten feet. Their job was to absorb the shock in case we hit anything. Believe me; the Captain wasn't taking any chances.

Getting back to the anchor, the Quarter Master of the Watch had calculated the swing, but what wasn't calculable was the extent of the drag. Granted, the Baffles was a large ship with a heavy anchor chain, but the bottom was soft and sandy. If the anchor teeth didn't sink in far enough, the Baffles could be dragged into harm's way. I once heard about a merchant vessel swinging with such force; it had taken out large sections of a wooden dock that was used to service oil tankers. The extensive damage required the rerouting of several ships to distant ports.

Regarding the fenders, the thick lines were difficult to handle. Salt water made them heavier than usual and without gloves, almost impossible to hold. Another problem was the pelting rain. It was driven by an unusually cold wind. I was wet and cold and shivering uncontrollably, but the fenders at Line 4 were tied off and deployed exactly as was ordered. Miraculously, no one at our station slipped overboard and drowned. Amazingly, as soon as the anchor was deployed, the rain stopped and the heavy winds subsided leaving only the cold air.

It was as if a switch had been turned off.

The temperature drop served as a beacon to the local inhabitants. Those remaining

142

outside adorned themselves with sweaters and wind breakers. European tourists, unaware of the temporal phenomenon, huddled together en mass, arms tucked inside short sleeved shirts to keep warm. Others, heading back from the beach, bunched together in small circles. Large bottles of rum were freely passed back and forth. For some, the numbing effect succeeded in warming them, for others, not so much.

By the time we secured from our sea and anchor station, the storm had completely passed. The island was now able to begin the slow process of recovery. Eventually, life would return to normal. Once liberty call commenced, I went topside to get a better look of the island. I noticed several odd shaped vehicles had gathered along the length of the pier. The motor whale boat was still be cleaned out, so I made my way up to the signal bridge to get a better look through Big Eyes. As predicted, debris was everywhere and I noticed the flickering of candles in several windows. Apparently, electrical power had not yet been restored. I was curious about the vehicles though, they were lined up single file and in a straight line, almost like a convoy. Once ashore, I got my answer. One of the drivers approached and stated the vehicles were there to take us to the top of the island. Apparently, that was where the "entertainment" was located. The vehicles appeared to be European, but I couldn't say for sure. Here's how I would describe them.

If you could somehow mate a Citroen with a Land Rover this is what their offspring would look like!

Honestly, I was quite surprised to see any vehicles at all. One would have thought the cleanup had taken priority but it hadn't. Business came first. As I reflected on the moment, it suddenly occurred to me these islanders experienced storms all the time. They were used to it. What they hadn't experienced was an American warship swinging at anchor in the middle of their harbor. Now that was something to talk about! The ride to the top was rather uneventful. The usual huts and dwellings so common to islands throughout the Caribbean were missing. There was, however, one rather impressive looking building near the edge of a short embankment. The locals referred to it as "The Queen of Peace Hospital." Our driver informed us the hospital was administered by an Indian doctor who was a very pleasant fellow. He smiled constantly and enjoyed injecting the word "serendipity" into almost every conversation. Unbeknownst to us, the hospital was to be our first stop. After exchanging pleasantries with the good doctor, he asked if we wouldn't mind repairing a storage facility adjacent to his office. The storm had damaged several book shelves, leaving hundreds of medical books lying on the floor.

Lieutenant Hutton, our Supply Officer, and a native of northern California, informed the good doctor that permission would have to come from the Captain before repairs could be rendered. Mr. Hutton assured the doctor he would have his answer in the morning. Emboldened by the response, the doctor wished us well but cautioned us regarding liberty call. Electricity was still out and would not be available until the following day. Without electricity, there was no air conditioning or refrigeration meaning wherever we went; we would have to sit outside. The thought of sharing warm beer with mosquitoes the size of marbles was not what I had in mind. I got back inside the vehicle and returned to the boat.

The next morning at Quarters, word was put out that Master Chief Howe was looking for a handful of volunteers to assist him in rendering repairs to the hospital. The Master Chief, also from Supply, had a good relationship with the Lieutenant. Not only did they work well together, but rumor had it the Master Chief was bucking to become an officer himself. Having Mr. Hutton in his corner was definitely a plus. Besides, building shelves was a piece of cake. The Master Chief worked as a carpenter before joining the Navy. I decided to volunteer for two reasons. First, I had a lot of experience building small wooden tables back in New Jersey. Twice a year our church held festivals to raise money. The tables were used to display food platters, refreshments and other handmade products available for purchase. Second, as long as I was volunteering, I was off the ship, and any time you're off the boat it's a plus.

The Master Chief, along with four volunteers, myself included, arrived at the hospital the following morning via official island transport. Apparently, the good doctor had informed the Mayor, who, wishing to express his gratitude, not only provided the free transportation, but also supplied us with the tools and lumber necessary to complete the task. Once on site, even though it was hot, the higher altitude and accompanying wind made the work bearable. Regarding the wind, I found it fascinating how it worked its way from the beach up to our location. According to the doctor, the wind began its journey on the calm side of the island before turning and twisting its way up and around the mountain ridge until finally reaching the summit. He said it reminded him of a giant anaconda that was curled around a massive tree, climbing higher and higher until finally reaching a spot conducive for good hunting. I thought it was a good analogy.

Personally, I was just glad we had a breeze.

Before starting on the shelving, we constructed wood horses. The horses provided balance and stability. Without the horses, cutting in a straight line would be next to impossible. And anyone who's ever held a hammer knows it's easier to drive nails when you have support. One of the first roadblocks we encountered was aligning the wood.

145

Since we didn't have a nail gun or a vice, it would have to be done by hand. The wood would have to be held firmly at both ends while someone else did the hammering. Fortunately, Master Chief found some crayons which were used to darken twine taken from a rusted toolbox. The darkened twine was turned into a rudimentary plum. Although not ideal, at least we had a straight line to go by. Once we began working, I noticed a group of islanders had gathered under palm trees not twenty five feet from where we were. They were a mixed group of males and females, perhaps twenty in number. Not long after they arrived, the smell of marijuana and beer filled the air. Someone in their party turned on a battery powered radio. The volume was turned up so loud, I thought the crackling speakers might burst. I smiled and shook my head.

It wasn't even 10 in the morning.

As I was sawing one of the planks which would later become a shelf, I became curious as to why these islanders decided to come and watch us work. The first thing that came to mind was the cleanup. Perhaps they were finished with what they had to do and decided to celebrate? Maybe the damage wasn't as bad as we had originally thought? In any case, they had come to watch us work. I for one was grateful for the company. A couple of women, feeling the effects of the smoke and the alcohol, began to move to the rhythm of the music. One of the girls got up and started dancing. She was young, in her late teens, and beautiful. Concentrating on my work was becoming difficult. I had one eye on the shelving and the other on her. She noticed I was looking at her and smiled. I smiled back but didn't say anything.

"Finished cutting that two by six Patterson?"

It was Master Chief Howe.

"Almost done Master Chief," I replied.

He walked over to where I was, and leaning over whispered.

"Attention to detail son…attention to detail."

It didn't take long before we were covered in sweat. The work wasn't difficult, but as the sun rose, so did the temperature. Even the wind was getting hotter. I asked permission to remove my shirt but the Master Chief felt it best I keep it on; something to do with representing the USA and all that. Disappointed, I refocused my attention on the dancing girl when I noticed another young girl had joined her. Both girls moved out from the shade of the palm trees and into the sun. The girl who smiled at me had light brown highlights in her hair which hung half way down her back. Covering what Mother Nature had given her was a small black bra. Much to my satisfaction, the design of the bra pushed her breasts together, accentuating an already lovely figure. She caught my eye again and I winked back, but, instead of winking or smiling, she blew me a kiss.

I almost lost it. A surge of testosterone overpowered me. Instantly, my legs became weak and my knees buckled. I thought for a second I might loss my balance. Had I not bent over to tie the lace on my boondocker I think I would have passed out? It took several minutes for me to fully recover. All this from a blown kiss. Unbelievable. By the time we finished, twenty new shelves had been constructed and installed and the good doctor couldn't have been happier. The dozens of scattered medical books had been picked up and placed alphabetically onto the new shelving. As an added bonus, a new front door was constructed and installed. The design pattern accentuated an already picturesque backdrop. The Mayor, along with the entire Island Council, bestowed upon us the ultimate expression of gratitude. We were allowed to sign the Mayor's Book which was considered the highest honor the island had to offer.

On our way back down the mountain, smiles and high five's were everywhere. The guys were pleased with the work they did. After all, it was a hospital. About half way down, a strong wind encircled us. Not only did it cool us off, it also dried our uniforms. I guess you could say it was Heaven sent.

Mr. Chamberlain, our driver and father of thirteen, was a dead ringer for Louis Armstrong. He even had the same smile. He knew about the motor whale boat and its tight schedule. He made it a point to drive faster than normal to get us to the wharf in time. We were grateful for his service.

Interesting fellow this Chamberlain. During the last leg of our trip, he told us he was the Senior Conductor for the Island Transport System. His eldest son also worked for the company but most of his children had left the island in search of employment in Europe and in the Middle East. He said he had twenty eight grandchildren and started talking about them but my mind was elsewhere. I closed my eyes and thought about the dancing girl. I so much wanted to meet her.

Back on board, Senior Chief Thompson, the ever present Master at Arms, informed us we would be weighing anchor the next day. The news came as a surprise since we were expecting seventy two hours of liberty. I wondered if the decision to leave was the Captains. After a quick shower and change of clothes, I made my way up to radio. The duty sparks was a friend of mine and even though he wouldn't answer me directly, the fact he was silent when asked about ship's movement spoke volumes. This was Commander Whitehead's decision. He knew we needed a little R & R but he didn't care.

His vindictiveness never ceased to amaze me.

And talk about being petulant! The good Captain had yet again found another way to punish the crew for his incompetency. Since liberty call was reduced from seventy two to twenty four hours, I decided to modify my liberty policy. Instead of resting and delaying departure till 2300, I left on the first launch. The motor whale boat was scheduled to make hourly pickups, so I had plenty of time to take in the sights. I arrived at the landing around 1800. A little early for partying, but, according to my driver, several small bars were open and ready for business. I instructed him to drop me off at The Queen of Peace Hospital. The heat of the day was beginning to subside making the outdoors bearable. I started walking and as I made my way, I was pleased to see that the electricity had been restored and most of the debris had been gathered and taken to a dump site.

Fifteen minutes later I arrived at a small blue bungalow. A worn and weathered red sign was swinging from two hinges attached to a wooden pole above the entrance. The white letters said Samson's Bar. I entered and was a little surprised at what I saw. The "bar" consisted of a thick piece of maple wood sanded and stained so many times; I was able to see my reflection. The maple top was supported by four empty beer kegs painted the same color as the bungalow. A few square shaped stools were lined up along the opposite side of the entrance. Each stool was stamped with the following message: PAYING CUSTOMERS ONLY. The table top was approximately eight feet long by four feet wide. The bar itself only slightly larger. I smiled. This is something my dad could have built in his garage. I sat down and ordered a cold beer which I never do. It would have to get a lot cooler before I could switch to shooters.

149

With the exception of the bartender, I had the place to myself. An air conditioner was installed, but it wasn't turned on. I thought about turning it on, but just then, I was surrounded by cool air. The afternoon wind had arrived. Instinctively, I unbuttoned the top two buttons on my shirt enticing the wind to enter. It moved quickly across my chest and then around to my back. It felt like Heaven. Not only did I stop sweating, I was able drink beer and have my shirt dried at the same time. I leaned back and closed my eyes. Soft music was playing from a speaker located on a shelf above the cash register. The moment was perfect. If only I had someone to share it with.

I finished my beer and another one came just in time for me to smoke a cigarette. I was completely relaxed. In fact, my mind was a complete blank. All of a sudden though, a brightly colored parrot flew in from an opened window on the opposite side of the bar. I hadn't notice when I came in, but a small white bowl was positioned on a table near where the bird was. In one giant swoop, it grabbed whatever was in the bowl with its powerful talons and flew back out the way it came. The bartender, Samson, smiled and whistled, enticing the bird to return. Although he had a pleasant demeanor, he was a powerful looking man with large hands. His salt and pepper hair suggested someone in their late forties or early fifties, but judging from the scars on his arms and across his forehead, he was not one to mess with. I wondered how many altercations he had been involved in.

About an hour later, the peace and tranquility I was enjoying was interrupted by three islanders. They appeared to be fishermen and may have smelled like fisherman, but I couldn't tell. The alcohol was interfering with my senses. They entered the bar and two of the men immediately sat down at a make shift table halfway between the door and the

150

serving area. As I looked over to acknowledge them, I realized I had seen them before. They were at the hospital this morning. The taller of the two was the one who brought the radio and the other gentleman, the one opposite him, was one of the men who brought the beer. The third man, the one walking over to where I was sitting was unknown to me.

"I gotta question for ya" he said.

He was standing close enough for me to smell the marijuana which had permeated the calico shirt he was wearing.

"Me friends say you look me sista today…danc'n…you like girl?"

"She's a good dancer" I said.

Ignoring my response he continued. "You want girl"?

"Do I want her? I'm not sure I know what you mean" I said rather defensively. Samson shifted over to my side of the bar but said nothing. I was sitting with my back exposed to his two friends. If anything was to happen, it was advantage islanders. I was completely blind-sided. I wasn't looking for trouble but that's usually when it happens. Worse, I was unarmed and if they carried weapons, even small knives, it would be difficult to defend myself.

"Patterson, I got your back!"

I turned around and faced the door.

It was Smitty from Deck Division. He had just arrived and was standing near the entrance. Petty Officer Smith was a farm boy from Iowa and stronger than steel. If he says he's got your back, he's got it. The three locals combined were no match for him.

I breathed a huge sigh of relief.

Smitty may have been a farm boy, but he had the whereabouts to recognize a

151

donnybrook when he saw one.

"So, you want girl?"

He repeated the question.

"Yea, sure, I want the girl…what do I have to do?"

"Give me 50 dollas and she's yours man!"

The man smiled revealing nicotine stained teeth.

"She's really your sister?" I said.

"Yea, baby kid sista, got four more just like her…so, whatya say man?"

I slowly lit another cigarette and took a long sip of my beer before answering. He sounded more like a pimp than her brother.

"Why do you want fifty dollars?"

"Cause I need to buy food for me kids and milk for dee baby! Dee money not for the girl man, if that's what you're think'n. Everybody poor here. Woman here cheaper than shirt. Dee money not for the girl man."

I stood up and faced the man. Samson slid out from behind the bar.

"If a woman is cheaper than a shirt, maybe I'll go find another girl and save me some money," I said.

The fisherman exhaled the tension that was building inside.

"Look friend, the woman is cheap yea, but where ya gonna take her? Hotel expensive. Charge you more than fifty dollas. You give me money; I show you where to take girl."

I have to admit for a moment I was tempted. The thought of having sex with his sister was exciting, but the neon sign flashing inside my head wouldn't go away.

Something wasn't right.

"Thanks for the offer, but no thanks," I said.

Immediately, his demeanor changed. The smile disappeared.

"WHAT! YA DON'T LIKE BLACK GIRLS!"

Both his arms dropped to his side. His two friends immediately stood up and turned to face Smitty. Samson moved out from behind the bar and stood between us like a referee.

"I LOVE BLACK GIRLS!" I shouted back. Everybody stood still.

"SO! WHAT THE PROBLEM....WHAT DO YA WANT MAN?"

The fishermen weren't backing down and neither were we.

"JUST SAY THE WORD PATTERSON...JUST SAY THE WORD!"

Smitty was itching for a fight.

I needed to defuse the situation and I needed to do it quickly. Whatever I was about to say better be good.

"What I want is for you and your friends to have a drink on me...what do you say?"

"A drink...any drink?"

"Anyth'g ya wan man!" I said.

The islanders, including Samson, roared with laughter at my feeble attempt to sound like them. The danger was over. Samson returned to behind the bar. The two fishermen sat back down.

"What your name friend?"

"William"

"And you?"

"Odane."

He turned around and pointed to his two friends.

"Dee tall one is Benton, and dee other is Trevor."

Odane leaned over the bar and grabbed three beers.

"It's on Willie!" he said, pointing a finger at me.

Samson acknowledged with a nod.

Smitty was still standing near the entrance.

"Smitty come and join us" I said.

"You buying?" he asked.

"Yea, I'm buying."

"Ok" and with that, the five of us gathered around one small table. We talked in general about a great many things but I could see from their faces they wanted specifics. They had many questions about the ship and how long we were going to be on the island. Benton told us he wanted to be a cab driver in Boston but didn't have the papers to go to the states. Trevor wanted to know if he could get a job selling hot dogs in New York City. Odane didn't ask any questions at all. He was happy drinking beer he didn't have to pay for. A few more locals arrived, shared a drink or two and then departed. I bought three or four more rounds for the guys and Smitty bought two before I realized just how late it was.

The Petty Officer of The Watch informed us the last shuttle back to the boat departed at 0000. It was 2330. Smitty and I finished our last drink and exited the bar, but before heading back to the transport vehicles, we passed the hospital where Odane's sister just happened to be sitting with one of her friends. I think it was the other dancer. As we approached, she got up and faced us. She looked even more beautiful than she did dancing. I finally saw her up close. She had light brown skin which accentuated her turquoise colored eyes. Long, chestnut colored hair obscured a small mermaid tattoo swimming near the middle of her back. Her legs were firm and shapely and she smelled like an angel. I don't think she was older than eighteen, it didn't matter; she was a sight to behold. Just as I was about to speak to her, I heard Odane's voice.

"Ya sure ya don't wan girl?"

He and his friends had followed us from Samson's Bar.

His smile had returned once again exposing his nicotine stained teeth.

"Want…YES! Have the time for…NO!"

I turned back to his sister.

"I would consider it an honor just to spend five minutes with you, but I have to leave now. I must return to the ship."

"I understand."

She spoke softly and alluringly.

"May I know your first name?"

"Shaniyah."

"Shaniyah. The name suits you. A beautiful name for a beautiful woman."

"And you?"

"William."

"A strong name for a strong man."

Shaniyah walked over to where I was and without hesitation, entered my personal space. Our eyes met for a split second before she planted a soft kiss on my cheek.

I was completely beguiled; she was a living, breathing intoxicant. I couldn't utter another word. I began to perspire and just like before, my knees buckled. I have to admit it was a little embarrassing. But I couldn't help it. I was mesmerized. For a moment, I even thought about missing ship's movement just to spend time with her.

"YEA, YEA, YEA THEY'RE ALL BEAUTIFUL SHIPMATE!! ALL BEAUTIFUL!! ALL THE TIME!!

Smitty had broken the spell. Slowly, I began to regain consciousness. I stood there a full minute composing myself. I never saw Shaniyah again but every now and then I think about her. The way we met. Her brother and his offer. You know, I've always been curious about that offer. Was he for real or was he just kidding?

I also think about her voice and the softness of her kiss. But mostly, I think about how she made me feel. Of all the women I have ever met throughout the course of my life, no one has affected me like that beautiful island girl living in the middle of nowhere.

Chapter 17

The Second Island

The unswerving and persistent winds which were so plentiful on the first island were nowhere to be found on the second. Lingering inside the harbor inlet was stale air and oppressive heat. Sweat poured down my back and legs as we waited for the tugs to complete the task of getting the Baffles pier side.

As we neared our mooring location, I witnessed something I had never seen before. From my sea and anchor station, I saw a frenzy of rats rip apart a sack of rice which had fallen onto the dock from a loading platform. The rats tore at the cloth bag with such ferocity; I was unable to count their numbers. All of a sudden, and from nowhere, I saw a human hand and then another begin to push the rats aside. Soon more hands joined in. The bodies behind those hands were thin and emaciated. Most were covered in shredded cloth. Only a few had shoes and most appeared too weak to stand. Using hands and feet, they scooped up the rice with whatever they could find. Some had bowls, but most just used the cloth they were wearing. The competition was intense and at times it looked like the humans had the upper hand.

But then the rats fought back.

Many screamed in pain from the relentless biting. Instead of concentrating on hands and legs, the rats, marshaling their forces, focused instead on the faces and necks of their victims. Their strategy was simple. Attack from all sides and overwhelm. One poor soul lost part of his check to a rather vicious group of vermin fighting separately from the others. Those that passed out were pushed to the side by those strong enough to continue. A uniformed policeman appeared from a small shack located between the two platforms. He was a tall, muscular man, perhaps forty years in age. Loosely sewn into his right sleeve were three tattered chevrons indicating the rank of sergeant. His official badge which was attached to his worn shirt glistened in the sunlight. He was impressive, but his most striking characteristic were his eyes.

He was a heterochrome.

When he first approached the ship, he moved cautiously aft until he came to one of the stern bollards. Once there, he straddled the big, black baton he was carrying over it. The morning sun was just high enough to illuminate his face as he gazed upon the ship. It was then I was able to see his eyes. His right eye was light green but his left eye was charcoal black. From a distance it looked like he was wearing an eye patch. Whether through birth or injury, the heterochromatia didn't interfere with his ability to carry out his duties as a representative of the government. Physically he suffered no impairment, but psychologically I believe the heterochromatia affected him. Although I didn't have any evidence to support this, I did notice one thing in particular.

The big policeman didn't like being stared at. The more you starred at him; the more irritated he became. Surmising the situation, he quickly summoned two rough looking stevedores who were working just above the landing. Their job was to salvage as much rice as they could. The big black baton would soon be put to good use.

The muscular policeman walked over to where the crowd had gathered and without saying a word, began striking people indiscriminately. As he moved throughout the crowd, I noticed he had a very unique style. He would first position himself over his victims then raise his baton high in the air. Taking aim, he would unleash his fury on or near the knuckle area of the perpetrator's hand. The sound of the baton strike was horrific, as was the wailing. The knuckle cracks reminded me of a bat hitting a baseball.

The stevedores weren't much better. Instead of hands, they kicked the rats and the beggars out of their way. I know those kicks were painful because stevedores wear steel toed boots. Once they made a big enough clearing, they lifted the torn bag vertically and began filling it with whatever remained on the street. At this point, the big policeman acted as a buffer between the stevedores and the beggars. He continued to swing his baton allowing the two men to complete their task. The whole time this was happening, I remained fixated on the policeman's face. He had the look of complete indifference, as if he were immune to their plight. In fact, I sensed he rather enjoyed it. His smile said it all. Whatever salary the government was paying him he earned with interest.

Once the rice was scooped up and the bag returned to the loading platform, the policeman disappeared back into his shack. The beggars and rats retreated to an area adjacent to the wharf. As they departed, faint cries caught my attention. I felt bad for them. Once we secured from sea and anchor detail, I made a bee line to my locker. The candy bars I had stashed away were spread out and unaccounted for. Some were tucked inside my socks while others were jammed inside my shoes. All in all, I had about twenty candy bars which I placed in the front of my locker. My plan was simple. The first chance I got, I would give them to the rat people.

Chapter 18

The Second Island

I was scheduled for duty.

Section Three was the last duty section assigned watch standing on the previous island. According to the bumper rotation set up by Mr. Calvin, Section Four was scheduled to stand duty. However, that responsibility somehow shifted to Duty Section One. Believe me, the guys in Duty Section One were not happy campers.

Mind you, I wasn't complaining, just curious as to why our duty section was skipped over. In all actuality though, I could have used the rest. I had just completed an all nighter. Two critical pieces of equipment had malfunctioned and my job was to get them working again before pulling into port. Remember, under this Captain, all equipment had to be working all the time. I thought about hitting my rack, but I was so wired from the ten cups of coffee I drank, I decided to hit the town instead.

By now, you're familiar with my liberty routine. I sleep first then go out later. However, this was a dangerous port and quite frankly, I was little surprised we even stopped here. What didn't surprise me was the granting of liberty call. As usual, political correctness superseded crew safety. So, instead of delaying liberty and resting like I normally do, I decided to bond with a coterie of like-minded individuals.

Honestly, it didn't take a genius to recognize a precarious situation. It's true, every port has the potential to be dangerous, but this place was unique. To begin with, the docking facility was brimming with onlookers. Normally, the only people we come in contact with are stevedores and government officials. Here, in addition to the rat people, numerous vendors had set up shop within ear shot of the ship. The truth is, there were so many people milling about, one had to be particularly careful just walking around. The chance of bumping into or stepping on someone was very real. This is what the crew had to deal with that first day, but I think the Captain had it worse. In fact, I never saw him looking more frustrated.

During our entire visit to the island, Whitehead never left the ship. Also, the redness which had saturated his checks never dissipated. There were times he got so red; I thought someone had slapped a uniform on a fire hydrant! Look, I'm no doctor, but I got to tell you, I thought the veins in his neck were going to burst!

For him, this island was a security nightmare.

Had good Captain Stewart been the skipper, I would have felt bad for him, but since we were under the command of the Son of Bligh, I felt nothing at all. Actually, during one of my private moments, I secretly thanked the island for doing to Whitehead what no one else had been able to do. For the first time, his emotions were getting the better of him and I couldn't have been happier.

Getting back to security, as a precaution, Whitehead increased the watch standing around the ship. The usual complement of watch standers assigned to the quarter deck doubled. The "additionals" were ordered to man the brow and prevent anyone from coming on board.

In addition, the motor whale boat was lowered into the water to prevent swimmers, and there were quite a few, from boarding the ship. Lastly, he increased the roving patrols and even posted a guard on the 0-3 level just to look for trouble inland.

I have to admit, I was a bit uneasy. I usually don't raise the yellow flag of caution standing on the quarter deck, but, like I said, this place was different. Since I was uncomfortable, I decided to team up with two guys I had befriended. Although twidgets, neither were sonar technicians which made it even better. I was tired of talking shop.

Besides, scuttlebutt had it we were leaving in three days anyway, so, as usual, I wanted to make the most of it.

Amazing isn't it? The nicer ports of call, we're lucky to get 48 hours, but places like this, 72 hours and counting!

Wind...Water...Whiskey...and Women!

Wasn't life grand?

"Hey Monsieur! Hey, you need cab?"

We were briefed at quarters about the local transportation.

Apparently, normal taxi service was unavailable on this island. What was available were small cars made to look like taxis. In almost all the vehicles, the front passenger seats had been removed. This was considered a courtesy. The islanders were well aware of the needs of western tourists. Allowing them to stretch their legs could only add to their bottom line. Unfortunately, these little cars came with a catch. If you wanted to be ferried around the island, you had to rent them for twenty four hours. I know it sounds crazy, but the drivers were used to it and as long as you gave them a good tip at the end of the day, they were happy.

"Monsieur?"

"How much for the three of us?" I looked him straight in the eye.

"Cab price for one passager, three passager–three price."

"No way Monsieur!" said Tommy from Minnesota. Operations Specialist Second Class Tommy Reynolds had a hot temper which he attributed to his paternal grandmother.

"I'd rather walk!" he shouted.

"And where do you plan to marcher?" the cab driver asked.

"Look around, Aimer! People live in garbage cans…no money…dirty…no food...no drink…no woman for you brave American Sailor! I take you around …show you good time…what you say?"

Tommy continued.

"Here's the deal Monsieur! You take three of us in one cab… charge one price or we find another driver! Savvy!"

The driver hesitated before answering.

"Je sais. Ok. Ok."

And with that Tommy, Tim and I squeezed into the back seat of a tiny little car.

"What you want first….drink….woman…what?

"Good food!" said Timmy. Tim Drake was the son of a coal miner from West Virginia and he was one of our better navigators. A crackerjack sailor who had stated on numerous occasions he was in for the long haul. A lifer. He had just completed his eight year of service and would soon be frocked to chief petty officer. He was much admired and respected by both officers and crew and I considered it fortunate to have him with us. He was Tommy's friend but we got to know each other playing backgammon in a small storage space located between the forward head and anchor windlass. I considered myself a good player; the game was my passion, but Timmy would beat me 7 out of 10 times, frustrating the hell out of me. I asked him once why he wanted to be a navigator and this is what he told me.

"William, (he always called me William) when I was 12 years old, both my grandfather and my father decided it was time for me to make my acquaintance with the mines. They said they would wait for school to end before showing me how they made a living. This was not uncommon. Many boys my age got their first introduction to the coal industry the same way. A lot of kids from my school and some from around the neighborhood joined me that first day. I was glad they were around because I didn't want to be the only one there my age. Not on the first day."

I nodded in agreement.

"Anyway, I stuck it out for two months, working six days a week alongside my dad and granddad and even though it was dark and the passage ways were pretty small, I enjoyed what I was doing.

Tim paused for a second before continuing.

And then it happened, we had a cave in on the north side of the mine and the weight of the dirt crushed an electrical conduit which was providing the power to operate the lift motor. So, we were stuck, about 40 of us, down at the bottom of the mine with no way out."

"Wasn't there a ladder you could climb?" I asked.

"Not that far down. This was a new dig and auxiliary equipment like that hadn't been installed yet."

"So what did you do?" I asked.

164

"We waited…we waited at the bottom of that mine shaft with no light except from our helmets and we had very little air to breathe."

"How long were you down there for?"

"My grandpa said almost 36 hours."

"With no food or water???"

"Oh, we had sandwiches packed in our lunch boxes, but not everyone had something to drink so we rationed the beverages. That was the first time I drank coffee."

Tim placed his hands around his neck signaling his disapproval.

"For me William, the worst part was the darkness, not being able to see the sun or feel the wind on my face. When I finally got out of there, I made up my mind; I was not going to be a coal miner."

"How'd you get out?"

"The guy's topside jury rigged the electricity. They bypassed the circuit breaker box which controlled the lift and were able to provide power. We exited ten men at a time as a precaution. After the fourth trip, everybody was topside."

"Wow!" That's a hell of a thing to go through as an adult. I can just imagine what that was like for a twelve year old?"

"Yea, even to this day, I still think about it every now and then."

"So why a navigator?"

"Why a navigator?"

A smile formed on Tim's face. I could see from his expression he was done talking about the coal industry.

"I work on the bridge. I'm surrounded by fresh air. I can see and feel the sun, wind and the stars, and sometimes, I'll get sea spray in my hair or on my face and for me, that's the ultimate freedom."

"Ok monsieur's, I take you up top of mountain to place that has casino, restaurant and bar…n'est ce pas?"

"Ya got a name friend?" asked Tommy.

"Sebastian…you can call me Sebastian…ok?"

"Ok…any girls in his place…you know…girls who like to party?"

"No, not this place…I take later to better place for girls." Sebastian continued:

"This place for rich and political people. Be careful what you say…you know no bad thing about government…the people…n'est ce pas?"

I jumped in.

"So why this place?"

"You want good food…this best restaurant on whole island."

At that moment, Sebastian made a sharp right turn and that's when we saw it. Jutting out from the mountain side was a stone castle complete with turrets and a draw bridge. It was a massive structure almost completely white in color. The only thing providing contrast were the black tiles spiraling around the roof tops. Even though it looked impressive, it didn't blend in with any of the surrounding architecture. Personally, I thought it looked out of place. Realistically, it would have looked much nicer in England or in Germany. Once we approached the entrance, Sebastian rolled down his window and spoke to one of the armed guards who was positioned in front of the castle.

"Give me 10 dollars please for guard."

Tim handed the money to Sebastian who gave it to the guard who waved us in.

166

Once inside the gate, Sebastian stopped the cab. I wait here" he said.

The three of us climbed out from the back seat and immediately stretched our arms and legs. I must say, it took us quite a while before we were comfortable again. As soon as we were ready, we climbed a dozen or so stairs until we came to a tuxedoed gentleman who was more than happy to open the door for us. Before entering, I quickly gazed at his uniform. Above his left pocket, the name of the restaurant had been embroidered in gold letters. It was called Lustre, but Sebastian later told us everyone knows it as the chandelier. Once inside, we were directed to the dining area by another tuxedoed employee who was also more than happy to seat us at our table. As we looked around, we couldn't help but notice the enormity of the room.

Without exaggerating, it must have been 100 feet by 150 feet with at least 100 tables, which, by our count, were mostly empty. At the far end of the room were large wood paneled doors separating our room from yet another room.

The doors to this other room were slightly ajar, allowing me to peek inside. What I saw was striking. A military officer dressed like General Patton was leaning over and lighting the cigarette of a woman who was seated close to the opening. Within minutes, two other uniformed men opened up the doors as if signaling the end of some kind of meeting. The woman with the cigarette looked to be in her mid thirties. She was dressed in a long gown and covered in jewels and diamonds. She exited the room first before her entourage quickly followed behind. I counted three women and five armed men.

Restaurant guests stood and politely bowed as the woman walked passed them. Other patrons followed suit and then a waiter quickly appeared at our table.

"Please get up!" he said rather authoritatively.

167

"The wife of the President…please get up and do like others do…and please…no talking!"

The three of us stood and politely bowed as Madame President walked passed our table. She was a thin woman but exhibited a firm body suggesting an active exercise regimen. She looked straight at the three of us but her face remained motionless, as if she had already dismissed us. The cigarette she held between her fingers was nothing more than a fashion statement. It never touched her lips. As her entourage approached the entrance to the foyer, a tall black man wearing African garb took a picture of her with his camera. Immediately, one of her armed escorts grabbed the camera and pushed the man back against the wall. With the man pinned, another guard came over and grabbed the camera. After a quick look see, he opened the compartment housing the film and removed it. Satisfied the camera and film were not a threat; he returned it back to the African. On the other side of the foyer, another guard was chastising one of the waiters for the apparent breech in protocol. After he finished yelling at the waiter, the guard punctuated the end of his sentence by whipping the man across the face with a small baton he was carrying. Madame President and her entourage continued talking as if nothing happened. Once they departed the restaurant, life returned to normal.

"Wow!" said Tommy.

"They don't mess around!"

"Her husband, Monsieur President must be a very strong ruler…did you get a look at their faces?"

"Fear" I said. "They have the look of fear. Imagine the secret service whipping a reporter because they didn't like a particular question. It would make the front page of

168

every newspaper in the country."

We found out later from our waiter people tend to disappear if Madame President doesn't like them…foreigners included. We quickly finished our meal and returned to the cab.

"Ready…so soon to go?" said Sebastian.

"Ready to get the hell out of here!" said Tommy.

"Where to next my friend?" I asked.

"Vesuvius…good night club….plenty women…you have good time."

"Ok. Let' go," said Tim.

We were about half way down the mountain when the cab stopped.

"You see that building?"

Sebastian pointed to a yellow building with pulsating lights. We nodded.

"The door is on back side. You walk down path to front…I wait here."

The building was maybe 200 feet from where we were but the path was well lit and it had guard rails. We walked around the building and entered from the front. Surprisingly, there was no one watching the door and no one to collect a cover charge. We entered and took seats at a small round table near the exit. There was a live band playing local music and several girls were dancing by themselves, but something looked out of place. Upon closer inspection, I realized the women dancing were racially mixed. Some were locals but others appeared to come from different countries since both their skin tone and hair were different. As I looked around, I noticed a lot of foreigners, tourists if you will. It's no secret European men like to fly to exotic places like this for vacation. They come to sample not just the food but other delicacies as well. Not

169

counting the dancing girls, every guy I saw had a woman with him. The only ones who didn't were us.

"Be careful with these girls."

Someone sitting behind us spoke. It was a strong voice with no accent. I believe the person speaking was an American.

"Even though they're dancing by themselves, they're already taken."

"Sir, if you could spare a moment would you like to come and join us?" Only Tim could be so polite.

"Sure," said the voice. A large white man moved over to our table and sat down in the only chair available.

Tim raised four fingers in the air. The bartender nodded.

"I'm Cap'n Noe, I run a fishing business."

"American?"

"Yes sir, born and raised in Michigan, but I've spent the last seven years here."

"So, you have your own fishing boat?"

"BOAT! HELL, I GOT MY OWN FLEET SON!" And with that, Captain Noe started laughing.

"How long you boys gonna be in town?"

"Less than a week…I imagine?" said Tommy.

"This is William, that's Tim and I'm Tom."

A waiter brought over the beers.

"Gentleman, your health!" said Noe.

"Now, what is it you're looking for?"

170

"Not sure yet, maybe women, maybe just a couple of beers," I said.

"Well, if you're looking for women, you've come to the wrong place."

Mystified, Tim and I looked at each other.

"Women aren't allowed inside clubs like this unless they're escorted. Believe me; every broad here is spoken for. Yea, you can try talking to some of them on the dance floor, but I would advise against it."

Captain Noe took a short sip of beer.

"Why is that Captain?" asked Tommy. Captain Noe's smile faded slightly. "You've seen all the poverty?"

We nodded.

"The girls who work in the escort business are well taken care of."

"How's that?" asked Tommy.

Captain Noe smiled brightly.

"PATRONS!!!"

"Don't you mean customers?" I said.

The Captain took another sip of beer.

No, not customers. Patrons. You see it works like this. These guys here, even before they get off the air plane, have made arrangements with the hotels. When they confirm their reservations, they're asked if they require "female companionship," or something like that. I forget how they're referred to now-a-days. If they answer yes, a woman is either waiting in the lobby to meet them, or for others, the restaurant or bar.

Everything is prearranged. Some of the guys even correspond with the girls, especially those who frequent the island on a regular basis.

"Patrons. Get it?" Captain Noe laughed.

"If you really want to meet women, best bet is to book yourselves into a nice hotel and tell the check in guy what you're looking for."

"Are these girls clean?"

"Oh hell yea! They got to be! Listen, they are carefully screened and are required to submit to weekly blood tests. Listen, mostly Europeans come here. If word gets out these girls are sick, there goes the tourism. No tourism means no money. No money brings more poverty, so the ones in control, the guys who run the operation, do everything they can to make sure nothing affects their income. If a girl gets sick, she is pulled off the circuit. In fact, I've been told some of the hotels are now requiring "guests" to submit to blood tests as well. Listen, these girls are the life blood of the island. Without them, the island would die. I'm surprise your driver brought you here. Maybe he gets a commission for every drink you guys buy. No fellas, this is not the place to pick up women."

"What about the other girls? You know the ones who look like they come from someplace else?" I asked.

"That's because they do come from someplace else. Listen, some of these girls end up in long term relationships. Their boyfriends bring them where ever they go. You know, they get used to having them around. That's why the dance floor looks like a rainbow."

We thanked the Captain for his advice, finished our drinks and headed outside. We retraced our footsteps and found Sebastian asleep in the back seat of the taxi, the radio's volume just loud enough to be heard.

"Time to go back to the ship," said Tim.

Sebastian slowly opened his eyes.

"You say night over…time for ship…pour quoi?"

"Because it's over Pour Quoi…that's why," said an aggravated Tommy.

Sebastian slowly made his way from the back of the cab to the driver's seat.

"The night…not start yet...too early…you wait…you see."

"Night over for us…maybe some other time," said Tim.

The drive down the mountain was very quiet. The only sound was the music playing on the radio.

"I do something wrong man…maybe I do something wrong?" Before Tommy could answer, I jumped in.

"No Sebastian, you see we are military sailors who go to bed early because we have to wake up early. It takes time to adjust to being up late…you understand?"

"Ok, I take back to ship…but you pay full 24 hours…that was deal." Tommy's face turned beet red.

"Ok, how much do we owe you Sebastian?" I asked.

"For everything, $100 dollars!"

I cut him off.

"One hundred dollars!!! Then we don't have money to give you a tip!!!"

The cab arrived just outside the pier entrance. Sebastian turned around and looked at us.

"Ok, fifty goes to company fifty to me." Sebastian was clever but I was one step ahead.

173

"Sebastian, do you really want to know why we left the club?"

"You say you tired."

"No," I continued.

"We left the club because there were no women and you promised us women after we left the restaurant. You told us plenty of women at Vesuvius but what you didn't tell us, all the women have boyfriends! What you didn't tell us is that single women are not allowed in that club by themselves...that they have to go with an escort to get in...that is what you didn't tell us...and the reason you took us to that club is because you work for that club...you make money from the sale of alcohol...that is what you didn't tell us!!!

"Alright! Alright! Next time I take to different club!" Tommy jumped in.

"There ain't gonna be a next time sport and as far as your tip goes...here's a tip...don't screw with the U.S. Navy!!!"

And with that, we flung open the cab doors so hard I thought the hinges were going to snap off.

Tommy finished with this.

"Here's thirty bucks...you decide how much tip to give yourself!!!"

And that was how our first day ended on island number two.

Chapter 19

Day Two

The following morning, the topic of conversation was yesterday's liberty call,
which was odd. We usually begin quarters with a look see followed by work assignments,
but today was different. I knew from experience what to expect. Whenever the Senior
Chief began his day off topic, a project of some importance was waiting in the wings.

"I hope you all had a good time last night. Interesting island isn't it?"

No one answered.

"Well, I hope at least the women treated you nice. Lord knows you all deserve a
little rest and relaxation."

Still no one said a word. Instinctively, I tightened the muscles in my arms and
legs. I knew what was coming next.

"Alright then…I need two volunteers for a project and..."

"What kind of project Senior?"

The interruption came from Peter Bennett. Peter was a nice guy but he had the
reputation of being a pain in the butt. No matter the topic, he always asked a lot of
questions. He was our WHO, WHAT, HOW, WHY, and WHERE man. Many found him
irritating and wanted nothing to do with him, but I saw things differently. True, he was
worrisome and tended to sweat the small stuff, but he was honest and that was good
enough for me.

"Well, if you let me finish Bennett, I'll tell you. They just completed construction on a brand new building. The dry walls are in but nothing's been painted yet and..."

"Who are THEY and what kind of BUILDING?

"What kind of building? I just told you Bennett, a brand new building. They? Who are they? Is that what you asked me? Who are they?"

Bennett nodded.

"THEY are the ones in charge Bennett! That's who THEY are! Now, where was I? Oh yes, it's a brand new building located just outside the city. Just think you'll be off the boat and away from the boredom. Hell, you might even meet some women and..."

"It's not in the city then?"

Senior could no longer contain himself.

"Bennett, if you interrupt me one more time, you'll be pulling double duty every day until we leave port! No! It's not in the city!!"

"Sorry Senior. I promise I only got one more question."

Out of exasperation, Senior relented.

"WHAT NOW BENNETT?"

"Where outside the city?"

"IT'S IN A LEPER COLONY BENNETT!!! IS THAT OK WITH YOU???"

"A LEPER COLONY!!!!" shouted Bennett.

"That's right Bennett, a leper colony, now, besides Bennett, who else wants to volunteer?"

I'm not sure why I raised my hand but I did.

"Patterson! Good for you! I'm proud of you my boy. Real proud!"

You know to this day, I still don't know if that was sarcasm or not.

"Great! Excellent! You two report to the Quarter Deck in fifteen minutes. Go grab yourselves a coke and smoke if you want."

Peter and I quickly made our way to the passageway where the soda machines were located.

"Damn it! I don't want to go to some leper colony!"

"Well, what'd you expect? All those interruptions. You were begging for it!"

"I know, I know. I gotta learn to keep my mouth shut."

"That's what I keep telling you! You need to stop with all the questions!

I sensed Bennett was disappointed.

"Listen, it'll be alright, who knows, maybe we'll even have some fun there."

"Damn it! I don't have any quarters!"

"Not to worry Admiral...I got your back," I said.

The spare change I had in my pocket came to exactly $1.50, just enough for two cokes.

"C'mon, let's go to the fantail" I said.

Once we were topside, I turned to Peter.

"Hey, give me five smokes and we'll call it even."

"Five smokes! Are you nuts! That's fifteen cents each!"

"I know. What? You're gonna get cheap now? C'mon, hand 'em over!"

Peter pulled out a pack of cigarettes from his dungaree shirt pocket and reluctantly handed me the sticks.

"HERE!"

"Thank you...hey, start on the soda while I light my cigarette."

I handed the can to Peter and pulled out my lighter.

"Think it'll be safe at the colony?"

I could hear the nervousness in his voice.

"Listen, Senior said it's brand new, besides, if they haven't painted it yet, I'm pretty sure it's empty. I mean, why would they put patients in a wing that's not complete. Doesn't make sense to me. Does it make sense to you?"

"No, I guess you're right."

His voice sounded better, the nervousness was gone.

We coked and smoked in less than 10 minutes then made our way to the quarter deck. Our Division Officer, Mr. Carson, was talking to the Officer of the Deck, Ensign Davidson from Operations.

"Bennett...Patterson!"

We answered with a hand salute. "Sir."

"I don't need to remind you two gentleman you represent the US of A, so, be on your best behavior. I know I can rely on both of you...

He was staring at us. Now I know what it's like to be in a police lineup.

... that said...do your jobs well and if they ask you any questions about ships movement...play dumb...you don't know anything."

"Yes Sir," we said, echoing each other. Mr. Carson continued.

"I will ride with you to the Colony but I am not going inside."

Bennett and I looked at each other.

"Don't get nervous...it's not what you think...the officers have been invited to a lawn party, their way of saying thanks. Oh, and before I forget, once you've finished

178

painting, the Colony will provide the transportation to take you back to the ship…understood?"

"Yes Sir."

At that moment, a tired looking Peugeot arrived at the dock entrance. Its misfiring engine sent black noxious smoke everywhere. I'm sure the guys working near the air intake vents really enjoyed that. It was a nice looking car even though the driver's side hubcap was missing. I thought about giving the car a passing grade until I saw the upholstery. Even through the windows, you could see it was torn and frayed. Actually, none of that bothered me. What upset me the most were the lack of ash trays. No ash trays meant no smoking. Bad news for me and Peter.

As to the exterior, I'd like to say the color was black but I wasn't sure. For starters, it had been repainted at least once. Add to that a plethora of scratches and years parked in the sunlight and the car could have passed for maroon. The only venerable feature were the two Red Cross flags mounted on the front bumpers. Which brings us to the driver? Talk about eye candy. The tall young man was dressed in an all white suit. Covering his head was a red fedora with matching handkerchief. His long sleeved shirt was adorned with coordinating cuff links complete with white socks and red shoes.

Honestly, he looked more like the Pope than he did a chauffeur.

"Good Morning…bonjour…I am your driver…I am Maurice."

"Good Morning…this is Petty Officer Bennett and this is Petty Officer Patterson. I'm Mr. Carson."

"Monsieur's Bennett, Patterson and Carson, thank you for your assistance...shall we go?"

Mr. Carson sat up front; Bennett and I sat in the back.

Unlike the cab, the front passenger seat was installed. Poor Bennett. He could hardly move his legs.

"How far is the colony, Monsieur Maurice?" asked Mr. Carson.

"Maybe one hour...depends on traffic...maybe forty five minutes." Peter rolled his eyes. He was definitely uncomfortable.

As we made our way from the harbor, I noticed something right off the bat. The night time ride with Sebastian had camouflaged the day time poverty of the city. Some people believe the Caribbean is synonymous with paradise. This place was the furthest from it. Once we cleared the docks, I saw thousands of people living in cut out garbage cans. It didn't matter the direction we looked, we were surrounded by deprivation. I saw many people and many families, but parents with small children had it the worse. One rummaged for food while the other slept and looked after the children. Even after switching roles, I believe it was impossible for either parent to get the rest they needed. After a quick look see, I came to a startling revelation. The poor people of this island, although individually unique, shared the same three things: Hunger, sleep deprivation and illness.

As we continued on our journey, we saw many dead bodies stacked along the road side. Maurice said this was how the government dealt with the dead. Dump trucks would make rounds twice a day. Their job was to collect and relocate the remains to an open field where they would be cremated. Another thing that looked out of place were the legions of sick people seeking medical attention. By my estimate, for every one doctor there were at least ten thousand patients. Maurice assured us the Red Cross stations were open, but in order to be treated, one had to get there.

Did I mention this was the Capitol!

Just imagine what the rest of the country must have looked like! Out of respect for Maurice, Bennett and I rode all the way to the Leper Colony in silence. Not so with Mr. Carson. He kept asking questions about the history of the island. I guess he felt it was the safest thing to talk about. We were never told why the island was in such dire straits or why there was so much poverty. I thought a recent storm might be the cause but I was wrong. This poverty was systemic. Many generations had suffered through it. These people were just the latest casualties. The deprivation kept us company until we were well out of the city.

"Ay! We are here! There is the gate!"

Maurice slowed the choking Peugeot, braking just feet from the front gate. A large sign adorned the top part of an awning. On the left side were the letters DEFAE and on the right side was CATIO.

"Defaecatio?" I asked.

"Qui, monsieur, Defaecatio," answered Maurice. The large black letters rested against a white background.

"A Latin word...to cleanse...to purify."

An inquiring voice interrupted our discussion. It came from the recently installed intercom system positioned just a few feet away from the entrance gate. Maurice pushed the talk button which was conveniently located next to his window. After a brief conversation, the gate opened electronically. As we sat there waiting to enter, I thought how odd it was. Here we were, just a few miles outside the city, about to enter a leper colony equipped with all the latest technology yet within the city itself, people were living in garbage cans! Once inside, Maurice drove down a narrow stone road until we came to a uniformed guard who ushered us to the back of the compound.

Surrounding us were signs of recently completed construction. Piles of wood were everywhere. A doctor wearing a white lab coat with a stethoscope draped around his neck approached us from an open courtyard. Maurice stopped the car, got out and walked over to greet him. The two men spoke briefly and then without turning around, Maurice gestured for us to get out.

"Remember guys, you are good will ambassadors…good luck," said Mr. Carson.

Bennett and I exited the vehicle and walked over to where the two men were standing.

"This is Doctor Villeneuve…he is in charge of the Colony."

"Welcome….welcome…my American sailors! Welcome to Defaecatio!"

"Thank you, Sir," said Bennett.

Mr. Carson exited the car and walked over to Dr. Villeneuve.

"Good Morning Doctor, I'm Mr. Carson."

The three of us exchanged handshakes with the doctor.

"Please to meet you Sir, will you also be staying?"

"No Doctor, unfortunately I have another engagement which I must attend to."

"Oh! That is indeed unfortunate! Perhaps next time then?"

"Perhaps," said Mr. Carson.

"Maurice, whenever you are ready,"

I sensed Mr. Carson wanted to leave as quickly as possible. Even though we were told not to worry, I don't think he wasn't totally convinced.

"Qui monsieur...we will go now."

"Good bye Doctor...it was a pleasure meeting you."

"Enchanter Mr. Carson...enchanter."

The two men once again exchanged handshakes.

Maurice followed Mr. Carson back to the car and they departed.

"Ok, are you two gentlemen ready to begin painting?"

"Yes Doctor," I said.

"Please follow me then."

The Doctor led us across the open courtyard to an arched passageway which turned into another courtyard. Surrounding the yard were recently constructed rooms not quite ready for occupancy. Some of the rooms had doors while others still needed framing. The rooms that had the doors were the ones we were going to paint.

"You'll find brushes and paint inside the room over there in the corner. Don't worry about the color; all the rooms will be the same. Let me thank you again for your assistance in helping Defaecatio become operational. Soon we will be able to receive patients...but before I depart, would both of you please sign our guest book...we would consider it an honor."

"The honor is ours Doctor," said Peter.

Doctor Villeneuve exited the courtyard, but returned shortly after. A thick brown book was tucked under his left arm. He placed the book on a piece of plywood which was supported by two saw horses. He removed a black pen from his white coat pocket and handed it to Peter.

183

"Please sign your name here."

Peter signed his name then handed the pen to me. I was about to sign below Peter but I hesitated. For some strange reason, the book signing on the first island popped into my head. Oh, I remembered the people and the ceremony, but what really made an impression was the Mayor himself. I mean the guy was the Caribbean Fred Astaire. He showed up to the ceremony in an opened tuxedo complete with purple sash and red cummerbund. Covering his head was a sparkling top heat that glistened whenever he moved. Complementing the pleated pants he wore were high gloss black shoes covered in white spats! Picture that! The only thing missing was Ginger Rogers.

I felt very proud when I signed their book. The work we did was necessary to get the hospital up and running again. They said it was an honor and I felt honored. Here, on island number two, I have an opportunity to sign another book. Even though there's no ceremony, I still felt venerated. I signed my name.

"Merci gentlemen," said the Doctor after closing the book and repositioning it under his left arm.

"I will send someone in later to check on you."

Dr. Villeneuve left the room. Peter and I walked over to where the paint was and got started. I counted five rooms; Peter said there were four. Upon re-inspection he agreed with my assessment. He forgot to include an adjoining room which was attached to the last room we were going to paint. Working together, it took us about one hour to finish the first room. I painted the ceiling and Peter painted the walls. We could have finished earlier, but some of the dry walls needed spackling due to small nicks and tears caused by the installation. In the states this is known as tape and float. Fortunately, Peter was able to find some spackle in one of the paint lockers. After fifteen minutes of drying time, we started the painting. Since the floors hadn't been installed yet, we could afford to be a little sloppy.

The next room we switched assignments. Peter painted the ceiling and I painted the walls. After the third room was completed, a young man in his early twenties appeared carrying a silver tray containing two large glasses and a pitcher filled with water. He set the tray down on a make shift table then proceeded to pour the water into the glasses. I was surprised the water was cold because I didn't see any ice in the pitcher. The man could barely speak English but he knew enough to explain the mystery of the water. It was drawn from a mountain stream located within the complex. He assured us the water was tested daily ensuring its purity and freshness. We emptied our glasses quickly and the young man filled them up again. While he was refilling, I noticed he only had three fingers on his pouring hand. In place of the missing fingers were two thick black stubs which immediately raised the yellow flag of caution. Not wanting to embarrass the server or alarm Bennett, I kept quiet. After he left I brought it to Peter's attention.

"Are you kidding me? The guy's a leper!!"

"Or was. I don't think they would expose us on purpose."

"I don't know. Better ask the Doc when he comes back."

I could see Bennett was becoming uncomfortable.

"C'mon, let's finish these last two rooms and get the hell out of here."

Exactly two hours later we were done with the fifth and final room. It was about five o'clock when Dr. Villeneuve returned. He conducted a visual inspection of each room. I have to admit, Peter and I were a little nervous. When he exited the last room he was smiling. Both of us let out a sigh of relief.

"Gentlemen, I have inspected all five rooms and I am most pleased with what I have seen. The rooms are well painted thanks to your knowledge and skill. I shall write a Letter of Commendation andpresent it to Mr. Carson tonight when I see him."

"Thank you Sir," said Bennett.

"I will call Maurice to take you back to the ship."

"Thank you Sir," was my response.

"Ya got a minute Doc?"

"Qui"

"I just have one question, if you don't mind?"

"Yes of course Monsieur Bennett. How may I help you?"

The gentleman who brought us the water. I was just wondering if he was a patient here in the Colony."

"Ex-patient."

Bennett let out a sigh of relief.

"Don't worry Monsieur. Emile is not contagious."

I let out a sign of relief.

"Emile was lucky. He came to us when he first began to notice changes. Fortunately for him, the disease only took two fingers. Others who survived were not as lucky."

I could tell from the Doctor's expression he wanted to go into more detail but declined to do so. Before exiting the courtyard we exchanged handshakes once again.

186

After that, the Doctor took off. He disappeared into a building located on the opposite side of the campus.

That was our cue.

Bennett and I retraced our footsteps back through the arched passageway to the open area where we first arrived. I hadn't noticed when we first came in, but across from the narrow stone road was a rather large building with many windows. I believe the main offices were located there. Outside the building was a table with several chairs but since the shade was wider on our side of the street, we decided to stay put. While waiting for Maurice, we smoked a couple of cigarettes…and that's when I saw her.

Standing on the second floor balcony overlooking the entrance area was a tall woman with light brown skin. Even though the western sun was only inches above the top of the palm trees, the light shining through was more than enough to accentuate her characteristics. I squinted as I looked up to see her, but even with the sun in my eyes, I noticed a strong resemblance to Dr. Villeneuve. She had to be his daughter.

She leaned over the balcony to speak to us.

"Merci…thank you for your good work."

"You're welcome mam," I said.

"May I ask a question…why…why do you come here to work…there is no pay…why?

"It's what Christians are supposed to do mam," said Bennett.

"And we do it because we are Americans, its part of who we are" I said.

Bennett quickly added:

"We believe whenever someone does a good deed, good things tend to follow."

187

"Besides," I added. "It gave us a chance to get off the ship and see your beautiful country."

Ah! Finally the real reason!" she said amused.

We smiled back. I think she appreciated the honesty.

"Are you leaving soon?"

"Probably, we never seem to stay long no matter where we go," I added.

"Where do you go from here?"

"Don't know Miss."

I lied. Bennett and I knew exactly where we were going, but I remembered what Mr. Carson said about discussing ships movement.

"I guess we'll find out when we get back to the ship, or, maybe tomorrow at muster."

"Well, please be safe and take care of yourselves, and thank you again for all that you did here today. I must try this volunteering when I get back to Paris."

"We will mam…and thank you for allowing us to contribute to the project," Bennett added.

Maurice pulled up to where we were standing but in a different car. Instead of that old, choking Peugeot, he showed up in a brand new Mercedes.

"Wow Maurice! Where'd this come from?" asked Bennett.

He was definitely excited.

"It belongs to my father!"

The young lady took the liberty of answering the question.

I was correct in my assessment. She was the Doctor's daughter.

188

"Monsieur's…ready…finir?" asked Maurice.

"Finir en beaute!" The Doctor's daughter shouted.

"Ah, Mademoiselle…Como Sava!"

Maurice looked up to where the girl was.

"Gentlemen…please…please go inside car…merci."

We entered the car and closed the door behind us. Maurice walked over to an area directly below the balcony. The two had a brief conversation and then she went inside. Maurice returned and then we exited the way we came in, passing a couple of security guards on the way. Once we reached the entrance gate, another guard approached from his station, looked inside the vehicle, whispered something to Maurice, and then waved to someone inside the guard station to open the gate. As we were exiting the colony, I felt compelled to talk about the lady on the balcony.

"Was that Doctor Villeneuve's daughter?"

I already knew the answer.

"Qui monsieur."

"Would you happen to know her name?"

"Christine…her name is Christine. Maurice continued.

She is a medical student living in Paris. She will return to France when the holidays have finished."

"She is very beautiful." I said.

Maurice nodded.

Bennett leaned forward in his seat. I think he was getting ready to ask a question.

"What did she say in French?"

"What?"

"Miss Christine…from the balcony…what did she say in French?"

Maurice scratched his head trying to remember.

"Ah! Finir en beaute…Finir en beaute is a compliment…it means your work should be considered glorious…that you leave the colony like a champion!"

Maurice smiled; I don't know if he got the translation right, but from the grin on his face, I could see he was pleased with his answer. After that, we left the peace and quiet of the country side and slowly made our way back to the harbor. Maurice drove slowly. The last thing he wanted to do was damage the Mercedes.

I was a little tired from the painting, so I slouched back slightly in my seat and closed my eyes. The cold air from the air conditioner blew directly in my face. Bennett continued to stare out his window. None of us found it necessary to speak. The only noise I heard came from Maurice. He was softly humming to a catchy tune playing on the radio. It was all very peaceful until we caught sight of the harbor. Almost immediately Maurice lowered the volume on the radio and locked the doors.

"Maurice, I'm a little curious. Why the Mercedes and not the Peugeot?"

The question was on both our minds but Bennett beat me to it.

"To say thank you. Dr. Villeneuve couldn't pay you. This was the next best thing…yes?"

"YES!!! ABSOLUTELY!!!" Bennett said what I was thinking.

Before anyone could say another word, the reality of the moment was upon us. We had returned to the fields of deprivation. Within minutes, we were once again surrounded by legions of poor people.

"Monsieur's, please keep doors locked and windows closed…please don't look at people…just look straight ahead!!!"

Just as Maurice was finishing his sentence, beggars began pounding on the windows. Within minutes, we were overwhelmed. Wave after wave of desperation pressed against the car making it impossible to drive. Soon the Mercedes began to rock from side to side. Honestly, I thought we were going to tip over. For a moment, I even thought Maurice might have a heart attack. Dr. Villeneuve's Mercedes, the pride and joy of Defaecatio, was being mishandled and there was nothing he could do about it.

In a Hail Mary moment of panic, Maurice pushed down on the horn as hard as he could, but no one moved away from the car.

The rocking continued unabated for several minutes and then it stopped. Even the noise of the crowd abated. From a distance, I could hear someone shouting. Even though our windows were partially blocked, I recognized the heterochrome policeman as he approached. I guess he was alerted by the honking. Anyway, he showed up ready for action. His big black baton glistened in the setting sun. Unfortunately, this time, he didn't come to crack knuckles.

The first strike landed on an older gentleman's temple. The man was definitely unconscious when he collapsed outside my window. The second and third victims fell near the driver's door. Maurice shouted something in French which caused our hero to move to the back of the Mercedes near where Bennett was sitting. A woman who had climbed onto the roof was also knocked unconscious. I turned around to look at her, but all I could see was blood gushing from her forehead. After that, the heterochrome moved to the front of the sedan to clear a path for us.

The bleeding woman served as a deterrent.

Very quickly, people moved away from the vehicle allowing us to continue our journey. Once inside the gate, Maurice jammed on the brakes and exited the car. Bennett and I followed.

"Gentlemen, on behalf of all my people…merci beau coop…merci beau coop for all that you have done!" and before I could say anything, he planted a kiss on my right cheek and then on my left. He did the same to Bennett. After that, Maurice got back in the car and sped away in the same direction we had just come from. I thought he might inspect the car for damage but he didn't. I guess getting back to the Colony was more important. Once the car was beyond the harbor it disappeared once again into the sea of desperation. As for the policeman, reinforcements arrived and the beatings continued. I don't know how many people were killed or knocked unconscious, but it must have been many. The last time I saw the heterochrome his uniform was covered in blood, but he was still smiling.

The whole thing seemed surreal to me. Clearly the cops were outnumbered and could have been overpowered by the mob but they weren't. I wondered if the penalty for striking a policeman was worse than getting cracked on the head or maybe it was just the fear of defying those in charge which kept the masses in line. I never did get an answer but I do know one thing for sure. If our founding fathers had acted as passively as these people did, I would be speaking the King's English today instead of American.

As we walked back to the ship, I noticed two chiefs smoking on the fantail.

"Patterson…Bennett…is that your new boyfriend? Did you buy him that hat?"

It was Senior Chief Chesterfield, the same Senior Chief who was on the fantail when we transited the Pillars of Hercules.

"Ah, c'mon Senior you know it's their custom…men kissing men on the cheek," said Bennett.

"Yea, but from here it looked like the two of you were really enjoying it," said Chief Morris snickering.

"Love those red shoes!" added Chesterfield.

"Pay them no mind Bennett…they're just jealous!" I said. The four of us busted out laughing.

Back on board, I went directly to berthing, took a quick shower then ran to the mess deck just in time for spaghetti and meatballs. While I was eating, I tried to keep the heterochrome out of my head but it was difficult. That big black baton was seared into my memory. Fortunately, I still had the twenty candy bars in my locker. Tomorrow, if nothing else, I would make good on my promise. I don't know why I ran to the mess deck. The only guys on board were the duty section. Everybody else was ashore. Normally, I eat quickly but today I took my time. Since I had no plans to go ashore, I just sat there staring at the bulkheads. I thought Peter might show up but he was nowhere to be found. We were both tired; maybe he hit his rack early.

As I sat there contemplating my next move, I wondered about the evening forecast. Clear skies would definitely make me happy. According to my star chart, Venus, Mars and Jupiter would all be in alignment tonight. Hell, if I stayed up late enough, I might even get a chance to see Saturn.

Eventually I made my way to the fantail to have a smoke. I was so tired; I smoked the whole cigarette with my eyes closed. Even though the bitt I was sitting on was damp,

193

I was very much relaxed. Cool ocean air had mixed with the tropical heat of the day. A soft mist had formed and was looking forward to settling down for the evening. At first I thought it came from the windward side of the harbor, but I was wrong. It formed on the leeward side of the ship which obscured my view of the harbor. So, there I was, alone on the fantail with just my thoughts to keep me company. It didn't take long before I drifted back to the colony and replayed the day's events. I was proud of my contribution. How many people get the chance to work in a leper colony? Thinking about Dr. Villeneuve's daughter made me smile. She was captivating and beautiful, and even though I would probably forget her, at least for now I could savor the moment. I thought of a special monikor. Something to help me remember her by. Let's see, the first time I saw her she was standing on a balcony. She also spoke to us from that same balcony. Wouldn't it be appropriate to remember her that way?

Yes, Christine would be "My Lady of the Balcony."

I wondered how one would say that in French? No matter. The important thing was remembering everything about her; her long black hair and green eyes. The short white skirt that accentuated her long lovely legs; the matching blouse and high heels and the sweetest Caribbean smile you'd ever want to see. Yes, Christine Villeneuve, my Lady of the Balcony, may I remember you forever. Within an hour Venus became visible. Like Christine, she was captivating and beautiful. Mars appeared shortly after followed by Jupiter.

I decided to play a little game with myself.

Christine would replace Venus and I would replace Jupiter. Orbiting between the two of us was her father Mars. As Jupiter raced to catch up to Venus, Mars became

194

defensive and tried to block his path. All seemed hopeless until Saturn arrived. With magic sleeping powder borrowed from the Moon, Saturn was able to put Mars asleep. Jupiter caught up to Venus and the two were secretly married by the Rising Sun. When Mars finally awoke, at first he was furious, but after gazing at the couple's happiness, decided to bless them for eternity.

It was a wonderful game. I really enjoyed the role playing, but like all games, it had to end. The truth is, all I had was hope. I knew I would never see Christine again but I hoped I would. I closed my eyes and fantasized about a future encounter but the dream didn't last long. A big booming voice shook me back to reality.

The Petty Officer of The Watch had just sounded taps.

Chapter 20

The Third Island

The following morning prior to reporting to my sea and anchor station, I gathered

up my candy bars and made my way to the fantail. As soon as I arrived there, I was

greeted by two rat people who had positioned themselves close to the after most bollard.

Somehow they knew today was the day we would be leaving.

I waved my arms to get their attention and it worked. One of the rat people waved

back and moved closer to the ship. I pulled out a couple of candy bars and threw them in

his direction. They landed on the dock a few feet from where he was standing. He picked

them up and smiled. It really was wonderful to see. Who knows how long it's been since

he's done that. Immediately his friend came over and I threw two more bars which he

caught. Soon three or four other rat people joined in but they were scattered. Believe me,

I did my best to throw the candy in their direction but I wasn't always accurate. And

that's when the pushing and shoving started. Whatever bars I had left, I just tossed to the

gathering crowd. Unfortunately, the noise and commotion alerted—you know who. The

heterochrome popped out of his shack like a shark sniffing blood.

Thank God he didn't see anything.

By the time he began walking around; all the candy bars had been picked up.

Under my breath I whispered hooray for the rat people! They had won the round but it

was short lived. Even though he didn't find anything; his mere presence was enough to

disperse the crowd. Only the guy who caught the candy bars remained. He pressed his body against the security fence as hard as he could. For a moment I thought he might knock it down. He was still too far away to talk to but his message came in loud and clear. He was crying and smiling at the same time. I understood exactly. He was happy and grateful for the candy, but sad and despondent I was leaving.

Soon after, we set sail for island number three. This was to be our final port visit before heading back to Florida. Our heading was 270 degrees true which is about as due west as you can get. We were expected to arrive at our next port of call within forty eight hours. Once we secured from sea and anchor, out of habit, I made my way up to the signal bridge to have a smoke. The sky that day was unusually blue; I didn't see a cloud or even a hint of whiteness anywhere. Normally there is something to contrast the serenity but today was different. I felt completely relaxed. After I finished my smoke, I peered overboard in hopes of seeing dolphins but there were none. Staring at the green water my mind drifted back to Christine Villeneuve.

It saddened me I was never going to see her again. True, Pennie and Ana had their pluses, but Christine was different. She was beautiful, refined and well educated. Standing on that balcony she reminded me of a Greek Goddess. Tall, erect and with her head held high, she would have been a welcomed addition on Mount Olympus.

True, I never touched her, but I wanted her and when I say want, I mean I wanted our atoms to fuse together. Yes, she was different from Ana and Pennie, but lust doesn't differentiate. When men succumb to their cravings, everyone is fair game. After all, sex is sex and nothing more. And it really doesn't matter who the provider is.

Whether a Princess or a hooker, the name of the game is satisfaction. Now, deep down inside, I knew this type of thinking was wrong and self destructive; and I knew if I

197

continued down this path I would never find true love. But you know what? I didn't care. I was going through women faster than I was changing my underwear and I loved it!

But here's the problem. Once the wolf was back in his den, guilt feelings surfaced. I had come full circle and this is why I wanted to talk to someone. I had reached the point where sex trumped everything. Physical needs totally outweighed the emotional. At this point, any kind of relationship with anyone was impossible. Believe me when I say I knew this wasn't normal. At first I attributed it to my age. But other guys younger than me had steady girlfriends so it wasn't that. Whatever the reason, sex was becoming my own personal drug, and like all addicts, I was becoming insatiable. And since we're on the topic of women, here's what I've noticed so far. Contrary to popular belief, not all sea faring men think of women the same way. Sailors, you see, fall into three distinct groups.

Group one consists of the "Pious." These guys believe women, all women, walk on water and should be treated with honor and respect. A lot of the younger guys, especially those new to the world of women fell into this category. Now, even though I was young, I was experienced and knew better. I learned early on from my relationship with Diane, women are just as fallible as men, and I learned from my mother they sure as hell don't walk on water.

Group three, notice I skipped group two. Group three belongs to the "Users." These guys believe women exist only to serve and to satisfy. They have no other purpose. It is the reason for their existence. In their minds, women should be barefoot and pregnant and chained to the kitchen sink. In the 1960's they would have been called male chauvinist pigs. A lot of guys who were divorced or separated fell into this category.

Most, if not all, have been hurt emotionally, and I think that is why they were torn between forgiveness and wanting to get even.

Group two. Group two was my group. This is where I belonged. It was also the group most of the crew identified with. Think of it as a buffer between one and three.

Slowly, my mind returned to the present. Somewhere inside Memory Hotel was a place reserved for Christine. I made sure I had easy access to her room.

Surprisingly, I remained alone on the signal bridge. In fact, I didn't see anyone topside which surprised me. Hell, even the birds were absent. My good friend the wind had shifted from the stern to the port bow so I repositioned myself to enjoy what I was about to receive. As is customary, I unbuttoned the top button on my uniform. The wind found no resistance as it caressed my chest and stomach. And then it happened. Out of nowhere, I began to cry. I don't mean tears but just enough moisture to moisten the eyes.

I felt so strange. I wasn't lonely or sad but I was crying nonetheless. Good thing I was by myself. Had anyone seen me I'd never here the end of it. And then it hit me. The guilt was causing the tears. I wiped my eyes and tried to stop but I couldn't. I really needed someone to talk to but no one was there. I had so many questions and no answers. Sure I had friends but I wasn't going to bring this up. This stuff is reserved for family. Besides, talking about sex and emotions might be seen as a sign of weakness.

Better to keep this to myself.

So, let's review shall we. We have a twenty year old kid who believes he's just a hop, skip and a jump from becoming a "User" and is powerless to stop it. Powerless because he has allowed his emotions to rule over his intellect and two, frustrated because there doesn't seem to be any solutions to his problem. I had come to a junction: I was

199

rudderless, like a dingy navigating through a bad storm. I thought how like the ship I had become. Both of us were in search of a harbor, but unlike me, the Baffles knew where she was going. With her there was no guessing and no uncertainty.

Whatever questions she had would be answered in our next port of call. Two days later, I was back at my sea and anchor station ready to take on the world. As always, tug boats guiding the ship to the pier. The Jacob's ladder was rigged halfway between lines four and six to accommodate the Harbor Pilot who usually transfers from one of the tugs to the main deck. From my location, I had a bird's eye view on whom ever came on board.

Regarding the Harbor Pilots, I decided to play another little game with myself. By now you must know sailors like to play games. Mine was a game of imagination. I tried to picture what the Harbor Pilot looked like and then I graded myself on how well I did. Unfortunately, I was only accurate 50% of the time which isn't accurate at all, but I was correct about one thing. Sure, their clothes varied and some were taller and heavier, but the real story was hidden in their faces. Years of weathering had impacted them. When I looked at their faces I saw roadmaps. Lines and circles crisscrossed under their eyes and around their ears. Years of wind burn and tanning had camouflaged the numerous pockmarks which were inescapable in their line of work. Praise and glory always goes to the Captain, but the real unsung heroes are the Harbor Pilots who, like surgeons, guide and weave around potential hazards in order to safely cradle their children to sleep.

We moored portside with the forward part of the ship facing the ocean. Once the brow was in place, officials came on board to speak to the Officer of the Deck regarding working parties and the replenishment of supplies. Our mailman was off and running as usual but this time he was accompanied by the ship's medical corpsmen who needed additional supplies to combat a nasty strain of dengue which had devastated the local populace. Large hungry mosquitoes had descended upon the harbor and requests were made for our assistance. And when I say large, I mean huge. You could have thrown a saddle on any one of them and gone for a ride. Fortunately, by late afternoon strong winds had eliminated most of them but those that got through continued to probe for soft spots where they could sink their pointed proboscises into unsuspecting victims. When they swarmed, which was often, they formed huge black clouds creating moving pockets of shade. The concentrated whine was reminiscent of bombs falling on target. Yes, this was our third and final stop and I couldn't wait to bid farewell to those nauseating little creatures!

But before heading below, I was approached by my leading petty officer. Peter looked like he had something to ask me.

"Patterson!"

"Yea Pete."

"Were you planning on going ashore tonight?"

"Not really, I'm kinda tired…thought I'd stay on board and catch up on some sleep."

Petty Officer Healy pulled out a pack of non filtered cigarettes from his dungaree shirt pocket and, removing two sticks, offered me one.

"Sounds like a plan."

He pulled out his lighter to light my cigarette.

"I was wondering if you'd do me a favor. You got duty tomorrow, right?"

I nodded yes.

"Stand duty today for Barnes and he'll take your watch tomorrow."

"Why, what's up?"

"The XO said there's a backgammon tournament in one of the hotels tonight and the winner gets 500 bucks. I'd like to give Gerry a shot at the title."

Petty Officer Gerry Barnes was the best backgammon player on board ship and it was rumored he had won tournaments back in high school while growing up in Connecticut. The way Tim Drake beat me at backgammon, that's how Barnes beat him. He was that good. Besides backgammon, Gerry was super smart, a real techie, but a bit of an introvert. He kept to himself and usually sat alone no matter where he went. If you needed to speak to him, best bet was to find out what watch he was scheduled to stand and get there before him.

Unfortunately, his solitude came with a price. Like Peter Bennett, Gerry was also shunned by most of the crew but he and I got along well which was beneficial to both of us. Gerry spoke Spanish which was definitely a plus. We were always traveling to or coming from a Latin country so the language came in handy. He said he picked it up in high school and decided to become proficient at it.

That was to my benefit. How'd it help him?

I provided the friendship he so desperately needed. Even little things like having a cup of coffee went a long way with him.

"Sure and tell Barnsee good luck from me."

"You're alright Patterson, I don't care what anyone says about you, you're alright."

"By the way," I asked.

"What watch does he have?"

"Balls to 4."

"Yikes, I better hit my rack!"

I tossed my cigarette overboard and made my way down to berthing. What luck I said to myself undressing. Midnight to four in the morning and I'm already dead tired…oh well, I guess it's for the best, at least I'll be off tomorrow night when I'm better rested. The following morning I was super busy. I had to perform semi-annual maintenance on the Nikason Acoustic Processor which required me to get inside the unit. But before doing that, I had to get to the access hatch which was located two decks below the main deck.

Talk about mission impossible.

The hatch itself was thirty feet down a shaft so narrow I thought I might have to lather myself in oil just to squeeze through. The first ladder took me through a bulkhead just wide enough to accommodate my shoulders. The second ladder, if you want to call it that, was just wide enough to support my boondockers. And the equipment I had to bring with me? Don't get me started. As for space itself, since it had no ventilation, I had to install a portable air blower just to keep from passing out. And if that wasn't bad enough, I had to replace a pressure gasket which was located underneath the processor. By the time I was done, I was covered in cuts and bruises. After two hours of painstaking work, I heard someone climbing down the top ladder. It was Senior Chief Robbins accompanied by Petty Officer Healy.

"Patterson, how much longer son?" said Senior.

"About 45 minutes Senior, everything's done, except for the gasket underneath the NAP."

"I'll help you with that," said Healy.

"Thanks!"

"Hey, one good deed deserves another, besides; I'm a little richer today because of you."

"Barnes won?" I asked.

"Second place...but he still won money on a side bet with one of the locals."

"How much?"

"100 bucks, but 25 are mine."

"How's that?" I asked.

"I picked up the bar tab and I also paid for the food so Barnes could concentrate on playing."

"Sweet," I said.

"Ok, I'm outta here. Peter will help you with the gasket. Finish this and then you're done for today...see you topside."

Senior exited the space just as quickly as he entered it. With Healy's help, I was able to finish in twenty minutes. Liberty call was in one hour, so I made my way to the passageway where the soda machines were located. Once there, I grabbed two cokes and went topside.

When I got to the fantail, I sat down on my favorite bitt which was located on the starboard side. I peeled back the opening tab on the first can and lit a smoke. Leaning back on the life lines, I tried to visualize what the night had in store for me.

And then it hit me.

The pain and soreness was pervasive. Even my forearms hurt, and the cuts and bruises I acquired during the scheduled maintenance forced me to sit somewhat unconventionally. In other words, I had to support all my weight on one cheek. But the real killer was my left hand. It was red and swollen and difficult to open.

Now, the smart thing to do was take a hot shower and go to bed but the thought of exploring the town rejuvenated me. I knew the alcohol would deaden the pain and as long as nobody grabbed my arms or slapped me in the butt I would be alright. Sound medical advice, don't you agree?

As I sat there planning my itinerary, gusting winds emanating from the wayward side of the ship suddenly shifted towards the fantail. Its path was erratic. Normally, wind gusts crossing the forecastle don't make an about face and continue through the middle of the ship but this one did and was I grateful. The narrow bulkheads increased the wind's intensity, so when it blew past me, it dried the sweat on my face and in my uniform. It was like sitting in front of a giant fan.

Thank you Mother Nature.

A couple hours later, as I was preparing to leave the ship, we received word from the local authorities about a possible demonstration by pro communist students. Now, even though the university was miles from where we were, the skipper wasn't taking any chances. He gave orders to move the ship out into the harbor where we dropped anchor.

Speaking of the skipper, I hadn't seen much of Commander Whitehead since the first island. Oh, he was around, but every time we got ready to make another "pit stop", his term for island hopping, he would disappear. Like he said at the Change of Command ceremony, we should be out looking for subs instead of making port visits. Believe me, if it was up to him, we would never see dry land. Personally, I think he was struggling with all the political correctness that was coming from the higher ups. We were sent to this island for a reason and I was beginning to think the university demonstrations had something to do with it.

The motor whale boat departed at 2000. I sat as far aft in the boat as possible, avoiding even the slightest possibility of getting sea spray on my face and clothes.

Why the break in protocol you might ask? Honestly, you don't have to be a rocket scientist to figure it out. If I waited till 2300 to leave the boat and there was a demonstration, liberty would be cancelled. If I leave now and liberty gets cancelled later on, at least I got the chance to relax for a little while.

Joining me in the MWB were three fresh air snipes from A-Gang. I didn't recognize them at all and since they weren't wearing their uniforms, it was impossible to identify them. They were carrying on a quiet conversation amongst themselves avoiding any contact with me, the lone twidget, which was normal. The transit to the pier was rather quick though. We arrived there in less than five minutes. As soon as I had my feet firmly planted, I did a quick 360. I was hoping to see the demonstrators but there were none.

"They never showed up!"

It was Freddy Sherman from Shore Patrol.

"You mean the demonstrators?" said the shortest A-Ganger.

"All that for nothing…building up steam and pressure to move the boat…all that for nothing!" said the tallest A-Ganger.

206

"Well, better to be safe than sorry right?" said the middle A-Ganger.

"Guys," said Sherman, the MWB leaves every hour on the hour."

"Thank you," I said as I proceeded to walk ahead of the other three.

"HEY TWIDGET!"

The tall one was yelling at me.

"Where's your crew…you know...your buds?"

"Don't have any, besides, I'm bound to run into guys from the ship anyway."

"You're welcome to tag along with us, if you want," he said.

"Thanks, but I'm just gonna wing it tonight, and besides, I might get lucky."

I turned to walk away but the middle A-Ganger asked me a question.

"Sure you don't want some company?"

"I'm good, thanks."

Before I could say anything else, the tall one spoke again.

"You know twidget; we're on heightened alert right?"

I nodded.

"And we're supposed to travel together?"

I nodded again.

"And stick together?"

I nodded for a third time.

"What's your name shipmate?" I asked.

"Evan and this is Carl and the short one is Phil but we call him Tool; we're all

from Georgia."

"Please to meet ya. I'm William Patterson from New Jersey."

I began to walk up the landing and away from the pier. As I neared the first set of stores, I heard people's voices along with catchy dance music coming from an area directly above the wharf. I was about to enter into the business area when I heard Evan's loud voice once again. You see, engineers are used to shouting over engines and turbines. Sometimes it is the only way they can communicate with each another. He was yelling my name and waving his arms. I turned around to face him.

"WILLIAM PATTERSON!!!" he sounded angrier this time.

Even though we were a considerable distance from each other, I heard my name clearly. I believe the rocks used to build the sea wall helped amplify his voice.

"LOOK AT YOU! HEAD'N OUT WITHOUT A CARE IN THE WORLD!! JUST AS BRAZEN AND BOLD AS YOU CAN BE!!!"

He hesitated for a second before continuing.

"HAVE YOU BEEN HERE BEFORE???"

I yelled as loud as I could.

"NO!!! AND THANKS AGAIN SHIPMATES, BUT PLEASE, THE CLOCKS TICKING AND WE'RE WASTING TIME!!!"

Within seconds, I was out of view, but not out of earshot. I could still hear Evan shouting.

"FELLAS, SEE THAT MAN YONDER…HELL…HE'S LIKE A LOST SHIP IN SEARCH OF A HARBOR…A DAMN HARBOR!!!

Evan was correct. I was, am and will continue to be a lost ship in search of a harbor. It's what defines me. It's what makes me who I am.

I entered the business area but instead of proceeding forward, I stopped dead in my tracks. Above me was a huge canvass dome similar to one you'd see at a sporting event. It appeared to stretch from one end of the financial district to the other. It reminded me of a giant umbrella. I believe it provided protection for all the businesses operating below it. Obviously, centuries of inclement weather had taught them well. I couldn't tell for sure, but it looked like it was designed to keep out both the salt water and the wind. I did notice one thing though. The pilings supporting the canvass were made of galvanized steel, which in turn, were protected by reinforced concrete. Of course it wasn't impervious to damage, but at least it wouldn't break down due of rust.

Anyway, the business area opened to a square which was heavily populated. Customers and merchants were everywhere. Beyond the square was a black billboard which had a white arrow that pointed down. Directly below the arrow was a fancy bar which looked enticing. I made my way through the square and entered the club.

After a quick look see, I turned around and almost walked out. It was a nice looking whorehouse but a whorehouse none the less. I wasn't interested in that just yet. The night was young and there was still plenty to do. True, the women were good looking prancing around in their under ware, but I wanted something more.

I was about to leave when a beautiful Latina with an hour glass figure caught my eye. She was bent over a pool table getting ready to sink the nine ball into the corner pocket. However, the distance between her and the ball was considerable, requiring her to use a make shift wooden bridge. As she continued to bend over to size up the shot, her garment tightened. Her yellow dress, highlighted by red and silver trim, began to creep up her thigh revealing firm but shapely legs. Intrigued, I walked around the table to see her face which, by the way, was absolutely beautiful.

Now, this seemed a little strange to me. I've seen beautiful women in cat houses before, but this one was not just beautiful, she was beauty pageant beautiful which again raised the yellow flag of caution. Why was someone this good looking shooting pool in a whore house? Her opponent, also female, was just as beautiful, but her mannerisms seemed to suggest a slight flaw in her character. She lacked that certain "je ne sais quoi" that the other one had. Some would see it as a lack of refinement, or perhaps education. I thought I knew the answer but I couldn't quite put my finger on it. In any case, I wanted to talk to her but I was cautious. Surely, theses two goddesses were just killing time waiting for someone to show up. Well, fifteen minutes passed and the girls were still sans men. A thought occurred to me they might be lesbians but I quickly ruled that out. They weren't hitting on each other or on any of the other girls. I refreshed my drink and lit a cigarette before venturing over to the table.

I asked her in Spanish if she would like to play a game of billiards with me. She nodded yes and motioned to her girlfriend to vacate the table which she did. Wasting no time, I quickly racked up the balls and made the first shot sending the balls to the four corners of the table. After a couple of shots, one of her balls was tucked behind one of my balls making the shot difficult to hit. She asked me how I would play it, so, standing behind her, I placed my hand on top of hers and we made the shot together. The ball went in; the billiard ball that is. I let go and waved to the bartender for another drink.

"Can I have a drink too?" she asked.

"Drink? Yea, if you mean a real drink instead of colored water, yea, no problem." I walked over and sat down in a chair near a round table.

The little voice inside me was screaming.

210

What the hell is wrong with you? Have you lost your mind? The woman is drop dead gorgeous and all you can think about is colored water?

A male server arrived with my drink.

"Hey, want to buy the girl a drink, she likes you," said the server.

"Been through that with her, it's her move."

Against all logic, I remained adamant. If she wanted a drink, it better be a real drink, I was tired of being ripped off. Been there, done that in Europe. Made a promise to myself not to fall victim to that scam again no matter how good looking the chick.

The server approached the pool table and leaning over whispered something in the girl's ear. He seemed a little angry and as soon as he left she came over and sat next to me.

"Margarita, I'll have a margarita, but only one, I'm working you know."

Despite the heavy accent, her English was pretty good.

I raised my left hand; the server came over and I ordered her a drink.

"Oh, do you want it frozen?"

"Naturally."

While waiting for her drink, I lit another cigarette and inhaled deeply.

"May I?" she said.

"Help yourself."

She took a stick from the pack I left on the table. I lit it with my Zippo. Shortly after, the server arrived with her Margarita.

"Would you like to know my name?" she asked.

"No, not really, maybe later," I said as I downed my scotch.

211

I guess she wasn't used to being treated like that, being as beautiful as she was, but this wasn't my first rodeo and we were in a whore house.

"Do you like the club?"

"Club? Is that what you call it! I thought it was a whore house," I said.

"We prefer the word club, but yes, you're right, it is what you say it is. Why did you come here?"

"Just got here, you know—your country, don't know where to go, thought I stop in and have a drink."

"You didn't come here for a woman?"

"Came here for a drink."

"So, I should go then?"

"Your choice sweetheart, but before you do, I'd like to ask you something."

"What is that?"

"WHY, WHY ARE YOU HERE? With your looks and that body, why are you here? You should be a movie star or something."

She was about to say something but hesitated. She knew what she wanted to say but couldn't find the right words. After a long draw on her cigarette she spoke.

"You know…this isn't America…this place… not much for a poor girl to do here... school costs money... not many opportunities."

"Why don't you work in a restaurant, or a store?" She busted out laughing.

"A restaurant…a store! Are you serious? I make more in one night here than I would one week in those places!"

Still giggling, she motioned to a couple of her co–workers. Once they arrived she told them what I said. They also laughed.

"Silly boy, silly boy…this isn't America!"

I paused briefly. I needed to collect my thoughts.

"Ok, ok, no more serious talk then…how much?"

"One hundred dollars!"

"A hundred bucks! Are you kidding me? What, is it made out of gold?"

I pointed to her vagina.

"Yea! Mine is made of gold! You want it, its $100. You wanna be cheap and settle for bronze or silver…find another girl!"

I laughed quietly to myself. Clever using the Olympics like that.

I had seventy dollars in my pocket but I still had to take care of my bar tab.

"Who the hell can afford that?"

"Powerful men. Men with money."

"OK, maybe later, I'm not ready yet."

"Maybe I won't be here later, maybe I'll be with someone else."

"Can I make a reservation or something?"

"Look Joe, the clock is ticking. I have a good reputation and a good following… it's either now or never."

"Now or never huh? Ok, but I need to talk to someone first."

I should have left the place and continued exploring the city but my old friend Mr. Lust had arrived and he wasn't going anywhere.

A couple of guys from the ship had wandered in and were sitting at the bar. From what I could see, they were by themselves. They were both twidgets which was good for me, but they were also very tight when it came to lending out money. Those who knew them well said they squeaked when they walked.

I know mission impossible right, but I had to try. Mr. Lust really wanted the girl. So, I quickly came up with a game plan. Make some small talk, buy them a round of drinks, and then make the request. And that's what I did, but I was turned down quicker than you could say Captain Swizelsticks! I was disappointed but not surprised. They had lived up to their reputation. I went back to the girl.

"I have a slight problem."

"You don't have the money?"

"I can give you $60.00 right now plus my lighter and this watch."

The watch was worth about $50.00 but the ship's lighter was priceless. Selling military paraphernalia on the black market is big business. I knew she would get a good price for it. Besides, I could always get a new one at the ship's store. The cash plus the other items was more than what she asked for.

She motioned to the bartender. I guess he seconded as her pimp. The two of them had a brief conversation in their local slang making it difficult for me to follow. I could see he preferred cash and wasn't really interested in the watch but when she mentioned the lighter, he acquiesced.

He asked me if I wanted to pay for the drinks and was about to say something else but I cut him off.

"I'll pay for everything now. Tip included."

"Can I see the watch?"

I took it off and handed it to him. After a quick look see he motioned for the

214

lighter. At first I was hesitant. That lighter and I had been through a lot together but right now, Mr. Lust was doing the talking. I was thinking with my other head. He convinced me to hand it over.

Again the bartender did a quick look see.

"Ok, you got a deal my friend but on one condition."

"What's that?"

"You get forty five minutes, no more!"

"Oh hell, that's more than enough time!" I said.

"Good, because the clock is ticking my American friend."

The bartender turned back towards the bar. As he walked away, I realized everything I owned was inside his pockets. I felt naked but Mr. Lust was happy, so it didn't matter.

"Follow me."

The girl rose from her seat and I followed. Did I tell you she had the most perfect derriere I had ever seen? I didn't? Well, now you know. The hell with Rule Number 4 and the hell with the yellow flag of caution! I was at an impasse. I couldn't stop; I didn't want to stop.

"Worried about security? Don't. The army guards this place. Once we get to my room I will open the window. This will alert the guard that I am with a customer."

"So he gets paid too?"

"Not from you."

Cautiously, I followed her through an entrance way adjacent to the kitchen. On the other side of the doorway was a wooden passageway which connected our building to another. Adorning the walls were pictures of birds.

"Raptors."

"Oh, is that what they are. Why raptors?"

"The owner hunts a lot. He says the birds help him find game."

"So he uses them for hunting?"

"I think so."

Most of the birds were either hawks or falcons but there were others that resembled eagles. I remembered seeing odd shaped birds on one of those nature channels once. These must be them. Some had lots of hair on their heads while others were completely bald. All were multicolored with large talons. Some of the birds had partially eaten grape droppings near their feet. One picture depicted an eagle carrying another bird back to its nest. Curiously, all the raptors were lined up on the right side of the hallway. I didn't see anything on the left side.

Eventually, the hallway led to another door which was locked. My "date" produced a key, opened the door and went inside. I followed.

"Is this your room?"

"Yes, this is my room."

It was stifling. The room was very small with only a small wooden window above the head board. Unfortunately, the latched was closed. I had no choice but to sweat.

Without saying a word, she walked over to the window and opened it. Within moments, I heard footsteps. Someone approached wearing military boots. How could I tell? Every time he took a step he crushed the pebbles and stones which were on the walk path. And then, all of a sudden like, the window was pushed open. The first thing I saw was a gun nozzle. I found out later the nozzle was attached to an M-60 machine gun. Supporting the weapon was a soldier wearing a green uniform. I did manage to see his right sleeve. It was covered in yellow hash marks.

The soldier called out the girls name and she answered. They had a brief conversation and then he withdrew. I believe it was a godsend we couldn't see each other. After all, he could have been one of her clients and if he knew what I looked like, well, things could have gotten sticky.

She walked over to her locked closest and opened it. Sitting on the floor was a small white fan which she turned on.

"Want to get started?"

"Sure Irma," I said smiling.

"Ah! You caught that! I would have told you my name before but you said you didn't want to know."

"Irma is a nice name; my name is William and we'll leave it at that, ok."

"Ok."

She set the fan speed to high but it took several minutes for the room to cool down even slightly. As I undressed, the scotch and heat began to take its toll. I felt a little light headed. Had the room been air conditioned I could have cleared my head in an instant. But it wasn't. I must admit I was a little concerned about performing, but once Irma undressed, my dizziness went away.

"One hundred dollars gets me what?"

She pointed first to her vagina and then her mouth. Lusty was in heaven.

"Ok."

217

Even though the fans powerful motor pushed the hot air out the window, it wasn't able to repel the legions of hungry mosquitoes which had entered her room. Irma turned off the light in an attempt to discourage them but it didn't work. She then lit several lavender scented candles which helped for a while, but there were just too many of them. We soon found ourselves lying on the floor next to the fan.

The thin bed sheet which covered her mattress served as our mosquito net. I pulled the fan under the sheet and tucked the corners under us as best I could. It seemed to do the trick. We started to make love but every time the guard passed by her window it broke my concentration. His boots continued to crush the pebbles and stones on the walk path. Sensing I was uncomfortable, Irma told me to focus all my attention on her which I gladly did. Even though it was dark outside, occasionally the moon would appear from behind the clouds and illuminate her room. It was then I was able to appreciate the vision lying beneath me. One hundred dollars? Hell, I would have paid a thousand for what I was enjoying, and technique wise, she was well schooled. Irma was and remains the most beautiful woman I have ever made love to.

And then it hit me, a feeling of guilt, not because of Group three or the Users, but for something else. I don't know why or how, but I was both happy and sad for this young girl. In a way I began to feel sorry for her. I know it sounds crazy, and this never happened before, but out of nowhere I got religious. Yes! You heard me! Religious! Someone this beautiful; having to do this for a living! NO! This wasn't right! Honestly, I thought about helping her but how could I? Yea, I could give her money but for how long? As I think back to that night, I've often wondered what had become of her? Was she still a prostitute? Did she eventually get her own place, or, did she suffer and die from some horrible disease? I would like to think she met a rich guy who took her away from the life she was living. Maybe he even married her and had children with her. One can only hope. However she may have ended up, I have always wanted the best for her. I was at peace with myself. Relaxed, I closed my eyes and was about to fall asleep when…

"NO MAS!!!"

A high pitched sound followed her voice.

"NO MAS!! FORTY FIVE MINUTES!! OVER NOW!!"

Unbeknownst to me, Irma had placed a small cooking timer under her bed. She had secretly set it to go off after 45 minutes. Clever girl. I never saw it.

I sprang to my feet, dressed quickly, kissed her goodbye, and then returned to the bar. I plopped down on the first available bar stool and after downing two cold beers I left. I never saw Irma again.

Quickly, I made my way back to the pier. Even though the night was young, I was done. I just had the best sex ever but my clothes were drenched in sweat. Time to go back to the boat. Once I reached the landing, the stiffening wind provided much needed relief to my over heated body. Like the walk path outside the cat house, a uniformed soldier patrolled the dock area as well. I don't remember seeing him when I first arrived, but he also carried an M-60 machine gun.

Keeping me company were three other guys from the ship. Since there was nowhere to sit, the four of us sat down on the deck waiting for the motor whale boat to arrive. The soldier who was guarding us didn't say a word. He just stood there, starring at us with his assault weapon cradled between his arms. He would smile every now and then but his smile seemed detached and distant, as if he was concentrating on something else.

Physically, he was muscular and stocky, but running below his left eye to just above his chin was a nasty scar. The cut was wide and thick, indicating something bigger than a razor blade. If I had to guess, I would say he was involved in hand to hand combat. Hard to tell if he won or not. I guess the important thing to take away is he survived. Like the heterochrome, this soldier earned his pay.

The cooling wind continued to grow in strength. Sitting on the deck, we had front row seats to some kind of wind show. At first, it moved clock wise then switched directions, then back again and so on and so forth. It was like sitting in front of a giant oscillating fan. I couldn't have been happier. You must know by now how much I love wind. I don't know why, but powerful wind always seems to unleash something wild inside me. Think of it this way. The wind is my moon. The stronger the intensity, the more nonsensical I become, and cogent wind always seems to bring out the wolf in me. Honestly, I have never fully understood it. No one in my family reacts to the wind the way I do, so I know it's not hereditary.

Anyway, out of force of habit, I unbuttoned my top shirt button to hasten the cooling process. I was completely drenched in sweat. I truly believe Irma's bedroom was the hottest space I've ever been in. I don't know how she survives it. Anyhow, the joyous moment was cut short by the arrival of the motor whale boat. Needless to say, it wasn't long before we were back on board and inside our air conditioned spaces!

The following morning we left island number three and began our journey home. No more pit stops which I'm sure pleased Commander Whitehead. The happiest guys on board were the ones with families. It's always tough being away from your wife and kids. Some of the older salts broke into a shanty or two as they coked, or should I say coffee'd and smoked on the fantail. The next group glad to be going home were the guys with fancy cars and high maintenance girlfriends. We used to joke around with the ones who worried a lot. You know the guys paranoid about losing their girlfriends to someone else. The old out of sight out of mind dilemma. Actually, some of the Users were hoping their girls cheated on them so they could break up with them. And then there were the heavy drinkers. These guys couldn't wait to get back to their favorite watering holes. Believe me; some of them could drink their entire paychecks!

Which brings us to the polyamors. A well known barfly I had befriended awhile back told me a story about a newlywed couple he knew. He said the husband's ship hadn't even cleared the harbor when the wife was out looking for a replacement. At least she kept it all in the family. She could have gone bar hopping in town but instead decided to sink her hooks into some poor unsuspecting slob who was just relaxing and drinking beer in the enlisted club. As for me, I had mixed feelings. Even though I enjoyed being out at sea. You know I love astronomy. I needed a break from the monotony.

We were going home and that's all that mattered. It had been a long time since I'd seen so many smiling faces. By the way, this was my last adventure on board the Baffles.

SO— LONG—SON— OF— BLIGH— AND— GOOD— RIDDANCE!

I was headed back to school. Comforting me were all those wonderful memories. I knew I could count on them to get me through the tough times. And the beauty of it all, if one didn't work, I could always fall back on another. After all, I was returning to California with a treasure chest of adventures.

Chapter 21

WEST COAST SAILOR

Asia 1

Twenty two months—fifteen countries—five islands.

This is what I took with me when I walked down the brow for the last time. The
Baffles was a great ship with a great crew. I will miss her dearly. Next stop was San
Diego. According to the Navy, I needed additional sonar training before reporting to my
next boat. There were slight differences between the NAP unit and the new system I
would be working on. The good news, I was familiar with San Diego. I had completed
both recruit training and initial sonar school there. Knowing where to go to have a good
time would not be a problem. I also knew it was going to be a bit of an adjustment
coming from the fleet and all that, but this was how training was set up.

Surprisingly, I was assigned to a room with just one other sailor; a guy named
Kenny Wilson from Wisconsin. He was from someplace right on or near Lake Superior. I
asked him if he knew Doug Wilson, the boatswain's mate from the Baffles, but he didn't.
He said his father had done business with members of the Wilson family, but Doug
Wilson was not one of them. Anyway, he told me the name of the town but I couldn't
remember it because it was in the Chippewa language. After the third try I decided not to
ask anymore.

Anyhow, Kenny was a super nice guy from a rural community. His family was in the fishing business and we hit it off right from the start which was a good thing. We were both second class petty officers, but more importantly, we both shared a love for astronomy. I couldn't believe I found someone who enjoyed looking at the night sky as much as I did! Kenny told me he became interested at a very young age. He said it gets very dark at night and finding and identifying objects is pretty easy once you know what to look for. Indeed, his knowledge of the stars, planets and constellations was very impressive. Actually, I believe he knew more than I did, which was fine. Where we differed was in the timing. I like to survey the evening sky just after sunset, but he would concentrate on things like meteor showers which were only visible during the wee hours of the morning. It wasn't unusual for him to pull an all-nighter, especially when the Perseids appeared in late summer.

On more than one occasion, I brought up the subject of women and how the two were connected, but Kenny would just smile and turn away, as if embarrassed. The only time I got him to smile was when I told him I discovered a new constellation which was shaped like a woman! I must say, sharing a room with him was like living with a boy scout. He didn't drink, smoke, curse or talk disrespectfully of women.

My complete opposite!

Oh, and one more thing. Kenny would say his prayers every morning when he got up and every night before going to bed, and I imagine before every meal as well. Clean in mind and body, he was the Navy's new poster boy. I think even Uncle Sam would have been impressed. A quick side note. One time I left my wallet on top of my bunk and when I realized it was gone, I returned to my room only to find it neatly folded on top of my tee shirts. Not only was all my money there but also my identification. Imagine a world, I said to myself quietly, imagine a world filled with guys like Kenny.

School started Monday morning and boy was it rough. I didn't realize it was going to be so difficult. I guess a lot can happen in twenty two months. Besides the obvious software changes, there were hardware changes as well. Even some of the tools were upgraded to accommodate the new equipment. I realized then and there I needed a new game plan. The old me would have to take a hike if the new me wanted to pass this course. A lifestyle change was definitely in order. No more drinking or going out Sunday night. Partying was limited to Fridays and Saturdays only!

When I entered the classroom that first day, I witnessed something I had never seen before. No one was talking. Normally you hear small talk or chatter or someone tells a dirty joke or two, but there was nothing. I mean you could have heard a pin drop. The room was quiet, too quiet if you ask me. I guess I should have suspected something was wrong when I showed up ten minutes early and realized I was the last one to be seated. Obviously, these guys couldn't wait for class to begin. I did a quick head count and came up with fifteen. I was a little disappointed I didn't recognize anyone. Not one guy from boot camp or from my operations school was there. In fact, the only guy I recognized was Kenny and he was sitting all the way up front. Next to him was an empty desk which he had reserved for his roommate.

I hate sitting up front but I had no choice. All the other desks were taken. I took my seat and starred at the empty black board in front of me. That got old real quick, so I turned around to face some of the students. After a quick look see, I noticed most of them were second class petty officers and judging from the ribbons on their uniforms, most had been out to sea. There were four guys who didn't have any ribbons at all and that's

224

because they came directly from operations school.

Now, depending on one's point of view, coming directly from school could be considered a positive. On the plus side, the boat you're assigned to is the boat you'll be discharged from. No more having to transfer to another ship unless you request it. The downside: If you end up with a skipper like Whitehead, your gonna have a rough ride, but even then, there's light at the end of the tunnel. No matter where you go, you're never permanently assigned to anyone station. Sailors transfer from here to there all the time so even if you've got a lousy skipper, it's only temporary. Hell, I'm living proof!

Shortly thereafter, our instructor entered the room.

He introduced himself as Petty Officer Pierce Bloodstone and from the insignia on his uniform; I could tell he was a "bubble-head," a submariner. He had a red beard with piercing black eyes and from the moment I met him until the day I graduated he never smiled. Frame wise he was short and stocky but underneath his uniform were hidden "hulk muscles." He had bulges everywhere. The only explanation I could think of he was a weight lifter. He looked tough and I want to say he was tough, but looks can be deceiving. Then again, those muscles weren't a mirage. I did notice something right off the bat; during the entire course of study, he only wore long sleeves. At first I thought he did so consciously to detract from his physique, but then again, he may have had tattoos that needed covering up. I never did get an answer. I will say this, whenever he moved, the thread holding his uniform together seemed to be on the verge of splitting. Honestly, one time, I even thought his skin turned green.

Anyway, like I said, the course was arduous and the more we got into it, the harder it became. There was very little wiggle room for error. If you weren't precise and

225

consistent in your answers, you weren't going to pass. There were a couple of guys who didn't take things seriously and they paid the ultimate price. Bloodstone had a particularly effective comment about the churn rate. He said those unable to pass the course might as well stick their heads between their legs and kiss their assess goodbye!

A word or two regarding military training. It is difficult by design. The courses have to be. Imagine you're in a life threatening situation where every second counts. Who do you want to rescue you, the village idiot or the guy who aced his final examination? I'll take the guy who aced the exam. As for me, I studied hard and kept my word regarding the weekends. Eventually, the hard work and dedication paid off. I finished second out of thirteen. Elated, I phoned my parents with the good news and even wrote to a couple of friends. Once school was over though, I didn't have any time for lollygagging. Within forty eight hours I was en route to my next boat.

The U.S.S Pompton AR-30 was on deployment somewhere in the Indian Ocean. I had to fly half way around the world just to catch up with her. When I finally stepped onto the quarter deck I noticed there was a weather thermometer attached to the watch podium. Curious, I leaned over to see how hot it was but I couldn't believe my eyes. The needle pointed to 125F! Yes, one hundred and twenty five degrees and it wasn't even the hottest part of the day! Needless to say, my uniform was drenched in sweat. As I stood there waiting to be escorted down to berthing, I couldn't help but notice how quiet it was. In fact, I didn't hear any noise at all. No engines. No pumps. Nothing, which was very strange. Granted, we were connected to shore power, but still, I should have heard the wine of machines or at least felt the vibrations of electricity passing through heavy conduits. There simply was no sound. And something else, I didn't see any ships tied to

226

the pier or anchored in the bay. And where were the tugs? Normally there's at least one operating within the harbor entrance but there was none. Like I said very strange. What I did see and couldn't help but notice was water, lots and lots of water. Finally, I heard a pipe up near the forecastle. It was followed by another pipe but this sound was different. It lacked the crispness of the first whistle. The piping continued. The first whistle would pipe a command followed by a short pause and then a second whistle would try to mimic the call, but the sound didn't match. It sounded novice.

"Are they practicing?" I asked.

The Petty Officer of the Watch nodded.

"Captain's sort of old fashioned; he likes to hear bells and whistles."

"Wow, that's old Navy!" I said.

"Yea, it is, but the boat's old; the skipper's old and since this is our last hoorah, the old man wants to go out in style. Excuse me for a second."

The P.O.O.W. keyed the 1MC from the messenger shack and, with his free hand struck seven bells for 1130.

"So, the messenger pipes all the orders?"

"Not all, just the main ones. You know, side galley, away boats, all hands, chow, sweepers and carries on, but the POOW strikes the bells."

He pointed to the forecastle.

"That's what they're doing up on the forecastle. The chief boatswain's mate is working with a new transfer. If he can pass the chiefs test then he's ready to stand messenger of the watch."

"Jesus, I'm gonna have to practice striking bells if I'm gonna stand quarter deck watch."

"Yea, it's not hard. You start off with four bells for reveille and then add one bell every half hour till 0800 when you strike eight bells and then it starts all over again with one bell at 0830. Just remember your gonna strike eight bells four times a day. 0800, 1200, 1600 and 2000."

As he was speaking, I strained my ears once more to hear any noise other than our conversation, but there wasn't any. My curiosity getting the better of me, I had to ask.

Is it always like this?"

"Like what?"

"Quiet. I don't hear anything. It's as if we're in a bubble or something."

"Pretty much. You know, we're a long way off the beaten path. I know what you mean though. It took me a while to get used to it. I can't explain it. The chief engineer can't explain it. Whatever noise the ship produces is absorbed by the ocean; or something like that. It's like we're in some kind of damping field."

"Wow, that's a first. Hey, let me ask you a question. I know we have bases here, but do we own the island. I mean is this U.S. Territory?"

"Nope. Not ours. We just pay rent. I think the Brits own it."

"The British?"

"I think so, but its ok. Yea, it's small but it does have an Olympic size swimming pool to cool off in."

"What about the ocean?"

He took a long pause before answering.

"No. Not the ocean."

He answered cautiously.

"Why's that?"

"Shark city."

"Oh…ok thanks... good to know."

"Yea, we lost someone two days after we got here. You know, we all got the same warning, but someone thought he was invincible. Turned out he wasn't."

 "Sorry to hear that."

"Yea, I knew the guy pretty well. Glad I wasn't there to see it happen. Anyway, if you don't like the pool, you can always swim in the bay but stay close to shore."

Just then my escort arrived.

"Thanks, by the way, I'm William."

"I'm Freddie but everyone calls me Fish."

"Ok Fish, see you around."

"See ya William."

My escort stood in front of me with just a hint of a smile. He was short and thin and appeared to be a bit uncomfortable. The faded stencil on his dungaree shirt said Spencer. The two chevrons on his long sleeved shirt told me he was a second class petty officer but as to what he did or where he came from remained a mystery. I tried to make eye contact but was unsuccessful. He preferred instead to stare at the deck. Nevertheless, and despite his shy demeanor, we managed to exchange handshakes and pleasantries before leaving the quarter deck.

On the way down to berthing, he talked a little bit about the ship. It was difficult to hear him because his speaking voice was slightly louder than a whisper. The first thing he mentioned was the lack of air conditioning in berthing. Granted each rack had its own blower but since the air was drawn from vents located near the main deck it was very warm. He said I was lucky because I was assigned to a bottom rack. Had it been a top rack, I would have been smothered in hot air. He also said I was fortunate because my bottom rack blower was located near my feet. He suggested I reverse my sleeping position in order to fully enjoy the air. Before exiting berthing, he gave me some comforting news. He told me not to worry about the hot air. He said by 2200 it would be cool enough to sleep. I took great comfort in knowing that. The following morning I reported to muster at 0730 where I met most of the division. I was assigned to electronic repair which consisted of approximately twenty technicians three of which were women. Everyone was cordial, even my new division officer which I took as a plus. I was grateful for having the opportunity to work on so many different systems. On board the Baffles, I was limited to maintaining the NAP, but here I could increase my marketability by becoming proficient on everything I worked on.

Regarding women sailors.

This was a new experience for me. The Navy began experimenting with "mixed crews" a few years before I signed on and I was surprised to learn most of the women on board had been deployed prior to being assigned to the Pompton. It was nice to know I wasn't sailing with a bunch of rookies. Psychologically, having women on board helped us cope with the loneliness of separation, but more importantly, they were a delightful distraction. They were particularly pleasing after knock off ships work.

Unbeknownst to the officers, male crew members would assemble on the portside just forward of the fantail. This spot was considered holy ground since this was the closest we could get to female berthing. Every day, and without fail, an exhaust vent located just forward of their enclosure would send waves of perfume and shampoo in our direction. On rare occasions, a few females, recently showered, would huddle along the windward side of the ship hastening the drying of their hair while their uniforms clanged to their still wet bodies. Any sound from us would have sent the girls scurrying, so, we stood still like statues. Talk about being frustrated.

On Fridays, one shipmate in particular, Petty Officer Maria Martinez from San Diego, "skin tight" to the male contingency, would grace us with her presence. Fortunately for us, her uniforms were, shall we say "strained." Sensing this may become a problem, the order was given to establish a "wide berth" whenever passing Petty Officer Martinez in the passage ways. Granted, she had been counseled for the "tightness" of her uniforms, but in her defense, the restrictive military attire she was required to wear made it difficult for her to "pack-in" all of her natural attributes. She was, after all, just following orders. One of the nicest thing about Petty Officer Martinez; she was a creature of habit.

Everyone, and I mean everyone from the skipper on down knew exactly what she did on Friday. It began with knock off ship's work followed by a shower and then a trip to the weather deck to dry off her long, beautiful hair. It took 11 minutes and 43 seconds for Petty Officer Martinez to dry her hair but who's counting! After that, she made her way to the mess deck for evening chow. This was followed by a visit to the fantail where just about every guy who wasn't on duty was waiting. Petty Officer Martinez would always show up to the fantail from the portside and for reasons unbeknownst to the crew, would always have untied laces hanging from one of her boondockers. Her favorite spot was the after portside bitt but before she could sit down, one or two observant admirers would alert her about the laces. After graciously thanking the good Samaritans, Petty Officer Martinez would raise her arms above her head and stretch, placing additional stress on her already overworked buttons. Once done stretching, she would raise her foot in order to tie the laces. How she found the flexibility to place her foot on top of that bitt was beyond me. Anyway, as she bent over to tie her boot laces, imaginations ran wild. One particularly restless sailor was Petty Officer Brian Pennington. Brian was from Boston and very proud he was third generation Navy. He felt compelled to comment:

"Hey Martinez!" he yelled.

"Yes."

"Do you know who I am?"

"No, should I?"

"I'm Brian, Brian Pennington from Operations."

"That's nice…was there something you wanted to say to me?"

"I just wanted to say, well, I'm sure you've heard it all before."

"Heard what?"

Brian was doing great; I thought maybe he has a shot.

"Well, I just wanted to say…I just wanted to say…"

"Say what? Cat got your tongue?"

And then the laughing started.

It began with Alma Alvarez. Soon others joined in. Obviously, Brian was embarrassed.

Suddenly, his demeanor changed.

"I JUST WANTED TO LET YOU KNOW THAT YOUR GONNA LOOK AWFULLY FUNNY WALKING AROUND THE SHIP WITH MY TEETH SUNK INTO YOUR THIGHS!!!"

Oh no Brian you didn't! I said to myself.

Needless to say, Petty Officer Pennington had a lot of explaining to do at Captain's Mast.

Let's just say he's seen better days.

Chapter 22

Asia 2

Exactly one week later we weighed anchor and headed east south east towards our next port of call. I was kind of sad because I really enjoyed the exclusiveness the British island provided. I saw it has my own private heaven. It took me quite awhile adjusting to the Pompton. Although she was bigger and heavier, she was also much slower. Making turns for ten knots was the exception and not the rule. But perhaps I was a little spoiled. After all, I spent close to two years on board the Baffles, and since we were always in a hurry, I got used to moving at a certain speed.

Interestingly, this constant momentum provided an unexpected benefit for those who were interested. Staring at the water gets old real fast, but picking out a part of a wave and watching it move down the side of the ship is a real time burner. In fact, if you observe the ocean from the same spot every day, eventually you'd be able to predict how long it takes a wave to travel the length of the ship. There were two guys from Deck Division who were very good at this. They could pick out a wave forming near the forecastle and tell you within a second or two how long it would take that same wave to travel past the fantail. Now that's what I call efficiency!

But that's what I mean about getting used to a certain speed. I didn't have that feeling on board the Pompton. In fact, at times I wasn't sure we were moving at all. The only way to know for sure was by looking overboard at the oil leak coming from the starboard engine. It produced a noticeable slick as we made our way through the clean pristine Indian Ocean. By the way, that oil slick would never have been tolerated on board the Baffles. Whitehead would have kept the snipes working 24/7 until it was fixed.

All that aside, personally, I couldn't have been happier.

The more time at sea the more time I had for astronomy and since the Pompton was a lot more spacious than the Baffles, it allowed for greater separation between officers and crew. An important lesson I learned while serving on board the Baffles. It's wise to maintain a buffer zone between yourself and the khaki's.

As for the skipper, compared to what I had just been through, was an angel. I never saw him attempt anything crazy or feel the need to show off. I was saddened to learn he had submitted his retirement package days before the Pompton deployed. Yes, good Captain Lambert was calling it quits after thirty years of loyal service. Ironic isn't it? How both the skipper and the Pompton were being put out to pasture at the same time. Curious how "Fish" didn't mention that when he revealed the Pompton's fate. I know how hard it can be losing a good Captain. Been there done that with Captain Stewart. Perhaps it was just too painful to talk about.

On the first day, after dinner, I made my way up to the 01 level portside which was just aft of electronic repair. I smoked a couple of cigarettes until it was dark enough to recognize the constellations. I was lucky, the night sky was very clear. I was able to see the Andromeda Galaxy and Berenice's Hair for the very first time. I also saw the Southern Cross which was on my astronomy to do list since I was a kid. And let me tell you, the long wait paid off. It was like looking at glittering diamonds, you know, like the kind you see in a fancy jewelry store. I was excited and dazzled by all the beauty that surrounded me. If only the Pompton had Big Eyes, just imagine what I could see. That first night I spent close to three hours topside before going below. I was completely

alone. The whole time I was there I don't remember seeing anyone. Honestly, it was a

little bit unsettling. Anyone slipping overboard would be a goner. I'm talking about me.

I couldn't believe on a ship this size and with a compliment three times that of the

Baffles, I was the only star gazer on board! Granted, I enjoyed the privacy, but in order to

be appreciated, space must be shared. I repeated the process three more nights hoping to

attract like minded individuals, but once again I had the night sky all to myself. Imagine

being invited to a planetarium that seats three thousand and you're the only one who

shows up. That's what it felt like. I had plans to do it again the fourth night, but the lure

of a bikini beach movie persuaded me to go below and watch it.

We arrived at our destination the following afternoon at 1330. Scuttlebutt had it

we were to drop anchor in the middle of the harbor.

Seriously?

A ship this size swinging at anchor? You've got to be kidding? When was the last

time you saw an ocean liner parked at the mall? Exactly!

Immediately, I remembered the hell we went through with the Baffles, and we

had the whole harbor to ourselves! Here, there were small craft, fishing vessels and

merchant ships all over the place. And what about the unknowns? What about the sea

floor? Dropping anchor into water with sunken craft could prove to be dangerous. And

what about the water depth? How consistent was it? And then there's the problem with

the wind. It was gusting from the windward side pushing the Pompton towards the beach.

Allowing a ship this size to swing at anchor was a recipe for disaster. Wisely, after

looking at all the variables, Captain Lambert reconsidered. He ordered the ship into deeper water.

Good news for the Pompton. Bad news for the crew.

The five minute commute just became fifteen guaranteeing a wet ride. Now, the captain's gig and the motor whale boat were excellent water craft but not exactly built for comfort. Any kind of turbulence would send wave after wave of ocean spray into the boats. The gig provided a little protection because it had a cabin, but the motor whale boat was completely exposed.

Liberty call when down a little later than usual around 1830, but I was ready. As the motor whale boat approached the beach, the information given me proved to be accurate. There was no pier or dock to tie up to. I was about to notify the other passengers, but they were already having a quiet discussion concerning our predicament.

"Hell, there ain't no damn pier!" said passenger number one.

"Damn it! I'm gonna ruin my clothes!" added passenger number two.

Fortunately, I was prepared. I was given a head's up by a quarter master friend of mine who suggested I wear shorts with sandals since I would be jumping into waist deep water and wading to shore. I'm glad I took his advice. I made one more attempt to offer guidance, but my fellow riders were too upset for conversation.

Once the motor whale boat hit the sand bar, like pirates of old, we jumped into the surf and made our way to shore. Honestly, I can't recall the last time I heard so much foul language. Maybe when I was on the wrestling team in high school. But even then it wasn't as bad as this. The water was unusually cold and the bottom felt very squishy. I believe we were walking on discarded garbage that came in with the tide. Small fish darted in and out of our legs every time we took a step. And one of the problems with small fish is, they attract large fish. There could have been sharks there but by the time we found out, it would have been too late. Oh, and one more thing, the odor was enough to make you vomit.

Luckily for me, even though my shorts were wet my shirt remained dry. The snipes didn't have it so good. They both wore long pants and long sleeved shirts. As to why is beyond me. Perhaps they were concerned about the mosquitoes. Who knows? I will say this, I don't know how long it took the wind to dry their clothes but they must have stood on that beach for a very long time. Once my shorts dried, I donned my sandals and walked up to the landing stopping at the first bar I came to. Ok, why here? Why drop anchor in a harbor with no dock? Good question, here' the answer. Security. I mean, what else could it be? Like I said, Captain Lambert was nothing like Commander Whitehead.

I'm sure we could have gone to a different city, one with a pier and a dock, but then again, every time you moor, you increase the chances of public malfeasance. Captain Lambert knew what he was doing. I was just glad to be off the boat.

As soon as I entered the bar, I was surrounded by short thin women adorned in white swimsuits. Large black numbers tied to box string hung around their necks like basketball jerseys. Centered in the middle of the numbers were red characters written in the local language. Those women not working the bar were dancing together on a mirrored floor complete with flashing bulbs and strobe lights. Whenever a guy entered the bar, the girls would stop dancing and rush towards him. One or two would throw their arms around his waist enticing him to stay.

This is what happened to me.

I wasn't in the mood for a chick just yet, so I separated their hands dissolving the hug and immediately they ran back to the others and continued dancing. All this took place without saying a word. Normally, I have a drink and a smoke before moving on, but the women here where very aggressive, so, I decided to venture down to the central market area where I happened to come upon a most unusual restaurant.

In the middle of the restaurant was a boxing ring, but not the kind we're used to seeing. It was set up for kick boxing. I found out later the international rules regarding this sport didn't apply here. The fighters were allowed to kick below the waist and they were also allowed to clinch and grab the kicking leg without being penalized but that's another story.

Surrounding the ring were numerous tables and chairs used for dinning. Upstairs, on the second floor, was a huge room filled with wooden bleachers. Towards the back of the room was a disc jockey surrounded by several speakers that were evenly spaced apart. Two multi colored turn tables were positioned in front of him and behind him was a shelf filled with twelve inch records. Sitting in the bleachers were "numbered" women, however, these women were dressed more provocatively. They all wore string bikinis.

And they weren't there for swimming lessons!

Initially, I sat alone downstairs in the restaurant and had the most wonderful meal. It consisted of lobster and crab topped off with steamed rice and a long green vegetable I couldn't pronounce. I ate, drank and smoked and was visited by several bar girls and even girls from the street but, like I said, I wasn't ready for a chick yet. An hour later, I paid my bill then made my way upstairs to where the loud music was playing. When I entered the room I couldn't believe my eyes. Half the crew of the Pompton was there. You would have thought we were having a ships reunion! I don't know how I didn't see them go upstairs unless there's another entrance on the other side. It didn't matter. With the crew there my mood changed. Like I said before, I would die for any one of my shipmates, but stay the hell away from me when I'm on liberty. Getting back to the women, all of them were wearing string bikinis except for a small group of ladies standing near the exit. They were wearing long dresses and talking quietly amongst themselves. Every now and then one of them would blow a kiss or bat an eye but nothing more than that. At first I thought they were employees but then I remembered what was put out at quarters.

CAUTION...!!!

The women in the long dresses weren't women at all. No, they were the shims; the he-she's and butterfly boys we were warned about. For some strange reason, they frequented clubs patronized by U.S. servicemen. Expectedly, they posed a problem simply because of misidentification. And no wonder. They were extremely good looking and almost impossible to distinguish from real women. In fact, this particular port had a reputation for having some of the most beautiful transvestites in the world.

That's why the real women wore string bikinis. Got it!

It was right around this time two "shims" started dancing with a couple of guys from the ship. I didn't recognize the taller of the two but the shorter one was Petty Officer Meadows from Repair Four Division. A couple of his buddies saw what was happening and tried to warn him but he wouldn't hear of it. And then, all of a sudden like, Meadows started hugging and kissing the shim he was dancing with. Now, I'm not making excuses for Meadows, but he was pretty drunk when this happened. Perhaps there was something about him we didn't know. I'm just saying. And everything was fine until he pulled the

240

shim in closer. It was then he realized something wasn't right. I don't know if he felt

something unnatural or if it was something else, but whatever it was, he raised his right

arm as if to hit the shim and that's when his friends grabbed him and dragged him away

from the dance floor. And good thing too. Had Meadows hit the shim and hurt him,

chances are he would have been arrested and held in jail. And that my friend is something

that needs to be avoided at all costs. Meadows was able to save face by directing several

obscenities in the shim's direction but only after wiping his mouth and spitting profusely.

Believe me; he will remember that night for the rest of his life!

As for me, I made my way to the bar area which was opposite the disc jockey and

I noticed right off there weren't any seats. I was forced to sit at a table which was like

flashing a neon sign above my head. Bikini after bikini approached wanting to be my

"date" but I turned them all away. After that, two "butterfly boys" tried their luck but

they too were sent packing. After the last one departed, I noticed a very pretty girl sitting

by herself and away from the dance floor. She was dressed in a yellow bikini with the

number 27 written on her placard. I watched her for a few minutes and noticed right away

she appeared to be uncomfortable. She seemed reticent about joining the others so I

walked over to where she was and asked for a dance. It was clear she didn't understand

me. She just sat there smiling so I tried one more time.

"Number 27, do you want to dance?" I began to dance in place motioning for her

to join me when an older woman dressed in a white blouse and blue jeans appeared.

"You like girl?"

"Yes."

"You want girl?" I nodded.

"Pay bar fine; take girl."

"Actually, I just want to dance with her."

"Pay bar fine; dance girl all night."

A bar fine is money paid to the "boss" for taking the girl away from her job. In most cases, the fine is split evenly down the middle between the club and the girl but most of the time the girl will ask for a tip once you've finished with her. The rules and amounts vary depending on which country you're in, but that's another story.

"How much?"

"Forty dolla…pay forty dolla take girl."

"Ok."

I whipped out two twenty's and handed it to the woman.

She turned to the girl and spoke to her somewhat aggressively. The girl was looking down but nodded in agreement. She rose from the table and grabbing by arm made a beeline for the exit door. Once outside, she raised her right arm and a jeep the size of a humvee pulled up. The driver was wearing a uniform but I couldn't tell if he was military or not. He motioned for us to sit in the back which we did. We speed off but the ride was anything but smooth. Large pot holes forced us to hold onto the inside of the jeep. At times, I thought we were riding in a bumper car. We made no turns or stops. We just went straight, but the ride was so rough it caused me to rise up off my seat. Thank God it only lasted five minutes. When the driver finally stopped, we were in front of a hotel. I motioned to pay the driver but he waved me off.

"Bar fine pay ride," he said.

Wow, I thought to myself, an honest cab driver!

We entered the hotel and after paying for the room, I followed number 27 down a long hallway which eventually emptied into a small courtyard. Inside the courtyard was a Buddhist shrine. Upon seeing the shrine, the girl stopped dead in her tracks. She seemed mesmerized. Slowly she knelt down and grabbed a candle from a wooden box which was positioned along the base of the shrine. After she lit the candle, she knelt down to pray. I watched her without saying a word. As she was praying, I glanced at the room number stamped on the key. Honestly, I just wanted to dance with the girl but when opportunity comes a knocking, you take it. I wasn't going to pass this up.

The number on the key began with a one meaning the first floor but the remaining numbers didn't match any of the rooms we had passed. I was about to interrupt her but the beautiful sheen coming from her jet black hair distracted me. It was so black it looked purple. Competing with her hair was an Asian face imbued with French ancestry. Within seconds, she stood up and grabbed my arm as we continued down the hallway to our room. It was located at the very end of the hotel. Once inside we quickly undressed. She wouldn't let me kiss her, but I could touch her anywhere I wanted to. After a few minutes, we got into it. The whole time I was with her she didn't say a word, not one word.

I thought she might attempt to teach me a few key phrases but she didn't. We cuddled each other for awhile and then she made the peace sign with her fingers placing it directly in my face. I tried talking to her but to no avail, so I shook my head from side to side indicating I didn't know what she was saying. I think she understood because she patted the mattress and raised her index finger, then, she patted the mattress again and gave me the peace sign which wasn't the peace sign at all, but the number two. She repeated the procedure one more time and then I understood. The peace sign was actually a question and the question was would you like to do it again…you know…round two! I smiled and flashed the peace sign back at her. I knew it was going to cost me more money, but I didn't care. It was the happiest peace sign I ever made!

In a way number 27 reminded me of Gina. Here, in this Asian country, I got the peace sign. Back in Euro 1 I got four fingers. Apparently being fluent in finger language is a prerequisite for this type of work. Once we finished we dressed quickly, then we moved outside to the street. I looked around for the humvee but it wasn't there. The girl hailed a taxi but when it arrived, I didn't get in. I gave the driver enough money to take her back to the club plus a little something for his favorite charity. I thought for a moment she might try to persuade me to go with her but she didn't. In fact, she didn't show any emotion at all. Her face was as blank as when I first met her. I closed the taxi door and watched as it sped away. When I could no longer see it, I decided to walk around a bit before heading back to the beach.

So much for "keep girl all night." I knew it wasn't true so I let it go. By now my priorities had shifted. All I wanted to do was explore some of the hidden shops which were located off the beaten path but I was alone and tired so I opted instead to stay on the main drag. After an hour or so, I headed back to the spot where I had originally landed. While waiting for the gig, a thought occurred to me.

Once again I had broken Rule Number 4. I had foolishly followed another woman back to her place. I was playing Russian roulette with my life and I didn't care. I should have cared but I didn't. I had become a User with no desire for rehabilitation. The only thing I cared about was sex. At this point, nothing else mattered.

The captain's gig came as close to shore as possible which wasn't close at all. The outgoing tide made the beach water very shallow. The sandbar we originally embarked from was now several yards to our stern. We had to wade out quite a distance before we could board her. Fortunately, the squishy garbage and the smell disappeared with the ebb tide. Although the sea bed was relatively clear, it still contained hazardous materials. While wading, I noticed several pieces of broken glass sticking out from under the sand. For a moment I thought about donning my sandals but just then the bottom cleared. Had there been more glass I wouldn't have had a choice.

Accompanying me back to the ship were three machinist mates I had never seen before. Usually the crew gets to eyeball each other during chow but these three were unknown to me. As I've stated, snipes and twidgets rarely come in contact with one another. Remember the A- gangers from the Baffles? I didn't know their names either and that was a much smaller compliment. On a ship this size, recognition was next to impossible.

Anyway, they were sitting forward inside the cabin which allowed me to eaves drop on their conversation. Turns out they just came from a place called Nero's. I was curious because one of them had small traces of blood on his shirt collar. Not the drip kind, but more like the blood was rubbed on or smeared.

"Did you get into a fight?" I asked the one with the blood stain.

"Nah, not a fight, more like a tug of war."

"So nobody punched you?"

"Nope, no punches…but I did use my mouth."

Now I was curious.

"How did you use your mouth?"

"Well you see…what's your name?"

"Patterson."

"Well Patterson, it was like this…I was sitting naked on a stool."

Immediately his two buddies busted out laughing.

"Quiet now! Like I said, I was sitting naked on a bar stool in a room that had no walls."

"What do you mean no walls?" I said.

He continued.

"Well, not the usual kind of walls …these walls were round…you know, like the kind of walls motorcycle guys ride around in. You know, when they're in cages?"

"You mean a pit?" I asked.

"Yea…yea, more like a pit with me in the middle, well, there's this small door leading in and out of the pit…and I'm sitting there and all of a sudden like, these six girls come in wearing nothing but sneakers!

"Really?" I blurted out.

"It's all true bro…six naked girls wearing pink sneakers."

"So then what happened?"

"Well, now comes the fun part. Each girl pulls on a thin piece of string which is rolled up like a ball tucked inside their vaginas."

"You've got to be kidding?" I added.

He shook his head no.

"And these strings they're just long enough to grab onto with your teeth. So, you

246

grab one, and then another girl positions herself in front of you and so on until you got all six strings in your mouth. Now, what they do next is amazing. Three girls begin moving to their left while the other three move to their right. Then one of the girls from the first group moves up one level by standing on one of those tiny stairs that are built into the wall and then one of the girls from the other group does the same thing, but on the opposite side of the pit. This is repeated over and over again by each girl until they're all standing one level above me. And you know what's amazing?"

"What's that?"

"They don't run into each other or knock each other over. They know just how much string to let out so nobody gets tangled. They're like freaking gymnasts!"

"So what the hell is the point of that?"

"They cocoon you bro, like you're some kind of a bug. All of a sudden like, music begins playing as the stool begins to move around and around. As you're moving, you keep getting wrapped in this string until they turn into a mummy. Once you're all covered up the music stops playing. It's sort of like a game…the trick is, once they're done cocooning you and you still got all six strings in your mouth…you've won…you get to sleep with one of the six for free.....but."

"But?"

"It's damn near impossible bro. They said maybe one out of a hundred can do it."

"Did you do it?" I asked.

The machinist smiled, revealing a mouth filled with dried blood.

"DAMN RIGHT I DID!"

"Why all the blood?" I asked.

At this point, one of his friends joined in the conversation.

"Nylon…the strings are made of nylon."

"Nylon?"

"Yea, nylon can cut and it's also very strong. Holding six at one time, I don't know how the hell he didn't slice his tongue off."

"Or his lips!" said the other friend.

"And, if that wasn't bad enough. Once they realized he wasn't letting go, the two girls closest to him crossed their legs and leaned backwards as far as they could go. That's when he started bleeding."

"Wow! That's amazing. How did they keep the balls tucked inside? I mean the movement of the stool should have pulled them out?"

"Don't know bro. Maybe the string was secured to something inside. I really don't know."

"The girl you chose…was she good?"

"Hell yea bro! Very good! I'll never forget her!"

We were almost at the boat when the first machinist spoke again.

"Hey Patterson, next time you see me, remind me to tell you about the wheelbarrel."

"Will do!"

We pulled up to the accommodation ladder which was rigged starboard side amidships. As soon as we left the quarter deck we went our separate ways. Three days later, I ran into the wheelbarrel man on the mess deck and reminded him about his promise.

"Let me get some coffee first…why don't you take a seat over there."

He pointed to a corner below the television set. It was a little bit out of the way but a good location to have a conversation. A conversation that is, if you're a snipe. Twidgets don't normally sit on the port side of the mess deck. That's their territory. Once in a blue moon, when twidget country is filled up, and all the seats are taken, do we cross over into their territory. But that's rare. The spot he chose was on the port side.

I knew I was going to take some heat.

Three snipes were sitting together at one of the tables and they didn't take kindly to me standing on their front porch.

"Are you lost?"

The question came from a first class boiler technician who had a long horizontal scar running across his forehead. He wasn't smiling.

"Yea, he didn't finish telling me about what went down on liberty call."

"Liberty call? You guys hung out together?"

"No, no, we meet in the gig on the way back to the boat. We were comparing notes but we didn't get a chance to finish."

"So, you're gonna finish it here?"

"I suppose, that's why he went to grab some coffee."

Sensing what was going on, the wheelbarrel man stopped off at the boiler table before joining me. I couldn't hear what he was saying though. He had lowered his head and muffled his voice. I do know this, whatever he said calmed the situation. Scar head didn't ask any more questions.

With coffee cup in hand, the machinist mate sat opposite me.

"What did you say to them?"

"That you're cool."

"Oh, ok thanks...what about later? They're not gonna bust your balls are they?"

"Nah, don't worry about it twidget—everything's cool."

I couldn't tell if he was being sincere or not. I guess it really didn't matter. He seemed eager to tell his story.

"Patterson, have you ever heard of the wheelbarrel? Not the farm kind, the sex kind?"

"No."

"Well. Let me start by saying it's not for everyone."

"How so?"

"Well, it's kinda like a race against other teams."

"Go on."

"Well, you have to get naked in front of other people."

Here we go again I said to myself. What is it about snipes and their need to walk around in their birthday suits? Do they have some kind of a psychological need for self expression? Maybe working in all that heat affects the brain? Who knows? I just found it amusing. Two machinists, who work in the same division, feel it's necessary to strip naked whenever they're around women!

"What people?"

"Guys and girls."

I let out a sigh of relief. At least it included girls!

Never can tell about a person.

At that moment his eyes shifted down towards the table. I could sense he was a little embarrassed.

"Ok, and then what?"

He paused to take a sip of coffee. After that, he exhaled deeply before continuing.

"Well, then the guys line up behind the girls."

"To do what?"

"Well, the girls aren't standing…they're lying flat on the ground…on their bellies."

"OK?"

"Now comes the hard part…well…it was for me…you see, you have to sort of get excited without touching yourself. You know, rubbing on the girl and stuff. I mean not just me, everyone does it at the same time…"

"You're kidding , right?"

His voice became a whisper.

"And once your aroused enough…well…you have to stick it inside her and then lift her so she's walking on her hands."

"You mean like a wheelbarrel?"

"Exactly…then all the couples line up behind a line on the floor…someone blows a whistle and you're off. The one who crosses the finish line first still inside the chick wins."

I have to admit, I never heard of anything like that in Europe or in the Caribbean. This was definitely an Asian thing. Maybe because of the size difference? I really don't have an answer. The fact he was able to do this in front of other people speaks volumes.

251

"Jesus! How far did you have to go?"

"About 100 feet."

"And the couple who won… what do they get?"

"Each other…you get to spend all night if you want…no charge."

He took another sip of coffee and wiped his brow. He was perspiring.

"So, how did you make out?"

"I BOMBED MAN…I COULDN'T STAY HARD!"

I couldn't believe he shouted it out. Thank goodness the television volume was loud enough to mask his voice.

"Take it easy bro," I said.

He went back to a whisper.

"I couldn't stay hard in front of all those people…I just couldn't! You know, I wasn't raised like that…I thought I could, but just when I was getting into it, I thought about Father Chadwick and Sunday School and then I lost it!"

I had to use all my will power to keep from laughing.

"Father Chadwick!!! Sunday School!!! What the hell made you think about that???"

"I don't know! Can't explain it. It just popped into my head."

"So, who won…somebody from the ship?"

"Hell No! Some damn European who's probably been walking around naked his whole damn life!"

That was it; I lost it. I started laughing.

The tension broke; my new found friend joined in.

"Hey Patterson, this stays between me and you…right?"

"You got it bro…not a word."

The snipe finished his coffee and left. I did the same. On my way back to berthing, I wondered if I would have acted differently. Realistically, it was a moot point; I wouldn't have tried it. That's not me. As for the snipe; at least he was able to realize his limitations. Why he opened up to me, a complete stranger, is mystifying. I'm sure there's a medical term for it, but here's my take: Since we don't know each other, I really can't judge him. In his mind, his failures and disappointments were safe as long as he confided in someone he didn't know.

Makes sense to me.

By the way, I never did catch his name.

Chapter 23

Asia 3

Three days later we were underway and heading east to our final destination. A tug boat

was dispatched to help us on our way but it wasn't necessary. Once we weighed anchor, the deep

water drop outside the harbor facilitated our departure. Seventy two hours later we were pier side.

Interestingly, Asia 3 was remarkable similar to Asia 2. For starters, the dollar exchange rate was

almost identical as was the climate. Where they differed was in the religion. Number two was

predominately Buddhist while number three was primarily Christian. There were other minor

differences between the two, but not worthy enough to mention. The nicest thing about Asia 3, she

had a pier the Pompton could tie up to. No more wadding through three feet of garbage just to get

to shore! I had duty the first day and couldn't get out of it. Nobody wanted to swop with me. You

see, Asia 3 had a reputation for debauchery. Had I something of value to compete with the

pleasures the city had to offer, I may have had a chance, but unfortunately I didn't. The lure of

what was to come coupled with the desire to get off ship was too compelling.

The following night I decided to venture out alone which was not unusual for me. True,

ship's policy suggested we buddy up and I got the safety in numbers speech more times than I can

remember, but I was used to going it solo. You know, travelling with a group can sometimes be

deleterious. Want proof? Recently a group of hard core snipes went out together on liberty call.

They ended up drinking heavily, and after awhile, started playing patty fingers with a troop of

married women. Well, needless to say, all hell broke loose, but instead of fighting, which they

knew was off limits, they decided instead, to flip over a Volkswagen and two other small cars which belonged to some of the husbands.

Need I continue?

Believe me; going solo has its advantageous. The most important being anonymity. As long as you're willing to get away from the harbor area and blend in with what's going on around you should be ok. Fortunately for us, the buddy rules didn't apply here. Since this port was sailor friendly, we could pretty much go wherever we wanted to. There were no off limit areas and as long as you didn't kill or rape anyone, the authorities pretty much left you alone. The "entertainment center" was located just outside the gate. In fact, I don't think it was more than 150 feet from the dock.

Although small compared to European cities, what it lacked in geography it more than made up in recreation. Bars, restaurants and clubs stood shoulder to shoulder as vendors struggled to accommodate the thousands of sailors who were out and about and looking for a good time. As I made my way down the main drag, loud provocative music pulsated from huge speakers positioned just outside the mega clubs. Intertwined and somewhat hidden were the smaller bars. Now, competition between the two was serious business. In order to entice patrons, the smaller bars offered live acoustic music played by local artists. Its audiences consisted of kumbaya couples out for a night of red wine and hand holding.

Hidden and tucked away in the seedy places were the dives. These were bars wall papered with semi naked women. They catered mostly to the poor and to the criminal element. Most of them only offered beer but some provided whiskey as well. Snipes loved places like this. It was their home away from home. In fact, the rougher the bar the more they liked it. I never could understand why. Perhaps it had something to do with being macho. I'm not sure. One thing I do know. Economically, they saved a lot of money hanging out in places like this. A beer here was

255

maybe one tenth the cost of a beer in the mega clubs and I'm sure the wall papered women were discounted down as well.

Now, drinking alcohol all night tends to bring on the munchies. Squeezed in between the mega clubs and the smaller bars were the food joints. Some of the eateries were as large as cafeterias while others were so small you had to stand up in order to eat. I walked slowly down the strip taking my time as I carefully observed each establishment. As in all countries, swindlers were omnipresent. What was different here? The con game was no longer new to me. By now, I was a seasoned traveler. I had just completed my fifth year of military service and was well schooled in the ways of the world. But I was bored and in need of a little excitement, so I decided to play along.

"Hey Joe, you want to taste good woman?"

The question came from a hooker standing a few feet in front of a poorly lit building. She was soliciting anyone who had a penis.

"What do you mean by taste?" I asked.

"You know" she said rolling her tongue across her lips.

"And where is this good woman?" I asked infuriating her.

"RIGHT HERE! I AM GOOD WOMAN."

I circled slowly, eyeing her up and down.

"Na, I think you're a used woman, a very used woman,"

Instantly, I was hit with a wave of obscenities which slid harmlessly down my back as I disappeared down the street. Soon I was standing in front of a rather unusual place. It appeared to be a combination pool hall and discotheque. I quickly stuck my head in and not seeing anyone from the ship, I entered. As I looked around the room, I noticed several women sitting at the bar

256

chatting while others were huddled around one of the pool tables.

"Hey Joe, you want to play pool?"

A woman standing closest to me poised the question.

"How much?"

A girl working the bar answered.

"You buy girl drink, play for free."

Here we go again I said to myself. Can't I ever just walk into a place and be left alone without being burdened with requests and favors and sob stories about how poor I am and my mother needs an operation and my sister's gonna have a baby and my father beats me and so on and so forth. I rolled my eyes.

"How much is the drink?"

"Five American dollars."

Expensive. In their money it came to 100 pethoras.

"Expensive for one drink, don't you think?"

"Oh, not for you Joe. America plenty money. You rich Joe. You buy girl drink, ok?"

Now, I knew they were going to serve her colored water but like I said, I was feeling a little frisky so I went along with the scam.

"After I buy her a drink, I want to be left alone... understood... I'll let you know when I'm ready for a drink...ok."

"Sure Joe, you boss."

I paid for the drink and was about to rack up the billiard balls, when I noticed something strange about the pool table. It was longer than a regular table and the balls appeared to be much smaller in size. Then it dawned on me, this wasn't a regular pool table at all but a snooker table.

Snooker is a game invented by the Brits way back in the 19th century. The game is played using twenty two balls instead of the usual fifteen and the table is approximately three feet longer in length. Sensing a challenge, I quickly racked up the balls and was about to break when the girl I had just bought the drink for approached me empty handed.

"Where's the drink I just bought you?"

"I drink later."

"Yea, sure you will."

I put the cue stick down on the table and walked out. To this day, I can still hear the screeching sound the empty handed woman made when I walked out of the bar. The rest of the strip offered pretty much the same and then I heard about a "special joint" which featured a woman who was able to smoke a cigarette placed inside her vagina. The guy telling me was a twidget from a sister ship who had just witnessed it himself.

"Come on! It's got to be a trick, no one can do that!" I said.

"Buddy, I'm telling ya, we checked ourselves, there's no hidden curtain, no glass, no sheet, no camera, no machine no nothing! You gotta see this for yourself! She stuck the cigarette in her vagina and then she blew the smoke out her mouth!!! "

"How do I get there?"

"Go straight down this street then turn left…can't miss it."

"Ok, I'll go have a look see."

The walk to the "special joint" took less than five minutes. Even though I didn't know the name of the place it didn't matter. Standing outside the club was the tallest man I have ever seen. He was like a glowing beacon guiding sailors to the Promised Land. All I had to do was follow the crowd. When I got there, I couldn't believe my eyes. The entire joint was filled with sailors, and not just from my ship, but from several ships, and some were from other countries as well. I saw French and Italians mostly, but there were also a few British and German sailors mixed in.

It was a regular United Nations!

I scanned the room quickly. I'd have to say there were maybe two hundred squids there. As for the "smoking girl" she was nowhere to be seen. I made my way slowly to the bar and ordered a scotch on the rocks before lighting my cigarette. I found out from the bar tender the "smoking girl" would be out in thirty minutes. Meanwhile, there was a side show just left of center stage which featured a totally naked chick who had the ability to pick up a stack of 50 cent pieces using nothing but the inside of her thighs. Once she was confident the half dollars were secure, she would walk around the stage and drop them into buckets. The sailors called it the "coin show" but the locals had a different name which nobody could pronounce. Just about everyone was drinking and gambling was not only permitted, it was encouraged. It was like being in a miniature Las Vegas. Sailors the world over had come here to bet their money against the girl's coin dropping ability.

Unfortunately, many came up empty handed. Some left broke while others returned to their ships without a pot to piss in. Towards the end of the coin show, an announcement was made via the stage speakers that management was ready to accepted any and all challenges. They said the girl could drop a half dollar into any glass at any time regardless of the shape or size. The cost to bet against her was twenty dollars. If she missed, the winners received the equivalent in alcohol. As soon as the money was collected the music began. The girl squatted down on a stack of 50 cent pieces and then carefully walked around the stage lining up over each glass before releasing the coins. How she managed to release only one half dollar at a time remains a mystery.

Every now and then she would miss, but this was done on cue to keep the gamblers interested. However, whenever the appeal began to wane, management would up the ante. The free

259

drinks were elevated to bottles of champagne, provided you were willing to bet fifty dollars.

This time, the girl had to drop a quarter into a two inch shot glass. I'll say it again. A 25 cent piece into a two inch shot glass! Due to her proficiency, I knew right away there wouldn't be many takers, so the club sweetened the deal by allowing the winners to pick out the champagne of their choice. Finally, an Italian sailor agreed to give it a go provided the lights were dimmed. He thought it would be more challenging. Management agreed and as soon as the room got dark, the music started up again. Slowly the girl circled the elfin glass and after the third time around stopped. Her concentration was amazing. The whole time she was there, I didn't see her blink once. All of a sudden, she arched her body low like a cobra ready to strike. Once the coin was released, the music crescendoed. The quarter hit the bottom of the shot glass and bounced nearly three inches high before resettling back down again. Needless to say, the club erupted in applause. Shouts and whistles filled the room. I will say this, it was one hell of a trick and it must have taken a lot of practice to get it right. I don't know how you would list that on a resume but that's for another day. The girl bowed before exiting the stage but the lights remained dimmed. Honestly, I've often wondered what would have happened to her had she missed. You know, champagne isn't cheap.

Within seconds, a stroboscopic lamp lit up center stage. There was an object in the middle of the stage, but because the flashes of light were so intense, it took some time for our eyes to adjust. Positioned in the middle of the stage was a large wooden chair which was turned around. The only thing visible to us was the back of the chair. Within an instant though, the chair began to rotate counter clockwise. The first thing we saw were two flat pieces of wood extending from the chair. If you've ever sifted through a gynecological journal, the apparatus resembled a device used to perform examinations. The chair continued to turn until it was front and center and then it

260

stopped. Facing us is what I would call the ultimate Kodak moment. Sitting in the chair was a beautiful naked woman holding a lit cigarette with a red velvet glove.

And when I say beautiful, I mean Cover Girl perfect. On a scale of one to ten, she was an eleven. The shouts and whistles lauded on the coin girl ended abruptly. The Cover Girl had our undivided attention. Once the room was quiet, classical music began playing from the stage speakers. At first I didn't recognize the piece but after hearing the violins, I knew immediately what it was. Strange to hear Vivaldi's The Four Seasons in a place like this. I just couldn't connect the two. Vivaldi with naked women. Who would have thought? But then again, I'm sure when he was alive he had his fair share of admirers. Perhaps management thought the classical music added respectability?

Anyway, the vision sat there with her legs crossed. The long cigarette she was holding produced the thinnest trail of smoke I have ever seen. For a second I thought it was frankincense, but the aromatic resin associated with the product was missing. Suddenly, she uncrossed her legs and placed them on top of the wooden extensions. A narrow light beam focused on what was to us the Holy Grail. Staring us in the face was a beautifully shaven vagina that glistened in the glow of its own photon particles.

Sighs and moans were omnipresent.

Slowly, she took a hit and exhaled the remaining smoke above her head. Then, very carefully, she moved the cigarette down between her legs. Before inserting it into her womanhood, she drew an imaginary circle around her vagina.

Believe me; she redefined the term "pop tall."

Once inserted, she placed the gloved hand on her right thigh. At that moment, the chair reversed directions and began to turn slowly clockwise. The change in direction prompted the

261

smoking lady to arch her back and stiffen her muscles which caused the long cigarette to decrease in size. I gotta tell ya, it looked like it was being pulled in from the other side. Suddenly, she took a deep breath and once her lungs filled with air she twisted from side to side as if she was possessed.

During the act, I tried to focus on her face but it wasn't easy. The urge to look elsewhere was very compelling. Her full breasts and pointy nipples were enough to drive anyone crazy. Add to that a perfect face and body and you end up with a visual tour through Pleasure City.

Anyway, the contortions lasted for about a minute and then she stopped moving. Exhausted, she dropped her head to her chest. When she looked up again, white smoke came out her mouth. Liked everyone else, I sat there mesmerized. Obviously it was trick but how was it done? Granted, hard to call it a fake when you can't prove it's a fake, but remember this: just because you don't see any trap doors or hidden wires doesn't mean they don't exist. She repeated the process three more times before pulling the cigarette out. Good thing she did. She was just seconds away from being burned. After that, the lights went out momentarily and the music stopped. When the lights came back on again, she was gone.

Seconds later she reappeared wearing a red velvet robe which matched the color of her red velvet glove. She bowed twice before exiting stage left. You can imagine the applause. It was defeaning. As I stood there clapping, my mind drifted back to the act. I think the chair rotation had something to do with it, but I couldn't say for sure. Perhaps the smoke came from a thin tube attached to her body but then again, I didn't see one. Honestly, I didn't see anything that could have assisted her in her performance. And then it dawned on me. Perhaps what I saw was real. Maybe she had a physical deformity that allowed her to do what she did. I know it sounds crazy but crazy things happen all the time that can't be explained. One thing I know for sure. I saw smoke come out of her mouth but I didn't see any smoke go into her mouth. If it was a trick it was the best one I've ever seen.

The next day I decided to forgo any distractions and focus on taking care of the family jewels. I was definitely in the mood for some female companionship. The first two bars I hit were carbon copies of the snooker club. Pool tables surrounded by posses of half naked women anxiously waiting to separate me from my money. No thank you. The next place I ventured into was a regular night club complete with chairs and tables. I decided a different approach. Instead of acting like a lusting miscreant, I decided to be a gentleman. You know, like the Venus Fly Trap.

As soon as I entered, I sat down at a small table quite a distance from the dance floor. I was proud of myself as I waved off females and he- she's alike. To make matters worse, I sat with my back to the action sending a clear message-leave me alone. Within moments though, I felt a tap on my shoulder. I quickly turned around to shoo away the intruder but I was caught off guard. Standing in front of me were two nuns dressed in their habits! That's right, two sisters of the faith!

"May we sit down?"

The taller of the two made the request.

"Please do."

They sat down next to each other. The small table struggled to accommodate the three of us.

"Would you like something to drink?"

"No, thank you, we don't drink."

Of course they don't drink! What the hell is wrong with you!

"Something to eat then?"

"No thank you."

"Ok. How then may I help you sister?"

The one who asked to sit down spoke first.

"I am Sister Rachael and this is Sister Evelyn. We are here collecting for our church."

I almost choked on my drink.

"Church! In here! You got to be kidding?"

"No, we are not kidding. We saw you sitting here and noticed you have good morals because you turned your back on that sex show and you refused all the women who approached you…perhaps I should ask you the same question….why are YOU here?"

Remember, my radar screen was zeroed in on taking care of the family jewels. Having a conversation with a couple of Mother Teresa's was the last thing I wanted to do. I reached into my pocket pulled out a ten spot and gave it to her.

"Here, I hope this helps."

"Oh! You're very kind Sir. I will say a prayer for you tonight before I go to sleep."

"Thanks, and about the good morals, all is not as it appears to be."

Sister Evelyn chimed in.

"No one is perfect Sir; we came to you for help and you responded. Whatever bad you may have done; the burden you carry is a little less heavy. Sacred Heart thanks you for your contribution."

"Amen to that sister," I replied.

The nuns got up, made their way to the exit and left. As I lit my cigarette, the possibility I just got ripped off crossed my mind. I mean I could have; these girls are all very good at what they do, but I didn't think so. They seemed sincere; but then again, who the hell knows! I wanted them to be legit, that was the important thing. I felt it best not to dwell on it. I had two more drinks before leaving the club.

Once outside, across the street, I noticed two women huddled together on a street corner. One was middle aged and the other looked to be in her early twenties. If I had to guess, I would say a mother/daughter combination. Standing behind the two women were two men who appeared to be drunk. Both men were heavily tattooed and they appeared to have markings on their faces. One of the men began talking to the younger woman and then, all of a sudden like, the other one grabbed her arm. Obviously the mother wasn't happy. She began yelling at the two to release the younger woman but her plea fell on deaf ears.

I believe the two men were trying to separate the younger woman from the older one. It's pretty obvious as to why. Anyway, the heavier one, the one doing the grabbing, released the girls arm preferring instead to concentrate on her shoulder. However, once he planted his oversized hand on her shoulder, he pushed down on it hard motioning her to walk. Sensing what was happening, I dashed across the street just as the second man grabbed her other arm. Without thinking, I punched the thinner one in the face knocking him to the ground. The heavier one released his grip on her shoulder just long enough for me to push him down. Moving between the girl and her attackers, I acted as a buffer. Both men reeked of alcohol and marijuana and the thinner of the two, the one I punched in the face was having trouble breathing. The heavier of the two rose to his feet, but before he could straighten up again, I pushed him so hard he fell back down.

And that's when I felt it.

Midway between my elbow and my wrist was a four inch line of blood. The line was razor thin, and upon first glance, didn't look like a cut at all. Honestly, it looked like someone had grabbed a red coloring pencil and drawn a straight line down my forearm. Truth is, I never saw what cut me. It may have been a knife or it may have been something else. The only thing I knew for sure. It was made out of metal and I was in pain. I moved backwards to reposition myself when my right hand brushed across a glass bottle lying on top of a garbage can. Just as the heavier man was getting ready to cut me again, I smashed the bottle across his temple knocking him down. A small crowd, reacting to the sound of glass breaking, appeared. The two men got to their feet and ran away. As I turned to face the women, something warm entered into my left eye.

An onlooker shouted I was bleeding. Sure enough, blood was shooting out of my forearm like the Fountain di Trevi. Immediately, I thought the son of a bitch had severed an artery. The older woman removed the scarf around her neck and applied it to the wound. Once the garment was secured, I applied pressure with my free hand. The younger woman pulled a white cloth from her shopping bag and began wiping the blood from my face. A small group of bystanders had formed a circle around us. The older woman explained to the crowd what had happened. Right after that, I was being patted on the back. It wasn't long before the police arrived and took statements from everyone, everyone that is, except me. Someone dressed in a police uniform took pictures with a flash camera and then I was loaded into the back of a police car and taken to the hospital.

According to the nurse in the recovery wing, I was taken immediately into surgery where I received twenty seven stitches. The nurse said the doctor would keep me for at least 48 hours, maybe longer, depending on the damage. I thanked her before mentioning I needed to contact my ship.

"The police contacted your embassy. I'm sure someone from the embassy will contact your ship."

"Embassy? Why the embassy?"

"Standard procedure. Whenever US military personnel are injured or killed the authorities

266

are obligated to contact the embassy. Someone from your ship will contact you, but, based on my experience, it probably won't happen until tomorrow morning."

Oh boy I said to myself. Oh boy. Standing orders are to maintain a low profile. Can anyone say Captain's Mast?

"Are you strong enough to make a statement or would you prefer to do it tomorrow morning?"

"Tomorrow morning, if you don't mind."

I was still feeling the anesthesia. Whatever had to be said would have to wait till then.

"Alright then, I'll check on you later."

The soft spoken nurse exited the room leaving me to my thoughts. Within minutes I was asleep. Around 0600 I was awakened and given pain medication by a different nurse. Apparently the shift had changed and the soft spoken nurse who attended to my needs the night before was gone. Even though I was hooked up to an intravenous bag, the pain medicine had to be administered orally. Normally, I don't have a problem taking pills but since my left arm was hanging from a sling, placing the pill in my mouth was somewhat difficult. To compensate, I chewed the medication before washing it down with water. The door to my room was kept slightly ajar affording me the opportunity to see the waiting area just outside recovery. Sitting on a long wooden bench were Mr. Zoran, my Division Officer and the Executive Officer, Mr. Reed.

"Two officers from your ship are here to talk to you, are you strong enough to talk to them?"

"Yea, I suppose."

"Ok, I'll go and get them."

My new nurse stepped to the edge of the room and leaned forward. This caused her uniform to rise slightly up her thigh. When she motioning for them to enter, her arm waving caused her butt to move gently from side to side. Now, even though I wasn't in the mood, I was grateful for the show. Once inside the room, the XO spoke first.

"How are you feeling Patterson?"

"Not too bad, Sir, a little pain in my arm."

"I spoke to the emergency room physician; he told me you're a very lucky man."

"I am?"

"Yes indeed. He said the knife cut was very deep; in fact, it severed your artery, but because the blade was sharp, the cut was clean. According to the attending surgeon, the reattachment was completed with minimal invasiveness."

"Well, that's good news," I said.

"There's more," the XO continued.

"What's that Sir?"

"The unknown…hopefully there's no permanent damage to the arm. Before he reattached the artery, he had to cut away a small portion of muscle. Also there was damage to one of the tendons as well. The surgeon doesn't think there is any nerve damage, but it's too early to make that call…did you make a statement yet?"

"No, not yet Sir."

"Well, just be honest about what happened. Attention to detail Patterson is all we're asking for. Mr. Zoran will get a copy of your statement from the police investigator. Alright son, you take care and get well. We'll be leaving in a few days which means you'll have to catch up with the ship. I haven't worked out all the details yet, but should have an answer by the time we get underway…alright Patterson, you rest easy son."

268

The XO patted my good shoulder but it sent ripples of pain down my side. I don't think he did it on purpose, but then again, who knows? I will say this. The XO is a very busy man. His plate's always full. Having to baby sit me only added to his headaches. As he walked out the room, a uniformed police officer entered, ready to take my statement. I told the investigator exactly what happened, providing a timeline of events. Since I couldn't write, a recording device was provided, complete with a miniature microphone which was clipped to my hospital gown. Mr. Zoran took a seat near a small window. I could see he was need of a little fresh air. My statement was followed up with several questions which I answered as best I could. The police officer informed me, based on my testimony; the two men were probably gang members and quite possibly drug dealers. He also told me I was very lucky to walk away with only a knife wound. He said guys like that usually carry guns and had they used them, he would be down at the city morgue conducting a homicide investigation, instead of taking a statement.

"The girl, is she alright?" I asked.

He nodded.

"And her mother, thanks to you."

"Ah, I thought so. A mom out with her daughter."

As we were finishing up, I asked the officer for the girl's name.

"By law, I am unable to give you her last name, but her first name is Mylene."

"Mylene," I whispered under my breath.

"Alright, this concludes the reporting phase of the investigation. If you should think of anything else, please contact me. Here is my card."

I looked at the card then quickly glanced at the name on his uniform. They matched. I was speaking to Officer Jaime Cabatuan.

"If you would please accompany me Mr. Zoran, I will provide you with a hard copy of the statement."

The police officer shook my good hand as did Mr. Zoran.

"Alright Patterson, hang in there, I'll pass the word you're here in case anyone wants to come visit. I'll be back later today, possibly early evening to check on your status...take care."

After they departed, I was alone again which was good. I really needed the rest. Unfortunately, I was beginning to feel some discomfort in my left arm along with a tingling sensation in my fingers I had not experienced before. I was hoping it was because the pain medication hadn't taken effect yet. But just to be on the safe side, I was about to press the call button and alert the nurse when all of a sudden I stopped dead in my tracks. Standing just outside my door was Mylene.

"Good Morning, I hope you don't mind," she said.

"Good Morning, and no, I don't mind."

Suddenly, I was feeling a little bit better.

"I'm Mylene."

"Yes, I know, the police officer told me... I'm William."

"I just wanted to thank you for what you did for me and my mom. You're a hero."

"Hero? Hell, I don't know about that."

"Well, that's what the newspapers are saying."

"Mylene held up the front page to one of the local papers. Squeezed in the top right corner was a picture of me swinging at one of the assailants. How they got that picture I have no idea. The caption below the photo said "American sailor saves local girl from gang—story on page fifteen."

"My mom would like to thank you as well."

Mylene turned around and walked out of the room. Within moments, she reappeared with her mother, who approached the bed and hugged me.

"Thank you for saving my daughter."

She had tears in her eyes as she whispered to her daughter.

"My mom wants to know how long will you be in the hospital?"

"At least two days, maybe longer. It all depends on how well the artery is doing. I feel fine but you know how doctors are."

"So, the artery was cut?"

"Cut in half."

"I'm not surprised. He had a balisong...very sharp and very dangerous."

"A what?"

"A butterfly knife... you know, the kind that are spring loaded, but can be opened with one hand...yes, you're very lucky...sometimes a butterfly knife is worse than a gun."

"Did you know those guys?"

"OH NO!!! I never saw them before in my life. No, I have no idea who they are."

"Well, keep a sharp eye out the next time you go shopping. You know what they look like and they know what you look like, so be on your toes. In New Jersey we have a saying...you need to have eyes in the back of your head."

Mylene smiled.

"OK. I will have eyes in the back of my head."

That was the third time I was told I was lucky. The first person to tell me was Mr. Reed. He said I was lucky because the cut was clean. The second person was Officer Jaime Cabatuan who said I was lucky they didn't have their guns and now I'm being told I'm lucky because they only cut one artery. Mylene relayed the information to her mother who became very emotional. More tears formed in her eyes. The mom whispered to her daughter again.

"My mom would like to invite you to our house for dinner."

"Oh! That's very kind of her, but once I'm well enough to travel, I will have to leave right away so I can rejoin my ship, but, please thank her for the offer."

"Ok, I will explain it to her later. We will visit you every day until you leave, is that ok?"

"Sure, I'd like that."

"Ok, you rest now."

The two women were practically hovering over me. In fact, Mylene was so close, had I stuck my tongue out I would have hit her check.

"Ok, we will come and visit you tomorrow," the mom said.

Mylene leaned over and kissed me on the check. I reacted to the kiss and to her perfume safely underneath the covers. So much for taking care of the family jewels.

"Thank you William. Thank you so much for what you did and I'm very sorry you got cut. You are my hero."

"Here, we will leave the newspaper; you can read the story later," said the mom.

"We will pray for you."

Wow, first the two nuns and now these two women. Perhaps there was hope for me yet.

Three days later I was released from the hospital but before I was able to leave my room, I was met by two gentlemen from the State Department. They were there to transport me from the hospital to a military airport where a C-140 was waiting to fly me to my ship. As promised, Mylene and her mom visited me every day and I believe I was beginning to develop feelings for her, but not the kind of feelings a pious man would have. No, I was way beyond that. I was thinking wind, water, whiskey and women. My piratical mind was conjuring up all sorts of things. Good thing I was leaving, the poor girl wouldn't have known what hit her.

The C-140 lifted off at 1400. By 0700 the following morning, I was standing on the Pompton's Quarter Deck. For some strange reason, I was treated like a hero. I thought it odd. What I did for those two women, anyone of them would have done. As I went around the ship thanking those who had visited me in the hospital, I thought back to Bartholomew Jones and the dive he made off the Baffles. I was receiving the same kind of adulation and like the Bart man; all I could do was smile. As for the arm, it was healing nicely but whenever I made a fist I could still feel some tenderness. The stitches would have to wait another two weeks before being removed. As for nerve damage, there wasn't any.

I thanked the Lord, the two nuns, Mylene and her mother for all my good fortunes.

Chapter 24

A few months after our deployment ended, the U.S.S. Pompton was decommissioned. Our forty five year old ship was regrettably put out to pasture. All that remained was her Folkvang journey to that big beautiful shipyard in the sky! Realistically, the U.S.S. Pompton, a veteran of World War II, Korea and Vietnam would be turned into a million razor blades. Sad when you think about it but practical. The decommissioning ceremony took place on the last day of March. Even though it was a somber occasion it did have its humorous moments. As for me, I was proud to be in attendance. Not many squids can say they decommissioned a ship.

Like the Baffles, I take away many fond memories of the Pompton. The one that burns brightest involved her main deck. You see, it was shaped like a hardboiled egg making it ideal for jogging. More importantly, it had two athwartship passage ways which were perfect for cooling down the runners. Brisk air currents would race through the corridors as if driven by powerful fans. Eventually, the strong winds catapulted themselves through the exit points. It was here where the tired sprinters congregated. Before returning to the fleet, I had to complete one more maintenance course. The class consisted of experienced sailors whose service commitments required them to serve at sea one more time. Like school number two, number three was also technically challenging. Once again, I had to limit my partying to Fridays and Saturdays only. As to the course itself, it demanded the upmost precision with zero tolerance for error. I gotta tell you, I had headaches the entire seven months I was there and when it was over, I just missed getting a perfect score by one point! Shortly afterwards, I was given orders to report to my third and final ship.

The USS Vailsburg DDG 153 was a fine ship with a good crew. She was skippered by one Commander Lively who had risen through the ranks the old fashioned way; first, as an enlisted man, and then as an officer. In other words, he had seen it all and was bullet proof. Oh, and another thing, he was quite content with his station in life. Whatever ambitions he may have had, he kept to himself. Honestly, I can't recall a time when he placed the ship in harm's way and from what I heard; scoring brownie points with the Admiralty was the furthest thing from his mind. He was the complete opposite of Whitehead. How refreshing! As for getting underway, he went by the book. Tugs were used at all times and those assigned sea and anchor stations were instructed to remember" safety first" whenever tying up the ship. I'm pretty sure Commanders Whitehead and Lively wouldn't have gotten along, and, had a fight broken out between the two, I would have given a year's salary just to watch Lively knock Whitehead on his ass. Anyway, I reported to the Vailsburg as a senior second class petty officer. Why do I mention this? If there was an available middle rack, I had a good shot of getting it. Remember, on the Baffles, I started off sleeping in the after top rack but eventually made my way to the forward bottom rack thanks to a certain senior twidget who didn't want an annoying torpedo man in our berthing area. On the Pompton, I also slept in a bottom rack, but now, now I had the potential to move on up. I was finally going to get the chance to enjoy all the comforts a middle rack had to offer!

And just as I had predicted, there was an available middle rack close to the scuttlebutt near the forward head, but I didn't care. The long wait was over and I was ecstatic! For the first time in my military career, I didn't have to bend down to reach for my clothes and no more walking fifty feet just to get to my tooth brush. Life was looking good but I was in for one more treat. When I became the leading petty officer some time later, I was able to commandeer the best middle rack berthing had to offer. It was spacious with a wonderful ventilation system and I even had my own privacy wall. Yes, the right side of my rack touched the starboard bulkhead. Finally, I didn't have to worry about neighbors eaves dropping on my conversations! Ah! The beauty of being top dog!!!

275

Within a fort night, we were underway heading west across the Pacific. I was lucky. The Vailsburg was scheduled to visit some of the same watering holes I had been to before. For once, I was going somewhere familiar, and, as an added bonus, would have the opportunity to sample life below the equator.

Our first port of call was the fiftieth state. Reflectively, we sailed past the eight battleships that make up Battle Ship Row. Donned in dress whites, we manned the rails to honor those who made the ultimate sacrifice for their country. As the Arizona came into view, I couldn't help but think about my own father who had fought against the Japanese during World War II. Seeing me there at Parade Rest, my medals and ribbons shining brightly in the late morning sun, how proud he would have been. Two days later, we were underway heading south by southwest.

It would be several weeks before we would see land again. The Vailsburg had received orders to participate in a variety of naval operations involving many of our allies. Working with other nations was a great way to keep our skill set up to date. Of course there would be language barriers to overcome as well as certain protocols and procedures, but that was to be expected. The exercises were designed to smooth out any rough surfaces wherever they may occur. After two weeks, we were given orders to separate from the task force and make our way to our next scheduled port of call. A week later we were pier side. Believe me; liberty call couldn't have come soon enough for the crew of the Vailsburg. Everyone and I mean everyone was exhausted from all the naval exercises and sleep for many was paramount. But, like sailors the world over, sleep would have to wait.

The Sirens were calling.

Wind, water, whiskey and women!!

As for me, I was going to stick to my routine of resting first, but before hitting my rack, I made my way to the fantail to watch the guys leave the ship. One by one they trudged down the brow like tired ants. You'd never know by looking, but many of them were walking around on empty, especially the snipes. In fact, truth be told, some of them hadn't slept in more than thirty six hours. So what was the big attraction? Why would the crew go out partying when they could barely keep their eyes open? Well, we were in an English speaking country and that made all the difference in the world. People just like us. What could possibly go wrong?

What could possibly go wrong?

Just about everything.

For starters, street fighting seemed to be a sanctioned sport. Not far from the landing, I spotted a huge fight taking place just outside the restricted area. Remember the nineteenth century boxing legend John L. Sullivan? He was considered the last of the bare knuckle champions. Well, bare knuckle boxing may be part of the history books, but here in this city, it was alive and well. From my vantage point, it looked like one group of brawlers was being challenged by two other groups.

Mind you, it was two groups against one.

The first group, I'll call them the young Sullivan's, appeared to be taller and heavier than the brawlers in the other groups. Almost like adults battling teenagers but not quite. I counted six young Sullivan's against maybe ten or twelve. Now, most guys I know would find that intimidating but not this bunch. No, they seemed ready and willing. The first thing they did was line up in a wedge. The leader stood out in front. Directly behind him were two others and behind them were the last three. There they towered, like bowling pins made from ironwood. And all of them had battle scars. Besides the obvious missing teeth and ring cuts, one of them even sported a large bump above his left temple. Obviously, he was no stranger to a shilalee.

Their opponents formed a circle around them. Believe me; they were just as mean looking as the young Sullivan's but their size disadvantage was striking. I was expecting weapons. Not necessarily guns or knives, but chains and broken glass but there were none. No, this was going to be settled the John L. Sullivan way. The attacker's strategy was simple. Charge from all sides simultaneously.

No Marquees of Queensberry rules here folks!

For the first minute or so, it looked like the larger group was going to prevail. The overwhelming numbers appeared to be too much, but when one of the young Sullivans's knocked out one of the challengers, the momentum shifted. You know the phrase don't kick a man when he's down, well, that didn't apply here. What happened next was striking. The leader of the Sullivan's knocked one of the attackers down. Before the man was able to get to his feet, he kicked him in the face knocking him out. I remember the look of satisfaction he had. Even though the Leader was bleeding above his left eye it didn't seem to bother him. He simply turned his bloodied blue shirt into a towel. When two other challengers could no longer continue, the fight was over. Rather than face total humiliation they gathered up their wounded and departed. Round one went to the young Sullivan's.

Now, in my experience, most fights happen for three reasons…women…alcohol…and money. Surprisingly, that was not the case here. No, in this city, men just fought for the hell of it. Think of it as a side show to their national pastime. It was no more complicated than that. So how do these fights start? They start with a punch. Someone walking down the street or standing at a curb gets sucker punched or cold cocked- take your pick. After they recover, honor demands they fight back, which is what they do. Now, I don't know if it's just boredom or if it's the alcohol talking, but there is an unwritten rule. Whenever you leave your house, make sure you're aware of your surroundings.

You could get hit at any time.

This is what the crew of the Vailsburg had to deal with that first day, and in case you forgot, we came here for rest and relaxation. Hours later, when I finally left the ship, the OOD reminded me about the consequences of fighting in uniform. Apparently, several crew members were involved in various altercations throughout the city. In fact, someone, and I still don't know who, ended up in the hospital with a concussion. Had the brawler not been taken into custody, I'm sure the skipper would have cancelled liberty call. I took this as my wakeup call. Avoid the bars, avoid the trouble. Really, a no brainer.

Or so I thought.

As I neared what looked to be the downtown area, I saw two women drinking coffee in front of a building that was just screaming for renovation. Cracked paint peels were scattered along the entire front entranceway as well as on the side walk. Although the windows were clean the latches appeared to be rusted. Yellow brown stains had formed on the sills, and small pieces of roof tile had somehow managed to find their way into some of the window jambs. The thick brown entrance door was adorned with small carvings of fish displayed in an elliptical pattern. The carvings were located just above the screened glass which comprised the top one third of the door panel. Intrigued, I decided to investigate. Surprisingly, as soon as I walked through the front door, I was in a coffee shop. Usually there's a buffer between the inside and outside of large buildings like this, but there was none. Had I an umbrella, there was no vestibule in which to stow it.

Behind the counter were two middle aged women. One was smoking a cigarette while the other was reading a newspaper. On the floor was a college aged girl who was waiting tables. She was pretty, but appeared to be more interested in her makeup then serving her customers. Besides the two women outside, the only other patrons were two small groups of college kids studying for midterm exams. All of them were drinking coffee. I decided to concentrate on the pretty waitress. She seemed to know her job and was polite and friendly but whenever she had a moment, she would stare into the mirrored glass behind the counter and touch up her hair or face.

I decided to go back outside and sit opposite the two women.

"Hello Yank!"

A woman in her mid twenties extended the greeting. She had blond hair, blue eyes and a very cute figure.

"Hello. Is it that obvious?" I said jokingly.

"Came in off that ship did ya?"

"Yes, but how do you know?"

"There's only one American ship in the harbor. So, out and about are ya?"

"We call it liberty call."

More like danc'n to the bosun's whistle if you ask me."

"I'm sorry, what did you say?"

"Danc'n to the bosun's whistle."

"What does that mean?"

"Good God man! Have you never heard of the hornpipe?"

"If he knew about the hornpipe, would he be asking about the bosun's whistle?

You must excuse her. She grew up around a bunch of drunken sailors who used to dance and drink the hornpipe until the wee hours of the morning. You see her dad, god rest his soul, was in the Royal Navy, and that's what they used to do when they were out and about—dance the bosun's whistle."

280

"When they had liberty?"

"Yea, when they had liberty."

So, the hornpipe is a musical instrument?"

"Yea, in a way. Think of it as a long pipe, you know like the kind you smoke from, but it has holes on the side."

"It's also the name of the dance," added Blondie.

The informative woman speaking was a bespeckled brunette who was considerably older and heavier than her blond friend. She wore thick black glasses that were so unappealing; they reminded me of birth control devices used in the 1950's. Even though she had a nice smile her yellow stained teeth suggested she was a heavy smoker. Years of tar and nicotine had taken its toll. Even her lips showed signs of damage. If ever there was an incentive to quit smoking, she was it.

"Come join us would you?"

I hesitated for a moment and even thought about walking away, but when Blondie asked a second time, I acquiesced.

"Thank you, "I said sitting down.

"Glasses" wasn't exactly pleased with the invite. I think she had a lot of things on her mind that required serious girl talk. Not one to be turned away, I quickly ordered coffee and told the makeup girl I would pay for the three of us. A nice gesture on my part since I wasn't eating and they were. Anyway, this small token did the trick. Glasses was impressed. She was no longer uncomfortable having me around. Notice I haven't asked them their names yet? This may sound a bit over confident, but by now, I had enough experience with women to know "names" just get in the way, especially in the beginning. Glasses was admiring my uniform and wanted to know what each ribbon stood for. As I was explaining, I realized my focus had shifted away from Blondie.

Granted, Blondie was younger and better looking, but she had the attention span of a squirrel. Every time I attempted to engage her in intelligent conversation, she would lose focus and change the subject. Glasses, on the other hand, although physically unattractive, possessed the sharper mind which, at this point, seemed to stimulate me more. Too bad I couldn't combine the two to make one woman! Now that would be one hell of a chick!

Eventually, Glasses suggested we take a stroll down to the shopping district which was only four blocks away. Blondie agreed as long as we stopped to get something to eat. Can you believe the girl was still hungry! Anyway, as we strolled down the promenade, I pondered my dilemma. My mind wanted Glasses but my body ached for Blondie.

How to resolve this? We decided to look for a restaurant near the shopping center. Once seated, Glasses leaned over and whispered her intentions into my ear. I reacted immediately. Blood began to surge from the bottom of my feet. Once it passed my ankles it increased in intensity as it moved up my legs. I began to shake slightly. Had it reached my pleasure center I think I would have exploded. It was clear what she had in mind. I was on the menu. The problem now was ditching Blondie.

After a quick dinner, we strolled down the main drag eyeing the various shops and attractions the walkway had to offer. Every now and then, Glasses would push her breasts into my chest. It may not sound like much, but a sizeable portion of her body weight was distributed across her head lights. I was very much aroused and couldn't wait for dessert. I was about to whisper that into her ear when I came to an abrupt halt. I thought I had just run into a brick wall.

"WATCH WHERE YOU'RE WALK'N MATE!"

Startled, I asked him to repeat what he said.

"WHAT? ARE YOU DAFT? YOU'RE IN MY WAY!"

I was about to say something nasty, but I hesitated. Staring directly into my eyes was one of the brawlers I had seen outside the landing earlier in the day.

And talk about bad luck!!

Standing in front of me was the head kicker in charge of the young Sullivan's. How could I tell? He was still wearing his bloodied blue shirt and just to make doubly sure, I looked for the cut above his left eye. Yep, it was him. I gotta tell ya, it was one hell of a situation. As soon as he crossed into my personal space, he began sizing me up. He must have been drinking because he reeked of alcohol. I thought for sure he was going to punch me but for some strange reason he hesitated. I looked around and he appeared to be alone. His mates were nowhere to be seen. Could be the reason why he hesitated. No back up.

I attempted to defuse the situation by smiling but he wasn't buying. Shortly after, I noticed he had both fists clenched but again, something was preventing him. It was most curious. At first I thought it might be my uniform. Then I thought since I was a tourist but that couldn't be it. No, something else was causing the procrastination. Funny now that I look back. He was at least ten years older and much bigger with a solid body. Underneath his bloodied blue shirt was a muscular frame and rock solid biceps. If I had to guess, I would say he was a day laborer. You know guys they hire to dig graves. Anyhow, along the length of his arms were tattoos depicting naked women. From what I could see, his chin had been broken at least once but no longer appeared to be a repository for pain. He had ring cuts all over his face and I believe he was missing one of his incisors. No mistake about it. This guy was a seasoned street fighter. That much was certain.

Distraught, I continued to look for ways to defuse the situation when I happened to notice the head kicker's eyes were fixated on the shine coming from my ribbon holder. He appeared to be impressed with the three rows of ribbons, but his real focus was on the three chevrons on my upper

283

left arm. That captivated him almost to the point of being startled.

Even though most people are unfamiliar with military rankings, they are able to associate three stripes with a specific rank. It doesn't matter the branch of service or even the country. Three marks on the arm can only mean one thing: S-E-R-G-E-A-N-T!!! And thanks to the movies, sergeants are always the toughest guys on the battlefield. They are the take charge guys, the ones carrying the wounded to safety. The guys, who never seem to tire, quit or give up. I believe this was the impression he took from our encounter. Whatever it was, it did the trick. He moved out of my personal space. That's right, he backed down. Had Blondie not grabbed his arm, he would have walked away. I don't know why, but for some strange reason, she felt compelled to add to his worries by telling him I was a war hero. Once she released her grip, he hastened his departure. As quickly as he had appeared, he melted into the crowd and was gone. I have to admit, I breathed a huge sigh of relief. Had we fought I'm sure he would have messed me up badly. I was indeed fortunate. Talk about being lucky. Had he approached from the right side, he wouldn't have seen the ribbons or the chevrons. An almost certain altercation was diverted because of plain luck. Once again, I thanked the man upstairs for all my good fortunes.

Continuing on our journey, we visited about ten different stores before finally sitting down for something cold to drink. It was right around this time Glasses whispered something into Blondie's ear. After nervously fidgeting around in her purse, she produced a crumpled piece of paper which she claimed was a doctor's appointment she had early in the morning. She rose, asked to be excused but before walking away, I kissed her on the check. I needed that. Ten minutes later, Glasses and I were in a hotel of my choosing, and brother, let me tell you, it was well worth the price of admission! What she lacked in physical beauty, she more than made up for in passion and sensuality. In a way she kind of reminded me of Diane. Both were warm, full of emotion and very

284

good at self expression.

Truth was, Glasses was a toe curler. You know, a woman who performs above and beyond the call of duty. They're rare, so when you find one, you want to hold onto them for as long as possible. Funny how technique trumped looks this time. Perhaps I was maturing after all. And one more thing, I learned a new expression—Danc'n to the bosun's whistle. I would have to add that to my ever expanding library of words, sayings and utterances.

The next day we were underway and heading to our next port of call. Same country but different coast. The city we ended up in was slightly larger than the one we just left. For a change, I decided to seek out like minded individuals, you know, people who share the same ethnic background as me. An almost sure fire way of finding these individuals is through the sense of smell and I'm not talking body odor! Since the city was a melting pot; I knew it would be awhile before I would be able to zero in on any familiar fragrances. I walked around for about forty minutes until I was inundated with odors I hadn't smelled since I was a kid. Inside a restaurant window was a vertical rotisserie of meat. It smelled like lamb, but it could have been pork. I was still a ways off. As I neared the restaurant, tantalizing aromas curled and snaked their way up from the street, circling my body before moving purposely past my face enticing me to stay.

Intrigued, I took a seat just outside the entrance way. Speaking in my mother's tongue, I placed an order and guess what happened? I got extra portions and a free drink! When I couldn't eat another bite, I paid the bill and continued on my journey. I needed time to digest the lavish meal I had just consumed. After I had walked North three blocks, I noticed the neighborhood had changed so I did an about face and, while walking back, discovered a little ethnic bar. Once again I spoke my mother's language and once again, I got a free drink!

As I was finishing my drink, out of the corner of my eye, I saw something scotch taped to a side mirror just outside the men's room. Small and rectangular, it was an advertisement for a church festival. I got up to read it. It said it started yesterday and would end tomorrow night. I was in luck! I committed the address to memory, had one more drink then made my way to the "Glendi" or festival. The advertisement stated any monies raised would go to the new building fund. Apparently, the church wanted to build a basketball court for its youth association. Had I known about the festival beforehand, I wouldn't have stuffed myself but, drawing on experience, I knew that if I moved around a lot and danced, my appetite would return, so, that's what I did.

When I arrived, I quickly joined hands with two young girls who were part of a larger circle moving counter clockwise to a Tsamiko dance. All those years of dancing in church had prepared me well for this moment, and being in great shape with youth on my side, I was soon attracting the attention of someone close to a microphone. After moving to the lead position where I completed a handkerchief flip, I heard the following:

"Look everyone, at that wonderful Sailor! He is visiting us from New York City, America!"

I bowed my head in acknowledgement as I continued to dazzle the crowd with my dancing. Soon, I caught the eye of a married woman whose drunken husband took offense. He walked onto the dance floor and grabbed my shirt just below my throat. I grabbed him back, but before I could get a punch off, several men rushed the floor separating us. It was obvious to all who the aggressor was, but, honestly, I started it, or to be more specific, his wife started it. Someone suggested I join their table to clear the air and that's when I met the wife. To reassure all, there were no hard feelings; her husband kissed me on the check before punching me in the stomach. His way of apologizing. I hugged him back and it was over. I sat down opposite the wife and was about to exchange a shot of whiskey with the stomach puncher when a thought occurred to me.

Why did they assume I was from New York? I presented it as an open question.

"That was just a guess? Are you from there?"

A woman at the other end of the table spoke.

"No, but you're very close; I'm just across the Hudson River; I'm from New Jersey."

"Ah see, we were almost right!"

Our eyes connected.

"I'm Voula."

"William."

The young lady was perhaps thirty five years old. Sitting on either side of her was a teenage boy of about fourteen and a pre-pubescent girl who looked to be about nine.

"This is my Georgie and this is my daughter Patricia."

I nodded at each, acknowledging them separately.

I didn't see a husband.

"Am I taking your husband's seat?" I asked coyly.

"No, I'm divorced," she said softly.

I felt a tingle run down my leg, not a surge, just a tingle.

The band playing the ethic music took a scheduled break. They were replaced by a DJ who specialized in modern dance music. The first song he played was an older song but it had a nice beat to it. I noticed Voula was swaying in her chair. Her body was in synch with the music.

"Would you like to dance?" I asked.

"I would."

Rising from her chair, I couldn't help but notice the lovely curves of her body accentuating the green and silver dress she was wearing. She stood about 5'3" and appeared to weigh somewhere in the neighborhood of 110 lbs. Not bad for a woman with two kids. I held her hand as

287

I made my way to the dance floor. Eyeballs were bouncing off the back of our heads.

"Can you feel it?" I asked.

"Feel what?"

"Eyeballs bouncing off the back of our heads."

"Oh, that. It's probably your uniform. Don't give it a second thought."

The song reminded me of the Latin hustle, so I grabbed her hand and spun her around which brought a smile to her face. We danced several more times that evening. When it was over, I escorted her and her kids outside and was about to say good night, when she suggested I ride back to her place for a cup of coffee. She felt the need to repay my kindness and besides, the kids were tired and needed to sleep. By the time we walked through her front door it was two thirty in the morning. After the kids went to bed, we talked for two more hours and then I got up to leave. It was late and I still had quite a ways to go before reaching the ship.

And then it happened.

She got up from the couch, reached out for my hand and began guiding me to her bedroom. Believe me, I wanted too but I just didn't have the time. Very quickly I asked for a rain check and to show her I was truly interested, I invited her and her kids to the ship. I had duty anyway, so why not kill two birds with one stone. Yes, the old bring them to the ship routine. Hell, it worked before didn't it?

Voula, George and Patricia arrived around 1600 which was perfect. I was scheduled to go on watch at 2000 which gave me almost four hours to spend with her. Voula reminded me of Penny except she was a little taller and had a better body. She walked up the brow wearing white shorts and a blue blouse so sparse, I could almost see through it.

As I stood there admiring her, a slight quiver in my leg muscles caused me to bend slightly, offsetting my balance. It was an awkward moment causing me to blush. Fortunately, the event did not go unnoticed. Her alluring smile said it all.

She understood; she wanted, she needed to take care of it.

After straightening myself, I motioned for us to depart the quarter deck. I gave them a tour of all the designated areas leaving the mess deck for last. When we arrived there I noticed they were a little tired from climbing all the ladders so I made a bee line to the ships store returning with cokes and chips. Around 1930, Voula and her kids departed the ship. I remember standing near the quarter deck watching them until they were no longer in sight. Before walking down the brow, we exchanged kisses as was our custom. Very discreetly, she tucked a small piece of paper into my closed hand. On the paper was the name and address of the restaurant she worked in. We were to see each other the following day.

As promised, I arrived at the restaurant twenty minutes before closing time. Once her shift finished, she asked me what I wanted to do and I told her point blank I wanted to make love to her. She seemed a little surprised.

"You want to make love to me?"

"Yes. I want to finish what we started the other night."

"I do too, but first a few questions, if you don't mind?"

Wow, why the ringer?

"Sure, go ahead. Ask away."

"How long has it been since you had sex?"

I paused before answering. Adding to the charade, I rolled my eyes like an innocent virgin.

"Four months."

I lied. It wasn't even two weeks.

"And you?"

"Six years."

No way I said to myself. Six years! The woman is going to eat me alive! I felt another tingle down my leg, but this time it was stronger.

"OK. Let's get a room; I know a place that's nice but not too expensive."

"Lead on."

Rule Number 4 didn't apply here because we had already spent time together. Remember, she did visit the ship. She hailed a cab. We sat together in the back but didn't talk to each other. The silence seemed strange so I spoke first.

"Why six years?"

Wrong question. Boy did I open up a can of worms. Voula proceeded to tell me her life story. She married young to please her parents even though she had serious reservations about her future husband. Soon after the birth of Patricia, she divorced him due to his addiction to infidelity. After that, she had a relationship with another man who turned out to be so abusive, she had him incarcerated. I could see she was a little uncomfortable, but she continued. While in prison, he picked a fight with another inmate who killed him.

"Why six years? She said. I'd rather be alone and safe then be in a relationship and have to worry about being cheated on, beaten or killed."

"Yea, but not all guys are like that."

I put my arm around her.

"I know, but right now, I'm happy in my comfort zone. I don't want to leave my bubble just yet."

She went on to tell me she hadn't dated anyone in five years which caused me to reassess the situation. This was all too easy. She was such an easy mark. Lonely and vulnerable. I almost called the whole thing off.

"I know you're ready physically but what about upstairs?

"Excuse me?"

You know, mentally. Are you strong enough to handle this or should we just go and get some ice cream or something?"

The ice cream made her laugh. She began to loosen up a little. I tried one more time to be a gentleman.

"Hey, listen. If you're not ready for this, we can call it off. I want you, but after all you've been through, well, I just don't want to cause you any pain."

"William, I've had three days to think about this. Even before you came over for coffee I've been thinking about spending time with you. I'm ready. Remember, it was I who led you to the bedroom. I wanted you, but you know what convinced me? You had the discipline to say no. That has never happened before. Because you put your commitment to your ship above me, it convinced me you were and are a man of honor and how can I say no to a man of honor?"

That was good enough for me.

We arrived at the hotel and quickly made our way to our room. Voula insisted we make love in the shower. Surprisingly, she needed little help standing on top of the soap dish. To better steady herself, she held on to a small shelf normally used for conditioners and shampoo. Her remaining weight was supported by my body. After we finished in the shower, we moved to the sink before finishing up on the toilet. As predicted, the woman was eating me alive! Six years of abstinence slowly melted away with each release of her womanhood. She had surrendered to me completely. After the bathroom, we ended up in bed for one final curtain call. When it was all over,

Voula stuck her tongue in my ear and told me the one thing in the world I didn't want to here.

"William, I love you so much."

Before I could answer she followed with this.

"I know you don't love me, but that's ok. I wish you could stay here and marry me, but, I know you can't. The only thing I would like…please write me every now and then."

I knew I wasn't going to write, but to appease her, I promised I would. Been there done that. After we left the hotel, we grabbed a bite to eat from a vendor whose food cart was located two blocks west of the hotel. We walked around for a bit holding hands like a couple of school kids on a first date. Soon after, I hailed a cab which took us back to her place.

"I'm going to get something from my bedroom; I'll be right back."

I waited in the cab for Voula to return. After a couple of minutes, she returned and handed me a piece of paper that had her name, address and phone number on it but what caught my attention was the amount of perfume she used to scent the paper. She must have poured half a bottle on the edges.

"So you won't forget me."

"Ride with me to the ship?"

"No, it's better this way. I love you William and I want to be your wife someday. I know it sounds crazy since we just met, and I know the years aren't right between us, but I just wanted you to know I'm here for you if you want me."

I got out of the cab to exchange goodbyes. We hugged and kissed and then she turned and ran back into her apartment building. I directed the cab driver to take me back to the Vailsburg. The following morning we set sail for home. Pearl Harbor, then San Diego.

During the voyage across the southern Pacific Ocean, I had a great deal of time to reflect on my Navy career. This was my last deployment; I was going to be honorably discharged from the military in less than sixty days. Normally, when we're underway, I like to spend my leisure time up on the signal bridge. I do this for two reasons. Privacy and Big Eyes. However, since this was the last time I would be out at sea, barring any new assignments, I decided to spend as much time as possible on the fantail. For some inexplicable reason, I felt the need to be closer to the ocean.

On the fifth day, around 1100, I made my way out to the fantail to have a smoke. When I got there I was really surprised. With the exception of the watch stander, I was completely alone. As is my custom, I made my way to the aftermost life line. Now, I do this for two reasons. First, I enjoy leaning on the line while I smoke my cigarette, second, I like looking at the rooster tail. What I didn't know, the skipper had ordered the engine room to make turns for twenty three knots. I don't know if this was done to satisfy some maintenance requirement or if he just wanted to hasten our return. Whatever the reason, we were moving quickly through the water. Suddenly, the rooster tail transformed into a wall of water. It's crest was even with the main deck. Not to be outdone, the wind increased in intensity. The combination of the two sent showers of cascading water down on me. Needless to say, I was completely soaked. Normally, I would have struck below to change, but since this was my last hoorah, I didn't budge an inch. Wave after wave of water descended upon me like a water fall but I didn't care. I was alive and free and enjoying every minute of it.

After a while, the salt water began to sting my eyes. The only way to escape it was by looking down at the deck. And that's when I saw it. A black shadow in the form of a cross lay in front of me. I didn't recognize it at first, but then it dawned on me. My old friend had returned. Sure enough, hovering not ten feet above me was Sunrise.

"DAMN PATTERSON! THAT SON OF A BITCH IS JUST ABOVE YOUR HEAD!!!"

293

The duty watch stander was staring at Sunrise. As far as the bird was concerned, he didn't

exist. It was just him and me. Sunrise continued to hover motionless above my head.

"NOT TO WORRY BOATS, WE KNOW EACH OTHER!"

Due to the loud noise we had to shout at each other.

"KNOW EACH OTHER! WHAT THE HELL ARE YOU TALKING ABOUT?"

"WE'RE FRIENDS, ALMOST SIX YEARS NOW-MET HIM ON MY FIRST BOAT!!!"

"SIX YEARS? HOW THE HELL DO YOU KNOW IT'S THE SAME BIRD?"

"I JUST KNOW. THE WAY IT MOVES AROUND. THE WAY IT LOOKS AT ME. I

JUST KNOW!!!"

"DIDN'T YOU SAY YOUR FIRST BOAT WAS ON THE EAST COAST?"

I nodded yes.

"HEY PATERSON, THAT'S ON THE OTHER SIDE OF THE WORLD!!!"

I nodded again.

"AND AFTER SIX YEARS! NO FRICKING WAY!"

"YEA. I KNOW IT SOUNDS CRAZY, BUT IT'S THE SAME BIRD. BELIEVE ME, I

CAN FEEL IT."

"NO PATTERSON, WHAT YOU'RE FEELING IS MENTAL ILLNESS!! THAT'S

WHAT YOU'RE FEELING!!!

I chuckled silently to myself.

The watch stander continued to yell at me but I pretended not to hear him. I moved out of

the water fall and shielded my eyes to get a better look. Sunrise had grown since our last

encounter- all those years ago. Suddenly, without warning, it backed off a bit allowing me to drop

my hand. Soon we were eye to eye but the distance between us increased dramatically. We stared

294

at each other momentarily before my friend disappeared below the rooster tail. Shortly thereafter, it rose up above the water spray and ascended skyward. I thought it might disappear into the clouds like it had in the past; but instead, it descended once again putting us at eye level. Looking directly into my eyes, it did the strangest thing. It dipped its rightwing then straightened out quickly. It repeated this two more times before finally ascending into the sky and disappearing.

Something wasn't right though. On board the Baffles, Sunrise would motion I look over the side for bow dolphins. And then it hit me. He was saying goodbye.

"DAMN PATERSON, DID YOU SEE THAT? THAT DAMN BIRD DIPPED ITS WING JUST LIKE AN AIRPLANE!!! WHAT THE HELL!!! IS THAT BIRD FOR REAL OR WHAT? IF I DIDN'T KNOW BETTER, I'D SAY THAT BIRD RECOGNIZED YOU, I MEAN, THAT DAMN BIRD KNOWS YOU!!!"

"THAT'S WHAT I'VE BEEN TRYING TO TELL YA!!"

"DAMN IT PATTERSON!!! NOW YOU'RE FREAKING ME OUT!!!"

"YOU SAW IT DIP ITS WING RIGHT?"

He nodded.

"WITHERSPOON, YOU'VE BEEN IN THE NAVY HOW LONG?"

"THREE YEARS!"

"EVER SEE AN ALBATROSS DO THAT BEFORE?"

"NOT ONLY NO, BUT HELL NO!!!"

"ALRIGHT THEN, AND REMEMBER—IT DIPPED ITS WING THREE TIMES."

"MAYBE IT'S NOT AN ALBATROSS; MAYBE I'TS YOUR GUARDIAN ANGEL. DAMNEST THING I EVER SAW! ABSOLUTELY MAKES NO SENSE!"

Like I said, I was soaking wet and had to get below. As I was changing my clothes, I

295

wondered if I would ever see my friend again. For the remainder of the cruise, I smoked all my cigarettes on the fantail, but Sunrise never came. As I look back now, somehow my friend knew I wouldn't be returning to sea. How he understood this was beyond me. The fact he did is what counts. Call it a mind meld if you will. Perhaps we communicate with each other on levels we don't fully understand. I don't know, but I will say this. The albatross had been a good omen. He had kept me out of harm's way many times. Six years is a long time to be out at sea; many things can happen and when they do it's usually in the blink of an eye.

I can't say this enough. I was grateful for all my good fortunes.

Fifteen days later we were pier side in San Diego. I was a free man, although technically, I was still in the Navy. All of the paper work had been signed and submitted, but since I still had vacation time I couldn't call myself a civilian until it was used up.

I must admit, walking down the brow for the last time was rough. It was a very emotional moment for me. I wanted to delay my departure, but the Vailsburg was getting underway so I said my goodbyes as quickly as I could. The Officer of the Deck was the Division Officer from First Division. Recently assigned to the Vailsburg, he was a boot Ensign out of Alabama. I didn't know him very well, but he had a pleasant demeanor and was soft spoken. His name was Conrad Coins, and he was the last officer I ever saluted. No more shipboard responsibilities for this civilian.

I was finally free.

I don't know why, but when I stepped off the brow, I thought about Chief Morris and the time he yelled at me for landing on my butt way back in Euro 1.

A smile came to me.

I was about to take my first step as a civilian and I wanted to savor the moment. I stood there in anticipation, but before I could move, I heard the call to single up all lines. The Vailsburg was getting underway, and she was getting underway without me. I turned around to watch her deploy. The tugs helped her into the harbor channel.

Once she cleared the break water, she was on her way.

Just as the ship was disappearing from view, something amazing happened. My friend reappeared!

Hovering just above the fantail was Sunrise! The albatross glided silently, moving from side to side as the wind currents supported its weight. It didn't flap its wings or move its head. I strained my eyes to see if anyone was on the fantail besides the watch stander but nobody was there. He was alone. I was about to turn and walk away when I noticed the watch stander was waving at Sunrise with both hands!

I couldn't believe my eyes! Somebody besides me was waving to my albatross! I couldn't make him out but it had to be Witherspoon! I mean, who else could it be?

And then I knew. The crew of the Vailsburg was in good hands. No matter where they went or for how long. They were safe.

Sunrise the albatross will look after them.

Made in the USA
Thornton, CO
05/25/22 03:47:32

d61dbab0-c33a-43fa-95e1-a9ebef510371R02